ISBN-13: 978-1451592870
ISBN-10: 1451592876

Library of Congress Control Number: 2010904964
CreateSpace Independent Publishing Platform
North Charleston, South Carolina

24/7

The First Person

You Must Lead

Is You!

Rebecca "Becky" Halstead

Book Dedication

This book is dedicated to the people who have affected my life immeasurably—especially the military men and women with whom I had the honor to serve. They influenced the person and the leader I am today, and they continue to influence my life, as I do my best to impact the lives of others. Each contributed to shaping the person I have and will continue to become. You and your Families touched my life in ways I can barely articulate. As an expression of my gratitude, you will find the words *Soldier* and *Family* capitalized throughout this book.

A new wealth of people have entered my life as a result of starting my company, *STEADFAST Leadership*. They have come from the corporate sector, not-for-profit organizations, colleges and universities, churches, and communities. To you, I am grateful for the new opportunities to share leadership with you and learn from you.

Finally, and most important, to my Family and friends who have unconditionally loved, supported, encouraged, coached, and guided me—*Thank you!*

I hope this book makes an impression upon the heart, mind, and soul of each reader. As you read, my hope is you will reflect, think, assess, learn, laugh, and maybe even cry along with me, and in the end, take new steps to always lead yourself first!

Table of Contents

Acknowledgments

Success is a Team Sport

A Special Thank-You
to
Sussman Consultants Ltd
for the
book cover design and artwork

A Special Thank-You
to
My Editorial Team
for your energy, enthusiasm, and encouragement

G. Isham and

D. Ahart	C. Halse	W. Sheffield
S. Alexander	B. Halstead	K. Torrance
L. Carabello	K. Kuhla	S. Thurber
S. Duffy	M. LeBoeuf	

Introduction
I Have Always Tried to Lead the Way I Wanted to Be Led

This book is about leadership—leadership principles based upon decades of practice and observation.

I begin with five simple leadership truths followed by thirty leadership principles. I offer these as a result of more than three decades of being on both the giving and receiving ends of leadership. These enduring leadership principles are not all inclusive or prioritized, as I intend *24/7* to be the first in a series of *STEADFAST Leadership* books.

What do I know about leadership, and why might I be worthy of helping others lead? The most obvious answer: experience. Instead of simply being a student of leadership, I have lived it; I have succeeded, I have failed, I have learned, and I am still learning and sharing.

The stories come from a diverse set of personal and professional experiences, ranging from childhood through college, to the challenges of serving and leading in the US Army for twenty-seven years. My experiences were gained during peacetime and combat, leading teams of as few as twenty-one to organizations exceeding twenty thousand men and women.

My *war stories* on leadership are based on successes and failures, mentors and tormentors, people by whom I was led and whom I led, and leadership lessons learned along the way. My simple goal is to inspire you to consider, or to consider more deeply, the importance of leadership in your life, and perhaps even ignite you to action.

I graduated in 1981 from the United States Military Academy with the second graduating class to include women and had the honor of becoming the first woman graduate in West Point history to achieve promotion to general officer. Although a historical achievement, one of my mentors recently reminded me that equally noteworthy was being the first officer on active duty from my West Point graduating class to be promoted to general officer. Being the first woman was a statistic, but being the first *person* in my class reflected my performance and potential.

Many refer to my military success as a *fast-track* career. I prefer to frame the journey as the result of faithfulness, a disciplined work ethic, a tenacious and grateful attitude, and an appreciation for the team of people who shared the journey with me.

Among the countless blessings and challenges, the privilege and honor to serve in Iraq from 2005 to 2006 as the commanding general for the largest logistics command was the most rewarding and life changing, especially as a leader. Being responsible for leading over twenty thousand military men and women, America's sons and daughters, as well as five thousand civilians and three Iraqi Motorized Transportation Regiments, brought new meaning and dimension to how I defined leadership and the principles I had to exemplify.

My combat experience also marked a new first for our nation, as I was the first woman in US history to serve as a commanding general in combat. It is humbling to know my military career is a bit of a historical collection of firsts and unique experiences. Another historical first was that my deputy commander and chief of staff, my top two officers, were also women. Our combined leadership experience and talent demonstrated it was time to move beyond gender stereotypes.

When I retired from the army, I confided in my father my intent to become a motivational speaker and author in order to share with corporate America the leadership lessons learned during my military profession. He was not impressed and criticized my new career idea based on his experiences of having been required to attend leader conferences and coming away entertained but unchanged.

He was convinced I would be much better off seeking employment aligned with my logistics and engineering background. He gently reminded me that offers in other fields were more financially lucrative, but I knew what I wanted to do. My main focus has always been on the human dimension. As we say in the army, "Mission first. People always." I wanted to deliver a leadership message that reflected my passion for people.

As I developed the business plan for *STEADFAST Leadership*, my dad's observation continued to drive my goals and vision. I kept asking the question, "If people go to these events and like what they hear, why doesn't anything change?"

The answer that made the most sense to me was they must not recognize the need for change in their own lives. Hasn't that happened to all of us? We listen or read, and we think to ourselves, "My spouse or boss or coworkers or kids need to hear or read this!" In reality, each of us needs to reflect, assess, and consider how we could live and lead ourselves better.

My goal is not just to entertain. I want to educate, provoke and stimulate new ideas, create hope, inspire, and stir leaders to action with my leadership messages. What better way to do so than to create a trademark tagline of *"The first person you must lead is YOU!"* and then add to it *"24/7"* as the title of my first book. The "24/7" represents leading ourselves twenty-four hours a day, seven days a week. Leadership is not something we should turn on and off when convenient.

The leadership premises discussed in this book helped determine my destiny and took an ordinary girl to extraordinary heights. I had to educate and develop myself, earn respect, and nurture more complex relationships. The first person I had to lead was me!

Numerous requests during speaking engagements for my leadership book gave me the final boost for writing *24/7*. I am consistently asked to discuss my hardest decisions, my loneliest times, my greatest victories, my favorite leadership roles, and other key points in my career. It is extremely difficult to single out one particular circumstance for each, but I share examples in the coming pages.

I have purposefully omitted names except that of one very special Soldier and American hero, Sergeant James Witkowski, and you will understand why when you read his story later in the book. Names are extremely important to me, but I don't believe they are necessary to understand the relationships or leadership roles described in these stories.

I am sharing authentic stories with you about real people, with real challenges and conflicts, with tough decisions, positive and negative outcomes, and rewarding, as well as less than rewarding, consequences. Using personal examples breathes life into the truths and principles presented and provides the framework for my leadership model. In doing so, I hope your leadership journey will be a little less bumpy than mine.

I encourage you to highlight phrases or paragraphs that strike *you*. Write *your* thoughts in the margins and make this book *your* own.

PART I:

Why Leadership and Why You?

Five Simple Truths

Truth #1
You Have at Least *One* Person to Lead—Yourself

It took me many years to realize life does not owe me anything but opportunities. Let's face it, opportunities abound. We are living in tumultuous times, and there is a crisis in leadership in many corners. What I do with those opportunities—the choices, the decisions, the attitudes—is up to me.

If I want to see change in myself, my Family, my community, and my workplace, I start by drawing a mental circle around my boots, high heels, tennis shoes, flip-flops, or Crocs; pick the shoes that work for you. Then, I take a deep, inward look at myself. If I want an outward change, I must start inside my personal circle.

In other words, "The first person I must lead is me!" I think Mahatma Gandhi's version of this concept was, "Be the change you wish to see in the world." Each of us must set the example first, before we demand it of others. Rising up the officer ranks, including as a general, I would never ask my Soldiers to do something I was not willing to do myself. I had to "talk the talk and walk the walk."

Throughout my career, I often asked myself, "Would I hire me? Would my boss consider me the 'must have' person on the team? If so, why? If not, why not? What are my personal ethics and what makes me valuable to the team? Am I fulfilling my purpose? Am I authentic?"

Many people have asked me why I think I was so successful. As I've reflected on my own leadership journey, I believe it boils down to having the foresight and discipline to lead myself first. If I'm not willing to be the example, then I should not be in a leadership position.

How are you doing? Are you an example of the change you wish to see in the world? Are you part of the problem or part of the solution? Do you come to work with a positive attitude and an expression on your face that communicates "Yes!" and "Let's make it happen!"? Are you a bridge or a wall to others? Are you leading yourself?

Leadership is a choice we make every day, and that leads us to truth number two.

Truth #2

Leadership Is Your Choice

That's right, leadership is a choice. My parents taught their children about character—who you are when no one else is watching. Translated, in all situations, I better respond in a way that would make my mother proud. I needed to choose to lead myself to do what was right.

Did I always pass the test? No. Did I miss some potentially incredible opportunities? I am sure I did. Why? I sometimes failed to make the best choices.

No one can force you to lead yourself, although the students at a Catholic high school recently tried to convince me the nuns could make them! Our parents, teachers, coaches, bosses, or even an upper-class cadet at West Point breathing orders into your face cannot make you lead yourself in a positive direction, although they certainly give it their best shot.

When I speak on leadership in the corporate sector, I have heard comments such as, "Leading in the military cannot be too hard—you just order people around" or "Everything in the military is about discipline and orders. Surely you don't want Soldiers leading themselves first!" Let me assure you, in the military as much as in the corporate sector, leading yourself first must be your foundation. It requires a huge dose of discipline, and oftentimes courage, to choose to do so. Fortunately, the choice is yours.

Have you ever wondered how children who are raised in the same Family and attend the same school and church end up turning out quite differently? Or, how people who work in the same organization, led by the same boss, under the same policies, respond quite differently? After years of observation, I am convinced the answer lies in the choices *you* make combined with *your* unique leader DNA, which is Truth #3.

Truth #3

You Lead Differently Because of Your Unique "Leader DNA"

Those who have studied leadership are familiar with the age-old question "Are leaders born or made?" Simple, deductive reasoning provides the answer: we are both born and made.

First, we are born with our own DNA. We are born with personality traits that are integral to the way we speak, act, and think. So, in essence, we are also born with our own unique *leader* DNA. Logically and naturally, this results in each of us leading differently.

Although our leader DNA may be created at birth, our leader identity is created and developed over time. Our identity is a combination of our personality traits and our learned skills that we develop over time as a result of experience, knowledge, responsibility, relationships, and exposure to different styles of leadership.

For instance, my DNA-related claim to fame has always been, "I'm just a country girl from a town with no traffic lights." I was born into a conservative, Christian family and raised in rural upstate New York in a small place called Willseyville. Our community was so small we had only a post office, which allowed us to boast our own zip code, and we traveled to Candor to attend school.

I was child number three of four. My parents both worked. Our home was disciplined but full of joy and fun. There were chores, demanding standards, and high expectations. There was always a Family vacation and quality time together. The focus on Family, faith, and discipline shaped my leadership style.

I preferred being outdoors, mowing the lawn or working in the garden. When I had to be in the house, I enjoyed playing office and, although it wasn't the norm at the time, I enjoyed being the boss! I was an athlete, a member of the National Honor Society, band, and chorus, and participated in numerous church programs. I was considered well-rounded and good at many things but not particularly great at anything.

My point in sharing my DNA with you is to demonstrate how ordinary I am. I think most of us are ordinary. I did not come from a Family with a tradition of, or expectation for, military service. I was not at the top of my classes academically, and I was not a person identified as most likely to succeed. I did not *look* like the stereotypical officer, let alone general. I stood 5 feet

1½ inches tall, and it was not uncommon for people to presume I was a junior Soldier or Soldier's child.

Although we may think of ourselves as ordinary, each of us possesses potential. How we put our skills and traits into action is what makes us unique. When we make the right choices, we are able to turn ordinary into extraordinary.

Take some time to think about your DNA. What skills and traits, values, and behaviors make up your leadership chemistry? Do you use them thoughtfully, graciously, and creatively to better lead yourself and others?

Truth #4

You Must Identify Your Strengths and Manage Your Weaknesses—You Have Both

No matter how successful we become, whatever our title, status, or rank, we all have strengths and weaknesses. The first critical step is recognizing this fact. Doing so requires a high degree of humility, honesty, and courage.

Recognition alone is not enough. I encourage you to reflect and identify what you believe are your strengths and weaknesses and write them down. Share them with a trusted agent, and then develop some ideas on how you can best manage the weaknesses and develop the strengths. Be mindful, strengths can become weaknesses when misused or left unattended.

Remember, no one is ever too old or important to stop learning. Identifying your strengths is the easier, more fun part of assessing the principles for daily living. But allowing yourself to discover your weaknesses will make you stronger and will also help you lead others better. Even as a general, I was still discovering my weaknesses but was willing to share them with those who worked for me so they could learn and perhaps not make the same mistakes.

The day you stop learning is the day you stop leading; for that matter, it is the day you stop really living.

What is holding you back? Have you identified your strengths and weaknesses? At the end of each day, can you name one new thing you have learned?

As you read through the thirty principles, stay focused on you, and assess yourself against them. If your thoughts wander to wishing your boss, spouse, child, or friends would read this book, bring the focus back to you because *24/7* is about learning about yourself and then learning how to make you a better you!

Truth #5

When You Lead Yourself Better, You Lead Others Better

Your personal development as a leader relies heavily on your attitude and willingness to continue to learn. You cannot know everything, but you can improve yourself daily. In the military, we call it, "Improving your foxhole every day."

By being willing to learn, remaining disciplined with your choices, recognizing your shortcomings, and deliberately identifying your priorities and values, you are leading yourself better. A better *me* is always a better *we*. Those you lead become the beneficiaries of a better version of you.

That's right, the great thing about leading yourself better is you will lead others better. Let's remember, leadership is, first and foremost, about those you lead. When you understand and internalize that leadership is about the led, not the leader, you begin to create a legacy of leaders who will do the same for the individuals they lead.

I am often asked, "What do you consider your greatest accomplishment in the military?" I suspect many expect the answer to be about "being first" with some accomplishment. This is absolutely not the case. My consistent answer is, "Leaving a legacy of leaders who choose to lead with character and competence."

By leading myself first and serving others, I believe I favorably affected the lives of those around me. My simple goal was, and remains, to lead the way I wanted to be led.

PART II:

Thirty Leadership Principles

for

Daily Living and Leading

Leadership Principle 1

Lead with Your Heart and Mind: Struggle Is Good

People will forget what you said. People will forget what you did. But people will never forget how you made them feel. ~Maya Angelou

Leadership is character and competence, not one or the other. ~Unknown

Have you ever struggled to make a decision? Your mind tells you to do one thing, but your heart leads you in another direction.

If you are a parent, I'm certain you have had many times when you wanted to grab your child and ask, "What were you thinking?!" Then your heart kicks in, you see the precious child you created, and you want to take a completely different approach to the situation. Fear not, you are normal. Not only are you normal, but also the struggle between your heart and mind is good.

Regrettably, most of us have been led to believe that when we struggle, we are weak, or we are indecisive. I believe the opposite to be true. We should experience a constant struggle between our minds and hearts. The struggle means you are paying attention to both, which results in coming to the best decisions and actions.

If you're struggling between your heart and mind, you are actually stronger, more caring, and more determined to achieve the best result. You are fusing that which you know and that which you feel in order to do what is right. I worry about leaders who lead exclusively with their head, or the opposite, lead only from an emotional vantage point.

Emotions are essential for a leader, but warning lights must go off when having emotions switches to becoming emotional. Emotions allow you to be a passionate leader, but being an *emotional* leader often leads to becoming a defensive, argumentative leader. True leaders learn to balance the intellectual response with the emotions appropriate to the situation.

When you think of heart and mind, I want you to think of character and competence, traits and skills, art and science, and emotional intelligence and intellect. Think of your heart as your traits—those qualities with which you are born and come to you more naturally than to others. Think of your mind as your skills—those characteristics, principles, and values you learn and develop over time.

Your heart possesses your emotional intelligence—the expressive impact you have on the people you lead. Your mind possesses your intellect—giving you a unique combination of creative, innovative, and scientific possibilities for all situations. Your traits and skills merge to give you the optimal response to each situation.

Your character fused with your competence will make you more confident. Confident, rather than arrogant or insecure, leaders are the ones we want to follow—not all-knowing, my-way-or-the-highway-type leaders. Confident leaders provide calm in the chaos; they build bridges, not walls. Leaders with character and competence assess situations before reacting. They are good "bad news" takers, make informed decisions, and trust their subordinates. Leaders who learn to fuse heart and mind are able to make the jump from a good leader to a great leader.

Leading and living your life using both your heart and mind are not easy tasks. Mastering the struggle, however, is incredibly valuable for making the best decisions and achieving the best outcomes. As I reflect on my life, I can identify situations when I failed to pay attention to both my heart and mind, and the result was far from the best. Allow yourself to struggle, contemplate, think, and feel. When you do, your best decisions will result.

Remember, leadership is defined by what is on the inside, not the outside, such as title, position, wealth, or gender. Let's take a moment to reflect on the subject of gender. I've read many academic studies, surveys, and blogs on leadership, and consistently we're being pushed toward stereotypes when it comes to male versus female leadership competencies. The six leadership competencies identified as being the most evident for leaders were: decisive, assertive, independent, friendly, unselfish, caretaking. Evaluate *yourself* and decide which three best describe *your* leadership traits.

I recently used this simple exercise at a high-level corporate women's leadership conference. After they chose the competencies that best described their leadership styles, I informed them that the survey had identified the first three competencies (decisive, assertive, independent) as male and the last three (friendly, unselfish, caretaking) as female.

They, like me, however, had identified with one or two of the male competencies as much, if not more than, the three female competencies. The prevalent competencies of many male leaders I have worked with, or for, definitely included some of the female traits.

When you take a closer look at the six competencies, I think you could assign the first three as being in the *mind* category and the last three as *heart*. Visualize three hearts and three brains

placed in front of you. The casual observer cannot id
ones are female versus male. The logical leap for m   ....,
men and women, need to focus on simply understanding the ba-
sics of great leadership, which is not about gender.

I would love for all of us to start challenging traditional culture and scrutinizing the stereotypes. Humans, especially in
business, military, and government sectors, created the culture;
therefore, we have the power to change it. Let's begin to do so by
removing the female and male leadership labels, and rather than
separating those traits into gender-based categories, let's grasp
the powerful concept that leadership is the fusion of heart and
mind.

★   It Is Not Making Sense to Me—Something Is Wrong   ★

In 1986, as a young company commander in my late twenties, one of the senior noncommissioned officers in my unit, a
sergeant first class, was not performing consistently. It was very
odd. He was intelligent, honest, and on many days reliable, yet
there were incidents when he seemed to be forgetful, late, and
lacking in carrying out his responsibilities. He was in a critical
leadership position, responsible for the quality assurance and
control for our ammunition accountability and safety operations at the largest ammunition operation for army training in
the Pacific Northwest.

The supervisors for this senior Soldier came to me and requested I relieve him of his responsibilities. They wanted me
to *crush* this person, because they were frustrated with the fact
he was at a senior level and was overlooking simple but critical

things. They interpreted it as him not caring about his job. Sometimes there is a tendency to take immediate action to punish or remove an individual who is not performing, rather than investing the time to either investigate or develop the person.

I was perplexed by the situation. My mind and heart were in a struggle. My mind clearly told me this was unacceptable behavior; he wasn't leading by example, and I needed to fix it. My heart, on the other hand, could not wrap itself around the *it*. My instincts, my heart, told me something else was going on.

I requested that he come to my office to discuss the situation so I could get firsthand knowledge to help determine the best corrective action to take. He and I spoke at length about many things. I dug into his many years of experience and his desire to be a Soldier and serve, and I asked him why he thought he was struggling to be punctual, thorough, and on top of his job. He seemed at a loss for words and almost helpless, uncertain himself as to the *why* of his behavior. After our discussion, my assessment was still that something was not quite right. So, I decided to send him for a mental and physical evaluation to see if medical experts could find what we were missing.

The result of my decision changed the situation drastically and, without a doubt, shaped the way I would continue to lead throughout the rest of my career. The medical professionals determined this career Soldier, not yet forty years old, had Alzheimer's. We discovered he knew very little about his Family history. As we investigated, we found that Alzheimer's was prevalent in his family. With this information, the next steps were to remove him from his duty position, help him receive treatment, and medically retire him with full benefits. This made a significant difference in his ability to care for his young Family for the long-term and gave him a better quality of life for the short-term, as he lived only a few years after his diagnosis.

When the situation doesn't make sense, ask questions, be curious, listen to your gut, and use your heart and your head. As one of our chiefs of staff of the army used to say, "If the horse is riding the cowboy, something is not right."

For me, this experience validated the importance of taking time to make sure I engaged both my mind and heart as I made decisions and led others. It may take longer to sort out the issues, but the results are far more remarkable and long lasting.

★ I Have Some Good News and Some Bad News for You ★

Do you hold on to your good people, or do you let them advance? Is it possible you may be more concerned about your own gain than what's best for your top performers and for the whole team (company)? I'll address more on "the betterment of the team" under Leadership Principle 24, but before you can take care of the team, your heart and mind must be challenging *you* to make the best decisions.

I found few things harder than giving up great people who worked for me by allowing them to move within the organization to where they would benefit the team at a different level. Every time this happened, I wanted to keep these individuals on my team because of the work they were performing and the benefit we were getting at our level, and, yes, because they were making me look better as a leader. Each time, I eventually recognized that by giving up these individuals, the larger team would be the beneficiary of their talent. Clearly, it was the right decision to recognize, reward, and advance the high-performing individual.

During my time as company commander, I'd suffered through several failed inspections of our vehicle maintenance operations. We had an incredible fleet of cranes, dozers, forklifts, trucks, and trailers, many of which had been in the army inventory over twenty years and were in rough shape. What we lacked was a senior noncommissioned officer (NCO) with maintenance experience and talent to spearhead our operations.

About six months into my command, a new NCO, a master sergeant, was assigned to me. His background, leadership experience, and expertise were exactly what we needed, and I immediately assigned him to take over the maintenance mission. Within weeks, he started to turn the operation around. He began to develop, train, and hold young Soldiers responsible for maintaining their equipment. He was technically competent and a motivator at the same time. He would drop by my office and have conversations with me about his training and goals. I was impressed with his goal to actually win a maintenance award, not simply pass the mandatory inspections.

Within a few months, my higher headquarters, the battalion, could see the visible change in our operations. I lauded the master sergeant and gave him all the credit when I was speaking to my boss, the battalion commander, about our improvements. It didn't take long for my boss to identify him as a leader among leaders across the battalion, not just within my company.

One afternoon the telephone rang. It was my battalion commander. "Becky, we have a first sergeant position opening up in one of the other companies, and I would like you to consider giving your maintenance platoon sergeant up to the battalion, and giving him the opportunity to take this key leadership position in another company."

I found myself experiencing a range of emotions as I listened to his request. I was thrilled my boss recognized the performance of, and the potential in, my NCO. I was excited for him to have the opportunity to advance and become a first sergeant, a coveted leadership position for an NCO. I was, however, distraught at the thought of losing him. For the first time, our maintenance operations were running successfully.

Talk about struggle between heart and mind! My *mind* was saying, "I'm crazy to let him go!" My *heart* was saying, "You can't hold him back. This is best for him, and it becomes best for the larger team."

I have no doubt I also considered, "What if we fail another inspection? It might hurt my career."

It didn't take me long to make a call and ask the NCO to report to my office at the end of the duty day.

"Ma'am, reporting as ordered."

"Take a seat. Good to see you. We need to talk. I've got some good news and some bad news for you, Sergeant. I want to thank you for the great work you're doing in the maintenance platoon. It has not gone unnoticed. As a matter of fact, the battalion commander is so impressed with what you've accomplished, he has requested I allow you to advance to the position of first sergeant for one of the other companies in the battalion. That's great news for you and the battalion."

"Ma'am, if that is the good news, what is the bad news?"

"Well, the bad news is, I just cannot let you go. What you have done in this organization has been the best thing I've seen since I took command."

There was silence in the room—a deafening silence. My face was serious, and I looked to see how he was responding to what I said.

"Yes, ma'am. I understand. Thank you for letting me know. Is there anything else, ma'am?"

"Yes. I'm just kidding. Not about the first part—the battalion commander did call, and you are doing a great job, and you do deserve to advance to a greater position of responsibility. I'm kidding about not letting you go. I hate losing you, but to hold you back would be the wrong thing to do for you and for the whole team. So congratulations, *First Sergeant!*"

Are you holding others back for *your* own good or *your* own gain, or are you making the tough decisions that result in the best outcome for the larger team? Are you leading from a position of just heart or just mind, or are you paying attention to both? Are you curious, and do you ask the hard questions? When you lead with both your heart and mind, it results in your making the best decisions for the greater good of the team.

Leadership Principle 2

Have Integrity: Choose the Harder Right over the Easier Wrong

I will not lie, cheat or steal, nor tolerate those who do. ~Cadet Honor Code, USMA, West Point

Oh God, our Father... Make us to choose the harder right instead of the easier wrong, and never to be content with a half truth when the whole can be won. ~Cadet Prayer, USMA, West Point

The only thing necessary for the triumph of evil is that good men do nothing. ~Edmund Burke

Many surveys I have read on leadership have revealed that integrity is the number one trait people want their leaders to possess. I agree: integrity is absolutely nonnegotiable. I learned the importance of integrity as a child; my parents were the consummate examples. Integrity was further reinforced as part of my West Point training, and it was an integral part of my leader identity. Every aspect of my being a professional officer in the military, twenty-four hours a day, seven days a week, was based on a foundation of discipline, trust, and integrity.

When leaders lack integrity, they destroy the environment around them. Likewise, if they recognize a lack of integrity with people on their team and do nothing, it spreads like a cancer throughout the organization. I often remind my listeners that you do not have to go all the way to Iraq or Afghanistan to find combat; combat is right here in our daily lives because of the lack of integrity.

What does integrity mean to you? If you are a businessperson, do you deliver a quality product or service on time and within cost? If you are married, are you faithful to your spouse? If a friend or coworker asks you for candid feedback, do you provide it? If you are given the wrong change when you make a purchase, do you return it? When someone gives you credit for an accomplishment that wasn't yours, do you give credit where credit is rightfully due?

Respect must be earned and is a result of the integrity we display in what we say and do. Integrity is admitting when you are wrong, having the intestinal fortitude to hold yourself and others accountable, being humble with your successes, and delivering consequences when trust has been violated.

At West Point we followed an honor code: "I will not lie, cheat or steal, nor tolerate those who do." This code set the bar high for leading yourself first, by being honest and trustworthy. It set the bar even higher by demanding that not only do you demand those standards of yourself, but you also demand them of others. Effectively, it meant we trusted each other until given a reason not to do so.

We also memorized the Cadet Prayer and were expected to live by it. One of the most demanding expectations in the prayer is choosing "the harder right instead of the easier wrong." This is particularly difficult when the *wrong* you may witness involves a friend, Family member, fellow teammate, or even your boss. When this happens, loyalty can often become blind loyalty, and the result is that our integrity becomes the casualty.

You cannot effectively lead others without integrity.

★ Integrity versus Blind Loyalty: The Lieutenant at the Entry Control Point ★

While commanding in Iraq, I was presented with a situation that underscored the importance of integrity at all levels.

The incident involved a lieutenant and was reported to me by one of my brigade commanders, a colonel with over twenty years in the military and one level below me in the chain of command. The colonel's headquarters was located in southern Iraq (my units were located across fifty-five different bases in Iraq, and one was located in Kuwait). One of his infantry battalions was positioned at Balad with my headquarters. The mission of that battalion was base security. The lieutenant in question and his security platoon were assigned to the colonel's infantry battalion and were in charge of one of our busiest entry control points.

For the most part, traffic entering and exiting through this entry control gate consisted of long convoys of large supply and security vehicles used for distribution of supplies and equipment. Before a convoy could depart the base, every vehicle had to have full tanks of fuel; functioning weapon systems; and Soldiers trained, armed, briefed, and ready for their mission.

Equally essential to smooth operations was bringing a convoy onto the base. This required convoys entering to be *cleared*— ensuring no vehicles had been interdicted or sabotaged with explosives along the route. This meant expeditious review of all essential paperwork, plus thorough and efficient inspection of each vehicle.

Convoy leaders understood their responsibilities and the need to keep the vehicles flowing quickly through the entry control point. As you can imagine, our goal was to minimize the amount of time vehicles remained idle—especially those outside the perimeter of the base where the enemy was ever present. Many systems were in place to ensure these operations were handled correctly.

Cameras, called J-lens cameras, which were operated by our Soldiers conducting physical security operations, provided constant surveillance to help improve the safety and security of the convoys entering and exiting the base, as well as the security of those who lived and worked on the base. This was no small mission for a lieutenant and his platoon.

This security platoon was a tight-knit, cohesive team. Army units train, live, and conduct their mission together with discipline, obedience, and a strong loyalty to each other; this is amplified in combat due to the life-and-death situations Soldiers face. There is an incredibly strong bond of camaraderie—a band of brothers and sisters. The chain of command or supervisory levels in this case consisted of the lieutenant (typically twenty-two to twenty-five years of age) in charge of the platoon (typically thirty to fifty Soldiers) and the platoon sergeant who reported to the lieutenant. The platoon leader and platoon sergeant formed the leadership team responsible for training and certifying their Soldiers, maintaining their health and welfare, and ensuring the good order and discipline of their platoon. Each platoon in the military has a specific mission. The mission of this infantry platoon was the security of the entry control point.

One afternoon, I received a phone call from the colonel.

"Ma'am, we have a possible disciplinary action involving one of my platoon leaders at your location in Balad."

The brigade commander was required to report this to me. Written combat policy, called *General Officer Order #1*, directs that any incident involving an officer be handled by the first general officer in the chain of command. The purpose of the policy is to provide visibility of all officer infractions and ensure a consistent standard across the organization.

The colonel let me know that his lieutenant had a physical altercation with an NCO in charge of one of the convoys trying to enter the base. The details were sketchy at first, but the overall scenario indicated the NCO did not have his convoy paperwork filled out correctly, slowing down the ability to get the convoy through the gate. The lieutenant became enraged at the incompetence of the NCO, got in his face, yelled at him, and then grabbed the NCO and pushed him against a cement bunker.

"Ma'am, based on my preliminary investigation, I am recommending a Field Grade Article 15 for this officer."

An individual receiving an Article 15 is authorized legal counsel and required to appear before the commander adjudicating the case. Before the actual proceeding, I received a copy of the investigation, sworn statements, and any other evidence for review.

The lieutenant was scheduled to report to me. As part of the process, his entire chain of command, the company, battalion, and brigade command teams, as well as the platoon sergeant and the J-lens operator, also reported. The chain of command reported first. I allowed them to enter the room and stand at ease, a more relaxed standing position. We discussed briefly how the proceeding would be conducted.

The lieutenant knocked twice on the door, at which time the chain of command in my office stood at attention. I directed him to enter the office, and he walked to within a few feet of my desk, raised his arm, saluted, and said, "Ma'am, reporting as ordered." I returned the salute. He lowered his arm and remained at attention, looking directly forward toward my desk.

I told the chain of command to stand at ease. The lieutenant remained at attention for the entire proceeding. He stood over six feet tall, with a strong build, square face. He had an intimidating presence. The expression on his face was one of anger and defensiveness.

As part of my normal process for Article 15 proceedings, I asked the lieutenant to tell me why, in his own words, he was summoned to my office. I asked this to establish if he had full understanding of the charges, as I had discovered early in my career that sometimes Soldiers were brought to my level for punishment, and they didn't know why they were there.

Apparently, junior leaders working for me had found it much easier to bring me the problem, instead of dealing with it themselves. I didn't catch on at first, and then one day I asked a Soldier why he was in my office—and was stunned to find out he had no idea. I dismissed him and reprimanded the chain of command for failing to do their jobs as leaders. I learned a valuable lesson, and from that point forward made sure those I led were doing their job: first by questioning the chain of command, and then by questioning the Soldier reporting. Do you recognize this kind of activity happening in your organization? Are problems being pushed to you that should be handled at a lower level? If so, how are you dealing with this problem?

I asked, "Lieutenant, please provide to me and your chain of command the reason for which you are standing here today."

"Ma'am, I am here because I have allegedly mistreated a noncommissioned officer." While he did so, his tone, bearing, and facial expressions demonstrated a strong defiance and arrogance. He rolled his eyes, threw his shoulders back, and refused to look me in the eye while speaking. When he was done, he looked beyond me.

"Lieutenant," I paused, waiting for him to move his eyes and look at me—although he made no attempt to do so. "Lieutenant, I am speaking to you. You better look me directly in the eye and keep your eyes focused on me." He finally complied.

"Before we proceed, let me remind you that your nonverbal actions, such as rolling your eyes, shrugging your shoulders, and tossing your head in disgust, are equal grounds for disrespect toward a senior officer as using words. So, if you do not want another charge added to your Article 15, then you better make some quick adjustments."

I clearly had his attention. The lieutenant's defense for his actions was that the NCO's incompetence jeopardized the safety and security of the convoy and put people's lives in danger. I agreed the incompetence of the NCO put the convoy at risk. Corrective action for the NCO and a review of the unit training protocol was definitely required.

However, the convoy was delayed even longer because of the lieutenant's response to the situation. Furthermore, his physical assault of a fellow Soldier was completely inappropriate and excessive. If he was capable of this sort of assault against a fellow US Army Soldier, what might he do to a local Iraqi man or woman who frustrated him? Lack of discipline and composure leads to further deterioration of good order and discipline.

The investigative packet had included a video taken by one of his Soldiers who was operating the J-lens cameras. The video had no sound, and it was in black and white. What you saw was a lineup of trucks in the convoy, the gate where the Soldiers were working, the cement markers for security, and the hustle and bustle of people doing their jobs. Then there was a circle of Soldiers who all came together. As you looked at the group, you saw a very tall individual get right up on top, and in the face, of another individual. You saw the larger individual shove the shorter person away from him. The taller individual, the lieutenant, started throwing his hands in the air, and you could surmise what was being said as he grabbed the other individual and pressed him down against a cement bunker. As this was occurring, some of the Soldiers began walking away. The camera panned away to the perimeter for just a few seconds and then returned to the incident that was unfolding.

After the lieutenant provided his defense, I informed him I had reviewed the video. I asked the young Soldier, a private who was operating the camera, why he had moved the camera away from the incident.

The young Soldier responded, "Ma'am I did not want to get my lieutenant in trouble. I was trying to save his a—."

"OK. Why did you then take the camera lens and return to the incident?"

"Ma'am, because my platoon sergeant was standing behind me, and he tapped me on the shoulder and told me to do so."

I looked at the LT, who was standing at attention and still looking straight at me. "Are you going to try to make me believe you really do not think you did anything wrong, when in fact, your own Soldier, who is younger and many ranks subordinate to you, knows that you, his leader, was doing something absolutely wrong? In fact, he turns the camera away in order to cover your a—! This ought to rip your leadership heart right out of your chest. To know that your own Soldier, whom you are responsible for leading, is willing to be blindly loyal in order to protect you. He knows all of this is wrong, and you don't? I refuse to believe you really think your actions were founded. This is exactly how small incidents become huge. This is how the Abu Ghraibs of this world happen."

I turned to the platoon sergeant and commended him for tapping the young Soldier on the shoulder and directing him to go back to the scene. I further praised him for having the courage to report this incident to his supervisors above the lieutenant.

I have no doubt he actually considered the impact of doing or not doing so. How difficult it must have been for the platoon sergeant to turn in his *battle buddy*, his boss. After all, they were the leadership team and depended on each other to do what's right and take care of each other.

He chose the harder right over the easier wrong. He led with integrity. Had he not reported this, it would have sent a message to the rest of the Soldiers that what the lieutenant did was acceptable. I reminded everyone in the room that taking care of each other should never turn into blind loyalty and concealing wrong actions to cover someone's butt.

Again, I looked at that lieutenant and said, "Can you imagine how hard it was for your platoon sergeant to have to do this, knowing it would probably destroy your career? Lieutenant, you ought to be ashamed as a leader for the position you placed him in. You have lost your privilege to lead Soldiers. You are relieved of your position as platoon leader. I will make sure you never have the opportunity to lead them again."

The platoon sergeant followed the standards and prevented the incident from spiraling out of control. He displayed incredible courage, because reporting it to his boss's boss could have backfired on him. We have all witnessed situations where people do what is right, only to have their superiors ignore them and take the easier wrong.

I didn't enjoy terminating the lieutenant's career. However, I had a responsibility to do so. He was a toxic leader, and if the situation remained unchecked, the probability of a more catastrophic event was high. If you find yourself enjoying delivering these sorts of consequences, then you are leading from a position of power and control and not integrity. It should be disappointing and disturbing for you to deal with these situations.

Use these situations to ask yourself what you could have done differently as a leader. What preemptive corrective actions could you have taken? You have the responsibility to listen to your gut, take corrective action, and deliver appropriate consequences— use the situation to give credit where credit is due and develop others, so incidents like this aren't perpetuated. You must lead with integrity and set the standard for others to do the same. You could share this event with other leaders to make sure it is not happening in their organizations.

On the other side of the coin, there are people in leadership positions who find these situations too difficult to deal with, so they opt not to deal with them at all. They know, in their gut, they should take action and deliver consequences, but they don't because it's hard and uncomfortable. They avoid the conflict. When they do not correct, they create a new, lower standard. Doing what is right is usually hard, but doing so demonstrates integrity to those you lead and builds trust across your organization.

If leadership were easy, everyone would be doing it. Leadership is a choice. Choose to lead with integrity.

Leadership Principle 2

★ When You and Your Boss Are in Disagreement ★

Prior to my deployment to Iraq, I was required, as were all other commanders, to provide a mission brief to our four-star general, the commander of US Army Europe. The requirement was to outline our combat missions, present the status of our training and certification of our units to perform those missions, and identify potential *war-stoppers*, such as shortages of equipment, weapons, and personnel.

The missions assigned in a combat theater of operations are often different from standard missions at home. Fortunately, excellent systems are in place to effectively transfer mission sets from one command to the next. We are aware of our new missions prior to deploying in order to organize, prepare, train, and certify our units prior to going into full execution within two weeks of hitting the ground in Iraq.

My boss in Germany, a three-star general, was in disagreement with one of the new missions being assigned to my command: to provide a reception, staging, and onward movement capability to all units going from Kuwait to Iraq. During our mission briefing rehearsals in preparation for the four-star briefing, my boss directed me to not include the Kuwait mission in my presentation.

This put me in a very awkward and unique position. On one hand, I had the requirement to brief the four-star general on all of our assigned missions. On the other, I had my immediate boss telling me not to brief my complete mission set, because of his personal disagreement. I tried discussing with him the importance of my giving a full account, but he refused to consider that option. Of note, neither of my bosses in Germany was deploying; I would have new bosses in Iraq.

I suspect my staff and subordinate commanders wondered what I would do, as I personally spent a great deal of time thinking about the best approach. Knowing my boss would be extremely upset if I went against his direction was intimidating. I was quite certain he might hold it against me and perhaps even reflect his displeasure in his performance rating and assessment of me.

I kept thinking to myself, "What is the right thing to do?"

I reminded myself that upon deployment from Germany, I was no longer assigned to the same chain of command. My new chain of command immediately became the Multi-National Corps—Iraq. I had already spent months dedicating the resources, people, time, and energy for making sure we were prepared to perform our mission in Kuwait, even though my boss did not want to hear about it.

I could have easily not briefed my mission, because the four-star general was not deploying with us either. It would have been transparent to him. I believed I risked much more than a possible poor performance report from my boss if I did not have the integrity and courage to do what was right.

The army regulations state, "The commander is responsible for all their unit does and fails to do." It was apparent to me that my responsibility was to brief my complete mission, and I did.

When you withhold the truth, is that lying? You decide. Would you agree withholding the truth is, at minimum, misleading? How often do you find yourself leaving out details to make a situation appear better than it is? If someone who worked for you did so, would your respect for that person increase or decrease? Do you trust the individual more or less?

Leaders must have the intestinal fortitude to do what is right versus what is easy. It would have been easy to be noncontroversial, not create any conflict, and please my boss. In my mind, the right thing to do was what I was asked to do by the four-star—present a full and complete wartime mission.

You must choose the harder right over the easier wrong. You must have integrity. When you leave out one small detail here or there to avoid a confrontation, it will eventually snowball into a situation far more difficult to lead through than the original dilemma.

Leadership Principle 3

Trust Yourself and Others

The essence of genius is spontaneity and instinct. Trust thyself.
~Ralph Waldo Emerson

If you do not tell the truth about yourself, you cannot tell it about other people. ~Virginia Woolf

I define trust as the result of integrity in action. Trust is the bond between others built on integrity and earned through respect.

Leaders nurture, enforce, and create 360 degrees of trust. What do I mean? I mean trusting the people on your right and left (your peers), the people you lead, those who lead you, and yourself.

When you practice 360 degrees of trust, you begin to have a better understanding of knowing when to lead, follow, or get out of the way, and you must be able to do all three. If you firmly believe everyone on the team is value added, then you must trust, respect, and empower the members of your team to do their job.

★ Practicing 360 Degrees of Trust ★

There is probably no place where this is more important than in combat. In combat, you are serving on a team where everyone has a specific duty and technical skill with a common responsibility to destroy the enemy, while at the same time taking care of each other. This is an excellent example of putting your trust and your life in the hands of your teammates. I was never in a firefight on the ground. I do not have the spellbinding, dramatic stories that many of my Soldiers who were on point every day have. I did understand, however, the significance of team and 360 degrees of leadership.

While commanding in Iraq, I traveled across the battlefield in a Black Hawk helicopter. With over twenty thousand people in my command, organized across two hundred units, operating out of fifty-five bases, it was the most prudent means of transportation to maximize my time and visit with as many of my units and leaders as possible.

A small team traveled with me—a senior NCO in charge of my physical security detachment (PSD), a captain who was my aide-de-camp (aide), a senior logistician (a warrant officer or colonel), and sometimes my driver, also an NCO. The top NCO in the command, my command sergeant major, typically navigated his way on the ground with the bulk of the physical security detachment. He would depart ahead of us and be what I referred to as *my eyes and ears on the perimeter.*

We operated this way as a team. We would divide and conquer and then meet with each other at least once a day, comparing insights, observations, and concerns. Working in this manner gave us a much clearer picture of what was happening across all of our units on the battlefield and also provided an immediate backup option no matter where I traveled.

I would sit in the back of the helicopter with my headset on, listening to the pilots as we maneuvered our way from one location to the other across the entire country of Iraq. Often we saw convoys on the ground, and at times we would witness explosions below caused by vehicle-borne improvised explosive devices (VBIEDs).

It was not unusual to fly at night in blackout conditions, with the pilots using their night-vision devices to fly. The first few times it was eerily still as I watched the terrain below me, sometimes seeing the shadow of the Black Hawk on moonlit nights. The heat coming through the open side doors was like having a hot hair dryer constantly blown in your face. My thoughts were all over the map on most of these flights. I wondered how my Soldiers were operating out on the roads, what our Families were doing back home, what might be the next serious incident with which I would have to deal, or how distribution of supplies across the battlefield could be improved. I often looked around the helicopter and took mental snapshots. I was so grateful for the team I was privileged to serve with and lead.

Seated across from me was my physical security NCO, a bulk of a man. When I stood behind him, you could not even see me. He was a great choice by the command sergeant major for leading my PSD. His primary responsibility was to lead a team whose only duty was to make sure the general lived—what a sobering thought and one that caused me great humility. He was a quiet giant who knew his job, and I needed to trust him to do it. He relied upon me to make sound decisions and provide necessary resources, while I relied upon him to have the team trained and ready. Part of my responsibility was to let them execute their duties. This meant I needed to be smart enough to know when to follow his lead. In a firefight, he would be in charge. He was the expert.

Then I'd gaze at the young men or women sitting behind the machine guns. They possessed a sharp focus as they postured themselves, weapons pointed out the side doors, scanning the horizon for movement below and making split-second decisions. Enemy or friendly? Shoot, don't shoot? Kill, don't kill? I knew if the bullets started flying, the 9 mm pistol strapped to my protective gear would be worthless from the helicopter. Our lives depended on the expertise of those gunners. I also needed to trust them do their jobs.

One night as we were flying in blackout operations, navigating our way along the Tigris River, I listened over the headset to the transmissions being communicated to the pilots. They were given the direction to move to the other side of the river due to enemy activity. It seemed to me we were not moving quickly enough to the other side the river, and I had an immediate urge to engage the pilots over the radio. What went through my head was, "What part of move to the other side of the river don't you understand?"

Just as quickly as those thoughts crossed my mind, I put the brakes on my tongue and said nothing over the radio. I recognized I needed to have tactical patience, trust them to do their jobs, and remind myself I am not a pilot and do not know what is required to move our formation of three helicopters.

In the military we are trained to have tactical patience and not rush to failure. I also learned a long time ago that part of trusting others was having the discipline to not say everything that crossed my mind. Did I have the right to say something? Sure, I was the senior person on the helicopter. Just because you have the right to say something, though, does not mean you should!

Sitting next to me on the helicopter was my aide, a junior captain. He, like my previous three aides, was a dedicated and brilliant young officer whose day began long before I showed up to the office and lasted long after I left. He was responsible for orchestrating every mission we flew in Iraq—no small feat. Although junior, he was respected among the most senior of officers, as they often networked with him when I was not immediately available. Most important, my aide kept me grounded. He was connected with what was going on in the lower-level ranks and served as an extra set of eyes and ears, sharing candidly with me the things I might not have otherwise known.

My aides made my life easier, and I always tried to be grateful for their selflessness, dedication, and commitment. I trusted them completely. In return, my goal for them was to have a year of unparalleled leader development. I wanted them to see how the army operated at a higher level and groom them for taking on more responsibility.

I understood the challenges of being an aide. In 1991, I was aide to a three-star general. It was one of the most challenging years in my career. I will never forget what a struggle it was, for the hours were long, expectations high, environment demanding, and learning curve astronomical.

I also never forgot how it felt to be completely trusted, especially by a three-star general—a senior leader in the military, a man with experience beyond what I could imagine and, in my case, a courageous leader who was, to our knowledge, the first three-star general to choose a female aide. Even when questioned by the chief of staff of the army about choosing me, he stood firm with his decision. For me, it was a year of significant growth as a leader, and trust was the epicenter of the experience.

I was careful to never take that trust for granted. I knew it would be quite easy to fall into a trap of thinking I was special or more important than my peers because of my access to the higher-level leaders. I focused on making sure others had the same privilege of access, while simultaneously respecting my boss's time and priorities. It was a delicate balance.

When selecting an aide, the best of the best are recommended by their bosses to interview. No matter whom I selected, I was getting a qualified officer. The interview allowed me a better idea of their personality, comfort level, confidence, chemistry, and desire to have the job. The tone and manner in which they responded to my questions were equally as important as their answers.

★   The Fine Line between Confident and Cocky Is Trust and Understanding   ★

I recently had dinner with my first aide-de-camp. He is a major in the Ranger Regiment. We were reminiscing about our days in Germany when I was a deputy commanding general from 2003 to 2004, and I asked him, "Do you remember your first day as the aide?"

"I'm not sure, ma'am. What exactly are you referring to?"

"Remember when I asked you to come into the office and take a seat, and I asked you if you would like to know why I selected you to be my aide-de-camp out of the five officers interviewed?"

He smiled sheepishly and replied, "Yes, I do."

Here's how the story unfolded. When I asked him that day, he sat right up straight, all proud, and said, "Yes, ma'am, I would like to know why you chose me."

"Because I was impressed with your confidence, and you were very comfortable in your own skin. Now, would you like to know why I almost did *not* choose you to be my aide?"

He lowered his head and hesitated, "Yes, ma'am, I guess so."

"Because you were very confident and comfortable in your own skin!"

I explained to him there is a fine line between being comfortable and confident and being cocky and pretentious. I had witnessed trust being destroyed because leaders became over confident. In this position he would interact with officers much senior, and they would depend on him as a valuable resource for information and for getting inside my head. I reminded him there would be times when senior people would treat him almost as if he were a peer, and it would be easy for that to go to his head. My guidance to him was to remain completely professional and never take advantage of the position of trust being given to him.

That was the first of many leadership discussions between us. My role was to develop, coach, and mentor him, and in some cases learn from him. In the process, we learned to trust each other.

Do you make sure the people who support you understand how you trust them to carry out their responsibilities? Are you willing to invest your time and energy to build trust up, down, and across your organization? It starts with trusting yourself, and then ensuring the people who report to you recognize the level of trust you have, or would like to have, in them as they represent you or your organization.

★ No-Confidence Vote by My Boss—I Had to Trust Myself ★

Have you ever struggled with trusting up? Perhaps there have been times when you have not liked or respected your boss. No organization in the world is exempt from bad bosses or toxic leaders. Although the majority of my bosses in my twenty-seven-year career were phenomenal, and I would have walked over hot coals to follow them, there were a few whom I did not want to emulate.

Yes, I was mentored, as well as *tormentored*, by some of the army's greatest. I learned from all of them—the good, the bad, and the ugly.

From the few who were toxic, I learned how to identify toxicity in those who worked for me, and there were a few of those along the way too. Rarely do we get to choose our bosses. Regardless of whether we like or trust them, we have an obligation to respect their position and be professional. I tried to look at those perplexing experiences as opportunities to lead up.

When there is a lack of trust, there is a greater burden to buffer the people who work for you. You must default to trusting yourself. Lead yourself and lead your team through the challenging environment without undermining the one in charge.

Prior to deploying to Iraq in 2005, while commanding in Germany and preparing my organization for war, I experienced one of the lowest moments in my military career. I had over twenty-four years of service, had worked all over the world and for a variety of bosses, but none compared with the environment in which I found myself. It was toxic and oftentimes demeaning. At first, I found myself questioning my own leadership capability. Then, I realized that attitude was self-destructive, and I needed to lead myself through the situation. I needed to trust myself, my experience, my knowledge, my leadership competency, and I needed to trust the people on my team.

The culminating point came just months before we deployed. My boss, a three-star general, made an unannounced field visit to one of my subordinate units to observe its training and preparation for deployment. When he arrived, members of the unit were already packing up their gear and returning to home station. Their exercise had ended.

To put this in perspective, think about when you go to a concert. The traffic is very orderly to get everyone parked and into the stadium. When the concert is over it is a free-for-all. It is no different when a unit is finished with its training in the field and headed home.

He was furious with what he witnessed and immediately called me on the phone. It was the ugliest phone call I have ever received. He ordered me to his office in Heidelberg. It was the longest ride of my life, and I was nauseous the entire way. My head was spinning. I was certain the conversation in his office would be direct and one-sided, as was his leadership style. I would not be given a chance to respond or explain.

I respected his rank and his experience, but candidly, I did not trust him. I feared him at times, which, unfortunately, I think he enjoyed. His secretary let him know I had arrived and directed me into his office. Although few generals actually *report* to other generals, I chose to be completely by the book, knocked twice on his door, waited to be invited in, walked to his desk, saluted, and reported, "Sir, General Halstead reports as ordered."

"Have a seat over there."

I took my place behind a chair at his conference table but didn't sit. Military protocol is senior people take their seats first. As I waited, he pulled a yellow envelope out of the bottom drawer of his desk. He threw the contents on the conference table, pounded his fist on the packet, and said, "This is what is going to happen to your units in Iraq. I have no confidence in your ability to lead in combat."

I felt as if I was suffocating. Had he really just said what I thought he said?

"If you think that unit is trained and certified, you are wrong. You will retrain and recertify all your battalion headquarters and come back to me with a plan to do so."

My head continued to spin. My thoughts were scrambling to grasp the gravity of the situation. I thought to myself, *We are within months of deploying. Is there enough time? How will I resource this? How do I explain this drastic change of training to my team? Vacations planned before deployment will have to be canceled, and how do I maintain morale on the eve of leaving our Families for a year?*

Justified or not, it was his decision, and any time or energy spent figuring out or defending the fairness of the situation would have been wasted. I needed to focus on resolving the training gap perceived by my boss and making sure my units were fully prepared.

There are times when no matter what you do or say, trust and respect are not received. Even without the trust, you still have the responsibility to be respectful and professional and to follow lawful orders. Remember, in every situation there is something to be learned. In this case, I learned to not treat others the way this leader was treating me and to be watchful for intimidating or threatening leadership styles in those I led.

When I shared this story publicly for the first time at a leadership conference, I began to doubt whether I should have done so. Typical of my routine after speaking, I sat quietly on the plane thinking about my presentation and critiquing myself as I flew from Las Vegas to Dallas. I kept wondering if I should have shared the no-confidence vote story.

As I got off the plane in Dallas, a couple with their child was waiting for me at the gate. They had been on my flight, and we had spoken briefly. As I approached them, the husband stretched out his hand to shake mine and said, "General, thank you for sharing in the seminar the story about your boss who had no confidence in you. I'm a CEO and at our last board meeting one of the directors told me he had no confidence in my ability to run the company. You have given me hope and a plan."

With his comments, I felt reassured that I had, in fact, made the right decision to share that leadership crucible. The most prominent outcome from the incident with my boss was reinforcing the importance of trusting me first. Throughout all the deployment training and preparation, I reminded myself I was the right leader to take this command into combat.

My boss essentially just directed me to fix it or else. He provided no additional resources, he never gave any encouragement, and he never allowed collegial dialogue. He actually discouraged me from approaching him. His philosophy was clear: if you bring something to his level, it means you cannot handle it at your level.

Would I have done it differently if I had this situation with one of my subordinate organizations? Yes. I believe leaders have the responsibility to shape success by providing guidance and resources; adjusting their leadership style and approach based on whom they are leading, developing, and counseling; and building trust across their organization. My boss obviously did not share the same beliefs, or if he did, it wasn't evident in his leadership execution. I will give him credit for being consistent, as he used the same leadership style with everyone.

If success can't be shaped because the leader is incompetent or lacks character, I would remove or relieve the leader, or at minimum, ensure the person does not have the privilege to lead again at a higher level. I would not allow the people or the mission to be in jeopardy. I had to trust myself to make timely, responsive decisions. I relieved and removed numerous leaders from their positions. My first choice was always to attempt to develop them and change undesirable behaviors. When that failed to be effective, I took action.

Do you lead through intimidation, or do you develop and mentor the people who report to you? Do you listen and allow collegial dialogue to determine the most effective steps forward, or do you direct them to fix it or else? Do you support with additional resources in order to own the solution with them, or do you leave them fending for themselves? Do you trust yourself to take the appropriate level of action? Trust is most effective when it is practiced 360 degrees. In the absence of trust in all directions, the mission must still go on. Therefore, trusting yourself is nonnegotiable.

Leadership Principle 4

Attitude: The One Thing in Life You Can Control

We are going to get along, or we are going to get along (remove you).
~Major General "T" Irby, Ret.

Your attitude determines your altitude! ~Chuck Swindoll

I love the subject of attitude. It truly is the one entity in life you actually get to control. When I wake up in the morning and plant my feet on the floor, my first choice for the day is my attitude.

For the most part, I have had a positive attitude and tried to see the glass as half-full versus half-empty. I believe the majority of the time my face should say yes. We all know what it feels like to work with people whose faces say no—typically, not the best work environments. We also know what it feels like to work where everybody else's mood is dictated by, "Is the boss in a good or bad mood today?"

Controlling your attitude is not just applicable at work. Stop and think about what your face and attitude look like at home, when your spouse bounces a check, or your child brings home a failing grade, or the dog chews on your chair. How about at the grocery store, when you pick up your pace to get in the short line for the cashier, but it turns out to be the slowest line. My greatest challenge for controlling my attitude is at the airport, from long lines at security checkpoints to canceled flights.

When someone brings you bad news, do you shoot the messenger? For me to control my responses, I take a deep breath and consciously tell myself to listen first. I make every attempt to respond with an attitude of being a good "bad news" taker. This doesn't equate to ignoring or not dealing with what went wrong. It does translate into keeping your attitude and emotions in check.

Just as leaders must adjust their leadership approach depending on whom they are leading, they must also adjust their attitude depending on the situation they are leading others through. There are also times when I just pause and write down my thoughts so I don't regret my words, especially if they were emotional and inappropriate. Remember, just because you have the right to say something does not mean you should. For over thirty years, I've chosen to write down many thoughts in my leader notebooks instead of speaking them aloud. It usually proved to be the better choice and was always great therapy.

I'm not suggesting you have to be a cheerleader, nor am I suggesting you have to be happy all the time. My point is that you have a choice. I tend to use quite a bit of humor. Each of us would be wise to figure out our strengths and weaknesses when it comes to controlling our attitude and practice getting it right.

★   Getting My Attitude Adjusted in "Beast Barracks"   ★

My first summer at West Point was appropriately called *Beast Barracks*, and indeed, those first two months—July and August of 1977—were a beast. I was eighteen years old and facing the greatest physical and emotional challenge of my young life. I was a pretty popular kid in high school. I liked to talk a lot, goof off, and make people laugh, but those practices came to a screeching halt my first summer at West Point.

I immediately learned that if I did not display the right attitude, the cadre would quickly ensure I made the adjustments! We were taught to have an attitude of *cooperate and graduate* and to appreciate the challenges facing us, because those challenges help build our character. I lost track of how many times, during an attitude adjustment, I bellowed at the top of my lungs, "It builds character, sir!"

West Point was extremely challenging. I was not accustomed to being yelled at and constantly corrected. We called it *hazing* in those days. It was never physically demeaning, but the upperclassmen were going to get your attention. You were on the receiving end of their orders. Life was pretty miserable, especially the first year.

The intent behind the rigor, of course, was to see how much you could handle. One of the tests was to see if you could swallow your words. Would you break down in the process, or would you be tough? The goal was to toughen us up. Although not fun, it was necessary. After all, West Point graduates become commissioned officers responsible for leading men and women in combat.

Tough love is required. You have to love your Soldiers, but you have to be disciplined, demanding, and by the book, with no shortcuts. Why? When you lead in combat, all Soldiers must understand their job, role, responsibility, and their task and purpose. They must also comprehend right from wrong. There is little room for error.

During Beast Barracks, we were allowed four responses when spoken to:

"Yes, sir."

"No, sir."

"No excuse, sir."

"Sir, I do not understand."

It was a full-time endeavor to keep my attitude in check, and I was constantly reminding myself it was all part of the tradition and discipline of the academy. There is great value in knowing when to speak and when not to speak, what to say and not say, and how to speak, using tones and gestures. Even today I am constantly adjusting my attitude.

★   Your Attitude Determines Your Altitude!   ★

When people see you, what do they think? When they look at your face, does your face say yes? Or does your face say don't bother me, get out of my way, or who do you think you are?

Often I have thought my face said yes, just to find out I was actually being perceived as intense, overconfident, frustrated, and even defensive. Sometimes it took holding my face, going to the mirror, and taking a double check of what others were seeing. I did not always like what I saw reflecting back.

One day an officer from my personal staff walked into my office and said, "Ma'am, may I tell you something?"

"Sure, what's on your mind?"

"Well, ma'am, I don't know if you realize it or not, but, when you start to get irritated in staff meetings, you start to puff air in your cheek."

"Yeah, right, you are kidding me."

"No, ma'am, really you do. I can always tell you are getting frustrated with us, because you puff air in your cheek. I thought you might want to know, especially since you're always talking about the importance of your face saying yes."

I passed it off. I didn't really believe him. Then, shortly after our conversation, we were in a meeting, and sure enough, I was starting to get irritated and caught myself puffing air into my cheek. I looked across the conference table at him and broke out laughing.

Unfortunately, there are many whose faces do not say yes. I have worked for some of those people. The *I'm large and in charge* kind of bosses. I have also had subordinates who worked for me who were the same—subordinates with poor attitudes are some of the greatest challenges for a leader.

It's always wonderful, and much more fun, when you work with people you like. Being liked, however, is not a requirement. It's the ideal situation, but it is hardly realistic that in any organization everybody will like you. We don't all see eye to eye, but disagreement does not have to equal disrespect. The leader must monitor the environment to make sure things don't get out of control or that toxic leaders emerge.

I've faced many challenging situations. In all cases, how I controlled my attitude determined my altitude. Some of the most difficult times for me as a leader were those involving subordinates who were borderline disrespectful toward me. In some cases they clearly just did not like me.

A few circumstances involved subordinates simply missing their old bosses (the leaders I had replaced) and constantly showing it with sarcastic comments and poor attitudes toward any change I initiated. On several occasions, the burr under the saddle was an issue of age and years of experience. A few people who worked for me had difficulty accepting that I was in charge, because I was either the same age or younger or had the same number of years in the army, or in many cases fewer. I forced myself to confront the conflicts and deal with the attitudes. I didn't let them bring me down to their altitude.

★ Having a Can-Do Attitude ★

Staying positive isn't always easy. Like others, my life has had its highs and lows, and I haven't always pulled myself up by my bootstraps. Thank goodness for others who were there for me.

When my coach was killed in high school, teachers embraced and encouraged me to keep looking up and forward. When I struggled through three major surgeries in my twenties and was told my military career was over, friends and Family supported me through recoveries and helped me have an attitude of *I can beat this*. When I faced divorce, my parents unconditionally loved me through it. When I was diagnosed with chronic fibromyalgia and had to make the tough decision to retire from my military career, many people requested that I tell my story. Even with all the external support and encouragement, there was still a requirement for me to choose the right attitude and lead myself through the challenge.

Success is a change of attitude from *I can't* to *I can!* Much of success is really having the right attitude. Unfortunately, in any given day, the *I can't* probably happens more often than you realize: "I can't stand this. I can't do this. I can't understand why."

Sometimes it seems as if all we hear is our boss telling us we aren't prepared to do something or a spouse or parent telling us, "You can't do anything right. You're never going to be worth anything." What happens is the wrong message gets ingrained in our heads. We actually begin to believe limitations that don't exist. Without realizing it, *I can't* gets inside our heads and hearts and becomes part of who we are.

Start turning the negative phrases in your mind into positive. Become the positive person who says, "I don't know how to do this right now, but I'm going to learn." I had to take on this frame of mind as I created this book. People would ask me how my book was going, and I would respond with, "Good, I *hope* to have it completed by the end of the year." One year grew into three. I should have been saying, "Good. I will have it completed this year and have it in your hands to read!"

For the next twenty-four hours, stop yourself every time you say or think the words *I can't*. Stop yourself and say, "No, I have a new attitude, and the new attitude is *I can!*"

You might have to practice. You might have to read a book or go to a class to get educated. It may take you longer, it may be harder for you than somebody else, but if you want to achieve it, you can. It's all about attitude. It's having what we in the military call *a can-do attitude*. Give yourself an attitude adjustment and then move out with your can-do attitude.

Remember to be able to laugh at yourself. You must take your job seriously but yourself less so. You must allow people to come to you and say, "Can I share something with you, boss?" You create the environment around you. How are you doing with your open attitude? Does your face say, "Yes, can do!"?

Leadership Principle 5
Have Tenacity: Don't Quit

It is better to have tried, and failed, than to have failed to try. ~Unknown

When the going gets tough, the tough get going. ~Popular Proverb

Instead of praying for the storm to go away, start praying to get through the storm. ~Chaplain, Iraq

How many times have you wanted to quit? I would not be able to count the number of times I have. My journal, when I first began at West Point in July of 1977, was a little three-inch spiral pad, small enough to stuff in my hat or slide down the inside of my black knee socks. My first three days are logged on one tiny page, and the main thrust of my thoughts was about wanting to quit.

What kept me going? I think there were many combinations of reasons why I didn't quit: not wanting to let people down; not wanting to be perceived as weak; desiring to test and find my own limits; being stubborn, determined, and disciplined; and maybe a touch of spirited competition. What keeps you going?

I was raised on a strong dose of discipline, which was reinforced ten times over in the military, and this played a huge role in my tenacity. It was extremely important for me to live up to other people's expectations, especially my parents'. Our parents taught us *two life rules*:

> ➤ *Rule #1—Don't quit.*
> ➤ *Rule #2—Refer back to rule #1.*

I also considered quitting as failing. None of us wake up in the morning planning to be a failure, but many of us take the easy way out by quitting. I understand the need to make adjustments in our life along the way; that's not what I am talking about. I am talking about choosing to quit and taking the short-term, quick, easy way out when things get tough.

My parents used to say, "When the going gets tough, the tough get going." When I signed up to play a sport, they bought me the gear I needed, and there was no coming home complaining that practice was too hard and that I was quitting. Quitting was not an option. You did not have to play the next season, but you finished what you started. Whether we played an instrument in the band, participated in a sport, or went to college, we were expected to at least try. It was better to have tried and failed than to have failed to try.

★ Our Obstacles Are Opportunities—Don't Quit ★

My parents were a great source of encouragement, energy, and enthusiasm as their children became involved in all kinds of activities, including chores, sports, and church. Their examples shaped my character, drive and determination, and future. The value system they instilled in me gave me the courage to pursue a rather nontraditional path for a young woman, although it did not start out as my goal in life.

You see, as I entered my high school years, I knew I was destined to be a coach and a physical education teacher. That was my personal dream. I played varsity sports all through high school, and what I lacked in height, I made up for with hustle. In the '70s, women's sports were not supported at the level they are today, but I was always assured of at least one faithful fan in the stands: my mother. I lived in the gym.

Then, in 1976 my mother read in our local newspaper about the military academies being open to women. "Look at this. They are letting women go to the military academies! I think this sounds just like you."

I looked around the room, and the only *you* in the room was me. After learning more about the academies and having many discussions about the future with my mother, I agreed to pursue it, but I felt certain my dream to be a coach was still on the table. My SATs weren't the strongest. I was not at the top of my class. If I had had to guess, I would have bet I would not be selected.

Applying to the military academies required letters of recommendation to be written on my behalf. I asked a variety of people to do so—my pastor, high school counselor, math teacher, youth group leader, and coach, who of all of them was the most influential person in my life.

On April 18, 1976, in the spring of my junior year, tragedy struck when my coach was killed in a sport parachuting accident. I was devastated. I withdrew. I was interested in nothing. I wanted to quit everything. This was in the midst of my application process for West Point, and I was scheduled to interview with my senator. My parents and my teachers convinced me to attend the interview.

The senator noted where I was from and asked me if it was my coach who was killed. He could tell by the difficulty of my affirmative reply I was deeply affected by her death. What he did after our conversation influenced my life forever. He asked his secretary to copy my entire application packet and mail it to me.

When I read my coach's letter of recommendation, written just twelve days before her death, there was a pivotal change in my view of the future. She had written of my enthusiasm, dedication, discipline, and trustworthiness. Her words were alive—they invigorated me, helped me pick myself back up, and made me realize that she believed in me. To quit was to let her down.

I had no idea at the age of seventeen how powerful that moment would be, but her posthumous encouragement kept me going during times in my life when I was discouraged and, even more important, gave me the courage to share with others and help others not to quit during their low points. In the spring of my senior year, on March 25, 1977, the day before my eighteenth birthday, I received my acceptance letter from West Point. I was going to be a member of the second class of women. The emotional range I experienced was off the charts. I was shocked. I was excited. I was scared.

The highest point in my life was my last day at home before leaving for West Point, New York. My town, the little country town with no traffic lights, seemed genuinely excited for me. We had never had an alumni graduate from West Point.

The worst day of my life was about twenty-four hours later—my first day at West Point.

★   You Can't Quit Before You Even Start!   ★

It was July 1977, just days after I graduated from high school. There was no time for a summer vacation. We arrived at West

Point the night before my first official day as a new cadet. I stayed in the dormitory side of the Hotel Thayer with other new arrivals while my parents stayed in a regular room on the other side of the hotel. I'd received numerous packages of materials about West Point and tips for preparing. They made it perfectly clear the first day was going to be the worst day of my life and encouraged a good night's rest.

I dutifully went to the dorm room early with the intent of getting the recommended good night's rest. Unfortunately, the three gals with whom I shared a room were more interested in talking and goofing off. One gal was talking politics, another of her desire to be an astronaut, and the third seemed mostly interested in partying. I felt totally out of my element. As I lay awake, petrified of what my first day would be like, I was frustrated with my future classmates—so much so, I decided I was leaving in the morning.

I went to my parents' room, knocked on the door, and said, "Let's go. I'm not staying."

My mom was perplexed. "What do you mean, not staying?"

I explained my night to her and how I felt: if those girls were an indication of "the cream of the crop," then it must be a different crop than where I was from. Once mom could see I was serious, she sprung into the coach role in which she is so gifted, sometimes much to our chagrin.

"Let's just get in the car and drive around and then see how you feel. You cannot quit before you've even started." I agreed quickly to appease her and minimize the discussion, because I was sure nothing I would hear or see was going to change this kid's mind.

Mom kept reinforcing, "You can't quit before you even start. Just give it an honest try." She was right. She always seemed to be right.

We lined up with the other Families, luggage in hand, and climbed onto buses that took us to a massive field house. We dragged our bags off the bus, made our way inside, and clumsily climbed onto the bleachers to await directions. It was the first of many "hurry up and wait" moments I would experience in the military.

They called us *New Cadets,* which meant we were the newest people to arrive at the school. It also meant we did not yet have the privilege of being considered part of the Corps of Cadets. We were quickly informed that New Cadets were considered lower than whale feces. I can't think of anything much lower. We were going to have to earn our status over the summer in Beast Barracks.

The introductory remarks were "blah, blah, blah" to me, until it was announced, "New Cadets, look to your right. Look to your left. Remember this, three out of four of you, four years from now, will no longer be here." It was not said as a threat; it was said as a promise.

Disheartened, I immediately started thinking, *Will it be me who fails? How long will it take?* I didn't know the answers to my questions, but I did know I wasn't going to quit. They would have to throw me out.

At the end of my first phase of Beast Barracks, I was rated ten out of ten in the squad. My squad leader was working hard to run me out. It was a horrible feeling. I had entered with the second class of women, but the sound of two hundred years of perfectly good tradition being broken could still be heard.

Admittedly, I struggled with some of the training. At 5 feet 1½ inches, drill and ceremony with an M1—a forty-three-inch, ten-pound rifle—was no easy task. I practiced endlessly in my barracks room to be ready for inspections. I grew up shooting gray squirrels and woodchucks with my brother. So, qualifying with my smaller M16 rifle on the firing range was no big deal, as long as I wasn't in a foxhole over five feet deep.

Over the next four years, there were many difficult challenges that made me consider quitting—academics and the strict discipline high among them. Several scenarios ran through my head: I would quit, attend a normal college, be with my friends, enjoy freedom, and leave West Point in my rearview mirror. As I would play through those pleasant visions, there was another voice in my head telling me I would regret quitting—for the rest of my life.

I eventually learned to tune out most of the negative, ignore those telling me I couldn't do something or that I was worthless, and surrounded myself with those who believed in me and engaged in healthy activities, like chapel. I had the most incredible sponsors who invited my roommates and me to their homes for dinner, football games, and just a bit of normalcy. Even with those outlets, I had to dig deep, gut it out, stay determined, and not quit.

This *stick-to-itiveness* probably made the difference between my graduating or not graduating. When I think of some of the reasons I wanted to quit along the way, words such as *too hard, inconvenient, you can't, you aren't good enough, you're a girl, I'm tired, I'm not ready* come to mind. In hindsight, those seem like weak reasons, but at the time they seemed quite rational.

If I had quit every time I wanted to, I would not have had the opportunities to help others that I have today. Not quitting opened doors to incredible adventures, valuable experiences, rich relationships, and rewarding moments of learning. Would I want to relive my West Point experience? No, I wouldn't, but no one can ever take away the fact that I successfully stuck it out and graduated. Remember the three women I shared a hotel room with the night before I started West Point? For a variety of reasons they didn't graduate, lending truth to the introductory prediction of "three out of four of you will be gone."

Each of us knows there's a difference between quitting when life gets tough and making an adjustment to your journey. Adjustments are necessary as we progress through life's experiences. We learn more about ourselves, we have different resources available to us, our knowledge increases, our position or opinions change, and so making adjustments in our life is not only OK, it is necessary.

I'm sure you can identify times in your life when you were tired, lonely, anxious, scared, or discouraged and wanted to quit. Reflect on the difference quitting or not quitting made in your life. Are there decisions with which you're struggling now? Will not quitting provide you with more opportunities or a better outcome? Minimize your regrets and resolve not to give up.

Leadership Principle 6

Commit Yourself Daily to Be the Best You Can Be

When we do the best that we can, we never know what miracle is wrought in our life, or the life of another. ~Helen Keller

Unless commitment is made, there are only promises and hopes...but no plans. ~Peter Drucker

Being better, being the best, going for the gold take commitment. Being good requires minimal effort. Your best requires engaging both your mind and heart.

I believe our commitment, like our convictions, grows stronger over time as we experience different types of relationships, advanced education, and successes and failures. This became evident to me as my positions of responsibility within the military increased.

As the distance between those I led and myself became greater, both in terms of rank and years of experience, I found myself speaking to my Soldiers about discipline and commitment. I encouraged them to serve honorably, and at a minimum, be committed to fulfill their enlistment contract or service obligation. I discovered that I was expecting their level of commitment to be aligned with mine, and it struck me that my expectations were unrealistic. Rather, what I needed to ensure was that my example of commitment was one they aspired to have themselves.

★   Commitment Manifests Itself in Your Preparation   ★

In my midthirties, with twelve years in the army, I was select-ed to serve with the famous 101st Airborne Air Assault Division at Fort Campbell, Kentucky. I was ecstatic about the assignment. Several of my friends, however, thought I was crazy.

"Becky, you are not air assault qualified. Do you know how physically demanding the air assault school is?"

From my cadet days, I was familiar with the requirements of airborne and air assault schools. I knew it would be extremely tough, but I also knew success would be worth the effort.

Air assault operations began during the Vietnam War with the use of helicopters to move people and supplies around the battlefield and take the fight to the enemy. The main purpose of the ten-day school was to train us on the missions performed by rotary wing aircraft, principles and techniques of combat as-saults, rappelling techniques, and sling-load operations. I would learn how to be a better logistician and leader, and yes, be pushed to my physical limits.

When I joined my new unit the summer of 1993, all I heard was how many people get kicked out of air assault school on the first day, called *Zero Day*. Zero Day consisted of a challenging obstacle course. The names of the obstacles alone would make your palms sweat: the belly over, the confidence climb, the tough one. If you didn't make the grade on Zero Day, you were auto-matically out.

As I heard horror stories of failures, I decided to find short Soldiers with the air assault badge on their uniform and convince one or two of them to take me to the course and show me how to negotiate the obstacles. Not only was the course tough but being short was also a huge disadvantage. I had to compensate by learning some innovative tricks. Preparation and making the commitment to pass would be my keys to success.

As I successfully maneuvered my way through Zero Day, I was glad I'd spent the extra time and energy getting ready. I learned it wasn't all about size and strength; it was also about how I used the talents I had to successfully get through the obstacles.

Are you proactively preparing and committing yourself to confront the tougher challenges you may face, or are you giving it less than your best and settling for whatever happens?

★   Committing Myself to Achieve My Personal Best   ★

Another memorable air assault experience came on the last day of the school—the twelve-mile foot march. I clearly remember the sign outside the bank as I was driving to the base at 0400 hours. The temperature ironically read *101* degrees. For a flash I thought it was kind of neat, since I was completing the school at the *101*st Airborne Air Assault Division. Of course it wasn't neat for long, as I realized I would be completing my twelve-mile foot march in extreme heat.

Walk, run, jog—however you do it—you have three hours to complete twelve miles with your full rucksack, M-16 rifle, marching uphill, downhill, and through woods on rough trails. It was an individual event. You were allowed battle buddies to walk with you, but they were not authorized to assist you in any way. Two officers from my unit, who had encouraged me every day, walked with me for moral support.

So off we started on the twelve-mile foot march in the brutal August heat. At about the nine-mile mark, a giant of a Soldier ran past me. And then the next thing I knew, I passed him. This happened because he would run by me, then stop and walk. Whereas I kept a consistent pace, a jog called the airborne shuffle—never walking but never really running either.

About the third time he passed me, he yelled on his way by, "Ma'am, you're killing me!"

I said, "Killing you? This has nothing to do with you. I'm just trying to finish."

He replied, "If you beat me across the finish line, my Ranger buddies will never let me live it down."

You see, as a Ranger, he was a member of an all-male organization, considered one of our elite units due to the extremely demanding physical training they must complete. The thought of me, a little 5-feet, 1½-inch female, beating him was more than he could handle.

I knew the only way I would beat him across the finish line was if he passed out or took a wrong turn. There was just no way it was going to happen. He had already completed Ranger school, and I was fully aware he had the physical ability to beat me. The question was this: Did he have the discipline and desire to do so? He had expected to be able, and I am sure had intended, to go slower. My pushing him seemed to irritate him.

We passed each other several more times. Candidly, I had a little fun knowing I was pushing him. If he wanted to beat me, he would have to earn it. When we crossed the finish line, he was first and I was second. I was more than satisfied with second place. Why? It was my *PB*—my personal best time—for a twelve-mile foot march.

I don't know if it was his best time for a twelve-mile foot march, but I do know this: he ran it much faster than he had intended on running it that day!

My first point is this: you are accountable for your attitude and your actions. Your goal should be to accomplish your personal best. Set your own record. Set your own pace, and then beat yourself. It doesn't mean you're always going to finish in first place, and that is all right. But the reality is you need to work every day to be the best you can be.

Secondly, if we had not been pushing each other, I know without a doubt I would not have achieved the time I did nor would he. So ask yourself: How are you pushing others to achieve their best? Iron sharpens iron. How are you sharpening others? Are you committed to high standards and a positive, can-do attitude? It's never too late to make that commitment.

Over the years, one method I have found to be helpful in committing myself to be the best I can be is to frame my plan with *I'm going to* instead of *I wish I could*. For example, if you want to run a six-minute mile, instead of saying "I wish I could run a six-minute mile," try saying, "I'm going to train so I will achieve my goal of running a six-minute mile." The way you state your goals to yourself reflects what you believe in your heart you are able to achieve and, ultimately, what you commit yourself to achieve.

When you frame your words as *I hope to, I wish to, I want to, I think I might*, you just kick the can of possibility and achievement down the road. When you frame it *I am going to, I am doing*, you actually visualize your goal as it will happen. Framing your goals as you believe you will achieve them ignites the energy, passion, and commitment to get them accomplished. You create and shape the standard, not just wish for it. State it, believe it, and make it happen.

★   Ground Yourself Every Day   ★

Grounding yourself is about committing intentionally to be the best you can be. This keeps you centered and focused. I would encourage you to create a daily affirmation and commit yourself to it every single day.

While serving in the military, I had a daily ritual during which I used to remind myself of my purpose and commitment. Each morning I would stand in front of the mirror and look myself straight in the eye and commit to being the best person, Soldier, leader, and American I could be. I firmly believed, and still do, if I could not look myself in the eye, then I could not look into the eyes of the people I led. Commitment starts with me. I must be able to trust and believe in the person in the mirror.

Then, before putting my dog tags over my head, I would recite the *Warrior Ethos:*

> *I will always place the mission first.*
> *I will never accept defeat.*
> *I will never quit.*
> *I will never leave a fallen comrade.*

Right next to my dog tags was what I called my shield of faith. I would grasp the shield in my hand and simply quote the Bible verse etched on the backside, Joshua 1:9:

Be strong, be courageous,
don't be terrified,
and don't be discouraged,
for the Lord thy God is with you wherever you go.

This daily ritual of commitment was a way of keeping grounded and focused on being my best. Nowhere was this more important than during my year in combat. While I was not terrified in Iraq, the emotion I had to fight most was discouragement—when people made poor decisions, when Soldiers died, when I found myself exhausted. Committing daily kept me from letting the discouragement take over and kept me attentive to carrying out the duties of my command.

Since retiring, I have a different but similar ritual. Before I left the army, I had engraved on both sides of multiple dog tags the names, ranks, and dates of all the Soldiers killed during my command in Iraq. I carry those dog tags with me wherever I go. Not only does looking at those names keep me grounded, but it also reminds me to continue to honor the last line of the warrior ethos: *never leave a fallen comrade.* The meaning this line carries for me is *always remember.* Always remember to honor the sacrifice of my fellow Soldiers. I owe it to them and to their Families to live each day in their honor and memory. I do so by sharing their stories when I speak and write.

Are you grounding yourself daily in some way? Find something meaningful for you, and commit yourself to it every day.

Leadership Principle 7

Be Authentic: Stay Real and Be Humble

Waste no more time arguing what a good person should be; be one.
~Marcus Aurelius

Take your job seriously, yourself less so. ~General Tom Hill, Ret.

Values do not lie. ~Unknown

The three questions people ask me most frequently are 1) Where are you from? 2) Should I call you by your rank or name? and 3) What did you do in the army?

I used to answer the first question by saying I was from Candor, because it is where I went to school. Then one day my mother said, "You are not from Candor. You are from Willseyville. We have a zip code." I chuckled about my mom being so adamant. She was right. We do have a zip code—but all we have is a post office. Neither Candor nor Willseyville have traffic lights, so my quip of telling people *I am just a country girl from a town with no traffic lights* remained valid.

When people ask me the second question, I simply tell them, "Do what makes you comfortable. I came into this world Becky, and I am leaving it as Becky."

It is important to stay real and just be yourself. When we get caught up in trying to be something we aren't, it doesn't work. I completely disagree with the statement, "Fake it until you make it." There is nothing more uncomfortable and personally destructive.

There is a huge difference between trying to figure out how you fit in and not being yourself in order to fit in. When we are comfortable in our own skin and in touch with our inner self and who we are, life is so much more enjoyable. Your authenticity will shine through, and when you are more comfortable, the people around you will be more comfortable.

To remain authentic, I think you must never forget where you started, and you must accept where you are today is a result of others helping you along the way.

When people find out I am retired, they ask me from what profession. I tell them I was a Soldier in the United States Army. Occasionally, when I have done this in the presence of someone who knows me, they jump in and clarify with, "She was a general in the US Army." I understand why they do so, as many consider achieving general officer quite a feat. However, my response to their comment is, "A Soldier is *who* I was, and general is *what* I achieved; soldiering is a matter of the heart, and general is a rank."

Stop and reflect about where you started. When I think about Candor or Willseyville, I smile at the thought of my Family, our old 1830s house, raising animals and growing gardens, lifelong friends, hard work, Family vacations, great teachers, close-knit community, and a wonderful church.

Remembering where I came from has kept me grounded. There is a tendency for some leaders, as they gain responsibility, success, and status, to get consumed with the glory, power, and control. This is dangerous territory, because they are allowing their focus to switch from those they lead to themselves.

To stay grounded, I kept a photo of myself as a young officer in a location where only I could see it. In the picture I am a twenty-two-year-old, brand-new second lieutenant in my dress green uniform, right out of West Point and basic training. It was a horrible photo. My hair was too long, my name tag was crooked, and my trousers looked wrinkled. It embarrassed me, but it also reminded me to never forget my modest beginnings. The photo prompted me to give credit to the people who entered my life and helped polish, groom, shape, coach, and mentor me. It also reinforced for me the importance of years of training, education, and diverse experiences, which developed my competence, confidence, and firm commitment to serve and lead.

Likewise, not only was the reflection on my own life important, but the photo also cautioned me to be slow to judge others and be vigilant in my role for developing leaders. To do so, I had to remain humble, authentic, approachable, and an example for others.

★   Teaching Sunday School to Four-Year-Olds   ★

Part of being authentic and staying real is not losing touch with your priorities in life, remembering what you are passionate about, and being willing to invest yourself in others. Volunteering your precious, limited time and energy may be one of the most effective ways of doing so. Yes, I used the *volunteer* word.

Are you investing in others, or are you too busy, too important? Let me assure you, if you want to stay real, volunteer in an area you are passionate about but uncomfortable with, and your life will be changed.

Ironically, when you first join the army, you are told never volunteer for anything. You would be asked if you would like to do something in a manner you thought was going to give you a little extra advantage or privilege. In reality, you were just going to be put to work. So it was drilled into us to sit on our hands and not volunteer.

Over the years, it became important for me to give of my time to others. I had been raised with the principle of tithing, and it was instilled in us that we should give back a portion of our income to the church to help others. The same concept is applicable to our time: giving our precious time to help others. I call it *heart work*. The higher we go in responsibility and status, the more important it becomes to give of our time, even though it is harder to find the time.

The tithing of money came much easier to me than the tithing of time. First of all, who has enough time? Let alone to give some of it up freely? Our minds quickly rationalize we barely have time to do the things we must do, so how could we possibly have time to volunteer? Or, perhaps, an attitude of *I'm too important* to volunteer creeps in.

I had to ask myself, "What is important to me? What are the priorities in my life?" If service to others, helping others, using my talents for others is important, then I must incorporate volunteer activities into my life.

When I was in Hawaii as a battalion commander, a lieutenant colonel in my late thirties, I was reminded there is more to life than work.

I was sitting in chapel one Sunday next to one of my best friends and her Family. The chaplain was expressing to the congregation they needed volunteers to teach Sunday school. I have gone to Sunday school most of my life, but I would not exactly say I was comfortable teaching Sunday school.

My friend leaned into to me and asked, "Becky, what do you think? Should we teach Sunday school together?"

"I don't know. I guess I'm willing to try it if you are."

My friend had two children. At the time their ages were four and seven. Her husband was a major in the army, and we had been friends for many years. She whispered to me, "What age do you think we should teach?"

My analytical mind went into play quickly. I did not want to teach older kids because they might ask questions I could not answer! I said, "How about four-year-olds?" I figured we could teach a class with her son in it, and I doubted four-year-olds would be very challenging.

She said, "Great! Let's do this!"

For the next year we taught together, and I often refer to our experience as the hardest hour of my week! My life was touched and my humor exhausted, and I was humbled more than once.

My favorite memory was sitting on the floor with all the kids, everyone being quite rowdy, and one little girl sitting on my lap and asking, "Miss Becky, where is God?"

I paused to collect my thoughts and prepare a profound, theological answer. All of a sudden, one of the other children could not wait for my answer any longer and blurted out, "Miss Becky, God is *everywhere*!" Oh, my goodness, talk about being humbled. Staying *real* is not for wimps!

Although I was humbled more than once, I also knew we were serving as examples to other adults by our willingness to do the heart work. I remember one set of parents picking up their child, and they were shocked to see a battalion commander sitting on the floor and teaching children.

Leaders must stay real, and few ways are better than volunteering. Volunteering where you are less comfortable is even more rewarding. When you step out of your comfort zone, you grow as a leader. When you volunteer, you most likely think you are giving, but what you will discover is you receive ten times more than you give.

Ironically, what happens is that instead of less time, you now have more energy, and you accomplish much more in the time you have. It is quite rewarding.

How do you stay real, authentic, and humble?

★   Be Yourself   ★

Staying real and being yourself requires self-assessment, reflection, and living by your core set of values. First, you must identify your values.

If I asked you to write down the five values most important to you, could you do it? Take a minute and try. My top five values are: discipline, faith, grace, integrity, and service.

Now, pause again, reflect on your values, and think about your behaviors, decisions, relationships, and daily activities—do those align with your values? You see, this is very important, because if your actions aren't aligned with your values, something has to change.

For instance, if you say a value, such as integrity, is important and yet you lie to your spouse, cheat at work, or hold back the truth and ignore mistakes, then you are not practicing integrity. You have two choices: change your behavior or pick a different value. When your behaviors don't match your values, then they are not your values! Why is this so important? Your values establish the foundation for your standards. Without values, you cannot be a standard setter.

People are always watching us, especially when we are in leadership positions. The behaviors we exhibit send messages to others. Your behaviors either demonstrate, or fail to demonstrate, your values to others. What messages are your behaviors sending?

When I was a newly commissioned lieutenant, I had to have all my wisdom teeth extracted at Walter Reed Army Hospital before going to my first assignment in Italy. I was dressed in civilian clothes for the surgery. My dentist was an army colonel and old enough to be my father. He said to me, "I understand you are going to Italy."

"Yes, sir."

"Great. Where will your father be assigned?" he asked.

I gracefully replied, "Sir, my father is not in the army. I am. I'm a lieutenant."

He was shocked to find out I was an officer. He made a judgment and presumed I could not possibly be old enough to be in the army.

Our behaviors and our responses reflect our values.

Almost twenty-five years later, just prior to our deployment from Germany to Iraq, I invited the Families of my staff over to my home for a large Oktoberfest celebration. I wanted to embrace and assure them we were ready to go to war and that we would take care of each other.

As the night drew to a close, I said good night to each Family as they departed my home.

One wife wanted her son to meet me before leaving. She yelled, "Son, come meet the CG" (short for commanding general).

He looked up at me, then looked at his mother and with shock responded, "Daddy's boss is a girl?"

His mother was mortified. I wrapped my arm around her shoulder and laughed. A mentor of mine once told me, "Take your job seriously, yourself less so." Stay real! It helps to have a sense of humor. The innocence made the moment a memory and allowed my authenticity to reassure the mother there was no problem.

Leadership Principle 8

Be Disciplined

Discipline...If you can't get them to salute when they should salute and wear the clothes you tell them to wear, how are you going to get them to die for their country? ~General George S. Patton Jr.

Commanders are responsible for the good order and discipline of their units. ~Army Regulations

In Leadership Principle 2, I mentioned integrity was identified on leadership surveys as the number one trait people desired in their leader. While I don't disagree that integrity must be a top leadership trait, I have to wonder if discipline was an option on the surveys. I am not sure why the subject of discipline is rarely included in conversations on leadership. For me, discipline has proved to be the most important leadership trait I practice. Why?

When I practice discipline in my life, everything else starts to fall into place. I make better choices. I respond more appropriately when I am bombarded by events out of my control. It takes discipline for me to stay healthy, respect and care for others, prioritize my time, preserve my character, and maintain my integrity. Discipline is a leadership principle woven into each story in this book.

I was raised in a disciplined but loving home. There were expectations for getting good grades, participation in sports, respecting your elders, doing your chores, and always telling the truth.

At West Point that foundation of discipline continued as an absolute expectation of cadets. Being a cadet was much more than just following rules and regulations—it was about developing character and respect. Our honor code, "I will not lie, cheat or steal, nor tolerate those who do," required us to embrace self-discipline, especially when it came to "nor tolerate those who do."

Discipline touched every aspect of our lives—physical, mental, spiritual, and emotional. We were taught discipline in preparation to be officers who were trustworthy, dependable, selfless, and, most important, capable of leading America's sons and daughters.

Of course, in the civilian world, your goal isn't to literally inspire your employees to die for the company, but you do want to inspire loyalty, a willingness to show up for work, and a commitment to engage fully in their jobs every day.

After twenty-seven years of leading Soldiers, I've concluded that self-discipline is a leader's most important attribute. When a leader gets discipline right, other attributes—integrity, honor, loyalty, selfless service, duty, humility—more easily follow. Discipline defines your character and determines your destiny.

★ Discipline Determines Your Destiny ★

Discipline provides the foundation for the difference between being a good or a great cadet (student), Soldier (employee), officer (supervisor), and human being. At the organizational level, discipline translates to the difference between a good versus a great team, school, business, etc.

Discipline provides the basis for your daily commitment to lead yourself to be the best you can be. When changes happen in your life, you must use discipline to respond appropriately to the shift. When you begin to feel your blood pressure rise, discipline allows you to control your attitude. When you feel like procrastinating on a project, discipline prods you to action and keeps you focused. Discipline allows you to make time for someone else, even when your own time seems so limited.

During our first summer at West Point, we were required to memorize an incredible amount of data, history, facts, and quotes. One of the toughest pieces for me to memorize, but the one which made the most lasting impression upon me, was Major General (Retired) John M. Schofield's definition of leadership:

The discipline which makes the Soldiers of a free country reliable in battle is not to be gained by harsh or tyrannical treatment. On the contrary, such treatment is far more likely to destroy than to make an army. It is possible to impart instructions and to give commands in such a manner and in such a tone of voice as to inspire in the Soldier no feeling but an intense desire to obey, while the opposite manner and tone of voice cannot fail to excite strong resentment and a desire to disobey. The one mode or other of dealing with subordinates springs from a corresponding spirit in the breast of the commander. He who feels the respect which is due others cannot fail to inspire in them regard for himself; while he who feels, and hence manifests, disrespect toward others, especially his inferiors, cannot fail to inspire hatred against himself.

What this definition means to me is that when you are part of an organization that is both disciplined and respectful, the environment will be demanding yet manifest trust and cooperation among its members.

On the flip side, if an organization is disciplined but *lacks* respect and professionalism, a demeaning, controlling, and toxic environment is created. Any organization, to include the military, can harbor pockets of demeaning discipline that destroys good order and trust.

At West Point there was a rule or regulation for everything—from how to place your toothbrush in the medicine cabinet, arrange your clothes in the closet and drawers (folding your socks with smiles), to displaying your textbooks from tallest to shortest on your bookshelves. You were expected to abide by the rules, even when no one was watching—although there was rarely a time you were not being observed.

Rooms were inspected every day, even Saturdays and Sundays. Everyone had a roommate. One person was the designated room orderly (RO), and this position rotated weekly. If there were any deficiencies during an inspection, the RO was given the demerits. This meant roommates had to be disciplined about working together to make sure the whole room was ready. When there were deficiencies, there was no blaming your roommates, even if they were the ones who were ill-prepared. Thus, our disciplined mentality was to *cooperate and graduate.*

Once, during my week as designated RO, I remember throwing my hands up in disgust and frustration. I raced to morning formation without my roommate, because I didn't want to get in trouble for being late. She had refused to help with preparing the room for inspection and wasn't dressed and ready for first formation. I didn't get in trouble for being late, but abandoning my roommate and not helping her get ready was considered a lack of discipline.

As a result, we were both given extra training and required to report to our upper-class squad leader's room. We were placed in opposite corners and spent an hour reciting quotes and singing songs in stereo. We were being disciplined to "cooperate and graduate."

The demanding environment of West Point over four years shaped my personal discipline, developed my tenacity, and formed my integrity and character. I learned that discipline and working together made my life more orderly, efficient, effective, and productive. I also learned, sometimes the hard way, the consequences of *not* being disciplined in my actions.

★   The Hardest Muscle in the Body to Discipline   ★

Which muscle do you think is the toughest one to discipline? I think it's the tongue.

I have probably ruined more days and hurt more people with reckless words than by any other means. In some cases I did so by *not* having the discipline and courage to say something when I should have. It takes discipline and discernment to refrain from saying everything you are thinking. However, it takes the same to know when to speak your convictions and not allow yourself to succumb to being politically correct.

How can you better control your tongue? First, understand that what you say is actually a reflection of who you really are, your character. What you say springs from your heart and mind. So, if you are not always pleased with what you say or how you say it, then take a step back and assess what was behind the words you chose. Second, understand that just because you have the right to say something doesn't mean you should.

I was interviewed by a journalist and asked my opinion, "What are your thoughts about the people protesting against the war in Iraq?"

"Well, the men and women I serve with, live and die for ensuring that protestors have those rights. However, I firmly believe that just because you have the right to say or do something does not mean you should."

★   Discipline Gives You Second Chances   ★

In the mid-1980s, when I was a lieutenant living in Italy, I became ill and was medically evacuated to the closest major military hospital in Germany. I spent the next three months out of work, recovering from major abdominal surgery.

I was told my career was over, but I refused to accept that verdict. I used the attitude of self-discipline instilled in me to improve my physical condition and return to work. I wanted to show my superiors I was capable of continuing to serve.

Within a year, I was promoted to captain, moved from Italy to the state of Washington, and given a company command. As I was successfully completing my first year as company commander, I interviewed for a second command.

It was unusual for officers to get back-to-back company commands, but I approached the brigade commander (my boss) and asked him to consider me. I wanted a challenge that would further develop my leadership skills. At the same time, I was going through a divorce and, after collapsing during a run, facing my third major surgery.

Once again, I was hearing predictions that my career could be over. My boss faced a key decision point that could affect my career. He was concerned about my health and ability to handle the responsibility of the larger company, so he held off on his final decision while I recovered from surgery.

My focus was to get through the surgery and then concentrate on my recovery, refusing to accept defeat. I was fully committed and doggedly determined to get back into physical shape. I began to work out—running laps, doing modified push-ups and sit-ups—on the parade field between my boss's office and house. I made myself visible to him, as he walked home from his office at the end of the day.

I needed to prove to my boss that I was trained and ready for that second command. I wanted him to see my tenacity, discipline, and passion for doing what I loved—serving in the military and leading Soldiers. He watched me recover and made the tough decision to allow me an opportunity to prove myself with the second company command.

I was blessed with his final decision. He was an incredible leader and became one of my most influential mentors. He invested time in me, cared about whether or not I was healthy and capable to command, and wanted what was best for me as well as the organization. He was a tremendous example of Schofield's definition of leadership.

Personal discipline gave me a second chance at moving forward in my career. The result was a successful second command and the honor, and unexpected announcement, of an early promotion to major.

Unfortunately, there are too many examples where a lack of personal discipline removes *any* chance, second or otherwise. This is particularly obvious in regard to safety. One incident that happened during my command in Iraq provided a heartbreaking example. A Soldier was killed in a vehicular accident because he failed to fasten his seat belt. Three others walked away. Sadly, and even more disappointing, the Soldier who was killed was the senior occupant in the vehicle. He was responsible for ensuring everyone in the vehicle was following the standards. He failed to lead himself. The result was tragic.

In the military, as in the civilian world, there are reasons for safety rules and regulations. Following them, or not, can make the difference between life and death. Sometimes the enemy is as close as our own personal lack of discipline. The difference between good and great leaders, good and great organizations, is discipline.

★   Conflict Management and Delivering Consequences   ★

It takes discipline to deal with conflicts, and when necessary, deliver appropriate consequences. Yes, deliver consequences. When things go wrong, you, as the leader, must address what went wrong, as well as why and who needs to be held responsible.

No one should enjoy disciplining people. If you do, I suspect you are more interested in power and control than in leading. Those who seek power and control are intimidators and tormentors, not leaders. They may have the title of leader based on a position in an organization, but that doesn't make them true leaders.

Why is delivering consequences a necessary function of leadership? If you don't, you establish a new standard, and it will always be lower. I doubt any of us intend to be mediocre, but lack of action leads to mediocrity.

Delivering consequences requires disciplined listening. You must listen to the full story. You must capture all the details and deliver a thoughtful response. Delivering consequences is a deliberate process and requires an investment of your time and energy.

Use caution and don't rush to judgment, but don't ignore situations. Nine times out of ten, someone's life, job, future, or income is at stake. You must get it right, as there is an impact on both the individual and organization when you do, and when you *don't*.

It takes discipline to be decisive and fair. The only thing worse than a leader who delivers consequences that weren't deserved or unfair is a leader who fails to convey consequences when they were deserved.

If you lead your organization without discipline and accountability, or the opposite extreme where you exercise power and control that are demeaning and intimidating, you get the same results. Both approaches create anxiety, mediocrity, lower standards, lower morale, people wanting to leave the organization, and stifled performance. Too much rigidity can result in creating an environment that is *zero defects*—meaning, no one can make a mistake or a wrong decision without fear of repercussion.

Whether demanding integrity, assessing productivity, or tracking compliance, you set the climate of the organization you lead. Without consequences for those who don't follow the rules, there will be no motivation for people to be creative, innovative risk takers and go beyond the minimum of what is expected of them.

Do you approach leadership in a disciplined and professional manner? When consequences are required, do you deliver them?

Start today and use discipline as your new habit to help you and your team reach higher standards of excellence.

Leadership Principle 9

Have Character: Be the Standard and Hold Yourself Accountable

Right is right, and wrong is wrong. ~Mom

The enemy of great is good. ~Jim Collins

We must reject the idea that every time a law's broken, society is guilty rather than the lawbreaker. It is time to restore the American precept that each individual is accountable for his actions. ~President Ronald Reagan

Leaders define, set, and enforce standards. If you don't demand that the standards be met, they won't be. This doesn't mean you automatically fire someone who doesn't meet the standard, but you must deal with it.

If consequences are needed, you as the leader must deliver them. If retraining is needed, you as the leader have the authority and must make sure resources are provided. Enforcing high standards leads to greater effectiveness, better morale, cohesiveness, and improved performance and productivity.

Few leadership principles stand alone or apply to only one area of your life; most are used in concert with each other, like the instruments in an orchestra. To be the standard you want to see in others and to always hold yourself accountable requires discipline, desire, obedience, and commitment. Your character will be reflected in the standards you practice and uphold.

When I was a junior officer, I would hear senior leaders say, "As you climb up that flagpole, remember, the higher you go, the further up your skirt everyone can see." Taken literally, this means to be careful what you do, because everyone is watching.

While I understood the intent of the saying, I disliked the insinuation that you need to pay attention to your actions only when others are watching. I believe your true character is who you are when no one else is watching. So, it should not matter when or if people are observing your behavior. If you consistently set high standards for yourself, you will not need to be concerned about who is paying attention or when.

What becomes critical is leading yourself twenty-four hours a day, seven days a week. You must be the standard and hold yourself accountable. Being ethical, moral, and principled is a 24/7 venture, not to be turned on and off for convenience.

I expected more scrutiny as I rose in rank. I was humbled by each promotion and advancement and reminded myself that to whom much is given, much is expected. After all, greater leadership responsibilities meant my actions and decisions would be more far-reaching and impactful. I wanted to be the example of what right looked and acted like, and I was committed to holding myself accountable. Doing so required being true to myself.

How do you feel when someone fails to tell you the truth? Not good, right? You probably feel angry, sad, or disappointed. Sometimes it can be devastating, especially when it is someone you unconditionally trusted.

So, if being the standard means being true to you, then *not* holding yourself accountable for being the standard is equivalent to not being honest with yourself. Shouldn't that disappoint and anger you just as much as when someone else lies to you? If you keep this in mind as you make decisions, develop relationships, and build teams, my bet is you will uphold higher standards than you might have otherwise.

When you look in the mirror, are you able to be proud of the person you are seeing? Or do you have to say, "I let you down." Until you are able to look yourself in the eye, you cannot look those you lead in the eye. Be accountable to yourself first, and then to others. Hold yourself to a higher standard of excellence, and others will follow.

All around us we witness people playing the blame game instead of looking inside at themselves. I've caught myself doing the same. Have you?

★   Avoid the Blame Game   ★

In tough situations, it's easy to let negativity overtake your outlook. A helpful exercise I do is to lead myself through an entire day, consciously trying to catch my negative thoughts and working to prevent those from becoming *outside words* and blaming others. Try it. If you are like me, you will probably find this difficult, but it will help highlight the point that we tend to see problems in others and not in ourselves and are quick to cast blame.

Being accountable for your actions and caring about your character means making it personal, not just with the big challenges, but with your normal, everyday activities and relationships.

Sometimes, when I have done something wrong, my first instinct is to find someone else to share or take the blame with me. Do you find yourself doing the same?

Wouldn't it be great if we loved to share our successes as quickly as we desired to share the blame? Let's face it, all of us make mistakes, but not all of us take responsibility and hold ourselves accountable for those mistakes.

I'll never forget traveling on Interstate 95 in Virginia on a beautiful summer Sunday afternoon. I was going home to Maryland along with everyone else, after a nice weekend, and all three lanes were heavy with traffic. If you've ever traveled on I-95 around the beltway in DC, you know what it's like. Everyone is exceeding the speed limit, and the tendency is to go with the flow. Most of us rationalize that if we slow down to the speed limit, we will cause more risk to the other drivers. That was my thinking as I traveled north in the far-left lane.

Looking ahead, I saw a policeman in the median. I did what every good driver does: immediately took my foot off the accelerator. After all, I didn't want to show my brake lights, indicating I was going too fast. As I started to slow down, I looked down at my speedometer and noted I was going 83 mph in a 65-mph zone. I comforted myself with the thought that everybody else was doing the same.

I looked in my rearview mirror and saw the policeman pull out. I thought, "Oh, goodness, he is going to get somebody."

I moved to the middle lane so he could pass me and catch those going faster than me. As I did, he followed me. I pulled over one more lane with thoughtful precision, kept my blinker on, and moved slowly and safely to the far-right lane. Again, the policeman followed me. It became obvious (you think?!) that I was the one he was after. His lights began to flash!

I pulled off the highway and waited for him to come to my car. I was shaking. I knew I was speeding and had no excuse. Well, except that everyone else was speeding too.

My mind was already rationalizing that I wasn't really wrong. I consoled myself with the fact I'd never received a ticket and that was going to be in my favor. The policeman knocked on my passenger window. I rolled it down, and he said to me, "Ma'am, I caught you going a little fast out there today."

"Oh yes, I'm so sorry. I was speeding. I looked down and saw I was going eighty-three miles per hour." (Who does that?!) "And, you are right—I was going fast. I was just going with the flow of traffic."

"Can I see your driver's license and your registration?"

I fumbled through my glove box. I couldn't find my vehicle registration to save my life. Me, the queen of organization! He was very patient with me. "Just take your time, ma'am. We really need that registration. If you don't have it, then it is an automatic fine."

"Oh, I know it's in here. I keep all my important paperwork in the glove box."

Thank goodness I finally found it. He took my paperwork and returned to his squad car. As the minutes passed, I wasn't concerned. I had a clean record.

Finally, he walked back to my car with a clipboard and handed it to me with a pen. "Ma'am, if you will just kindly sign where the yellow highlight is for me. I want you to know that when you sign, you are not pleading guilty to reckless driving. You are just stating you understand you must appear in court on the date that's stated above."

I flipped my head toward him, and with a shocked look on my face asked, "Excuse me, sir, did you really think I was driving recklessly?"

He calmly replied, "Ma'am, that's not for me to decide. That's for the judge to decide. In the state of Virginia, anything over eighty miles per hour is considered reckless driving, and for Virginia state residents it's an automatic three-thousand-dollar fine."

I was thanking the good Lord that I was a New York State resident! I was also feeling a bit overwhelmed, angry, upset, and mortified. Here I was, a general officer, going to court for reckless driving. Was this setting the example for my Soldiers? I don't think so!

I signed the paperwork, thanked the policeman (again, who does that?), rolled up the window, and pulled back out onto I-95. As I drove home, I kept thinking about what had happened, trying to rationalize that everybody else was doing it—everybody else was driving fast. I also rationalized that I was the one stopped because I had New York State license plates.

I had to take a vacation day to meet my court date. Reluctantly, I had to tell my secretary and my aide, who controlled my schedule. At first they were so impressed I was taking a day of vacation—that is until I confessed I was going to court!

My secretary and aide had quite a bit of discussion about whether I should wear my uniform or not. I decided not to wear it. I was humiliated enough without advertising my position.

The result of court, since it was my first offense, was attending an all-day defensive driving class on a Saturday. I rarely had an entire day to do anything personal on a weekend, and now I had to find time to attend this course within ninety days.

The entire incident was humbling. First, I broke the law. Second, my driving was, in fact, unsafe. Third, and most important, I was not leading myself first. I was not setting the standard for others to follow. I paid the consequences.

I held myself accountable. Not to do so would have been saying, "I don't take leadership seriously, and I don't care about my character." I do take leadership seriously, and sometimes I, too, need to make adjustments in my behavior.

I encourage you to enjoy your life through obedience (such as drive the speed limit) versus experience (losing money, time, and pride). It is usually much more pleasant. If you are going to have to learn something through experience, then learn it! Don't make the same mistake again. When you make the same mistake again, it wasn't a lesson learned—it was a lesson noted, and you didn't honestly take accountability for your behavior.

Our true character is who we are when no one else is watching. Upholding the standards and holding yourself accountable are nonnegotiable if you want to be an effective, inspirational, and influential leader.

★ Be All That You Can Be—Don't Focus on Minimum Standards! ★

It has always been disturbing for me to watch people remain content with working at the minimum standard. You should not settle for just getting by in life or having an attitude of *what do I need to do to just pass?*

As a leader, I want to influence, inspire, and convince people to be their best! The army slogan when I joined the military in

1977 was, "Be all that you can be." Isn't that a wonderful concept? Strive to reach your maximum potential every single day, in everything you do, and in everything you say. Be and do your best.

While I was in the army, we were required to take a semi-annual physical fitness test: two minutes of sit-ups, two minutes of push-ups, and a two-mile run. You were graded based on how many sit-ups and push-ups you completed to standard. The proper way to perform each event was read out loud to all Soldiers before taking their test. Each Soldier was observed closely to make sure each and every repetition was performed correctly. If not, the repetition was not counted. The number of repetitions required was provided on a chart, and there were minimum and maximum standards based on your age and gender.

I would go to morning PT sessions with my different organizations and mingle with the Soldiers. I would cheer them on, run with them, and check out their personal goals. While chatting with Soldiers, I would ask, "What are your goals for the PT test today?"

I could always tell by the way they answered if they were settling for just passing their test, the minimum standard, or if they were reaching for their maximum standard.

I would cringe when I heard someone say, "All I need is forty sit-ups, ma'am."

"You need just forty sit-ups? Is that your max?"

"Oh no, ma'am, that's not my max—that's my minimum."

"Why do you only want to achieve your minimum? What if the person grading you determines one repetition doesn't count, and then you fail by one? Why would you want to be one step away from failure? That's gambling with your career."

I wanted my Soldiers to have fire in their gut for pushing themselves to be the best they could be and to reach for the maximum standards. I wanted them to lead themselves to train harder, achieve more, and take pride in being the best they could be! I spent a lot of time talking with Soldiers and motivating them to push themselves for the maximum score. I demanded the same of myself.

As a leader, you need to be the best you can be, set the standard for others to follow, and encourage others to aspire to higher standards of excellence.

Are you reaching for your max or defaulting to your minimum standards?

★ Do Not Ask of Others That Which You Are Not Willing to Do Yourself ★

As cadets at West Point, we were taught to never ask of our Soldiers that which we weren't willing to do ourselves. If you want to achieve excellence personally and professionally, you must be disciplined and demand excellence of yourself first and foremost.

How can you achieve this? Give orders, guidance, or direction in your own name. Don't blame the boss, or the system, or corporate headquarters when directing your team. If it is a required standard, policy, or program, make sure it happens and track the details.

When a standard isn't followed, investigate and determine the reason. When appropriate, deliver consequences, making sure the punishment fits the crime. Don't prejudge or predetermine consequences. Be innovative in your approach for developing those who failed to meet the standards, and listen. All situations are different.

Leaders should look for opportunities to develop those they lead rather than destroy them. They ought to desire to be the force to help them change their behavior.

The same should be true in our personal relationships. We should desire open, candid, forthright conversations with our Families and friends. When they come to us with mistakes they have made, we must listen and appreciate that they trusted us, love them through it, and make appropriate, measured responses. The same standards of discipline, trust, and attitude that you would use in your professional life apply to your personal life.

The result of not holding yourself to the standard and being accountable is that you create a lifestyle of minimal, low standards. The message is clear and simple: you are either part of the problem or part of the solution. I want to be known for being part of the solution. What about you?

★   Freedom Isn't Free   ★

I seize every opportunity I have to remind people about the importance of being interested, educated, involved, and showing respect for the standards that made our nation great. It starts with me, and you, taking simple actions and leading ourselves. For instance, this includes voting, displaying our national flag correctly, and honoring our flag appropriately—such as removing your hat and placing your hand over your heart when the national anthem is played.

Aren't these standards the least we can do? Have we forgotten how our freedom was earned? Are we failing to remember the lives sacrificed and caskets covered with Old Glory?

Right after I arrived in Iraq in the fall of 2005, the first national elections were conducted. It was amazing and exhilarating to see what the Iraqi people were willing to sacrifice in order to have the privilege of voting. They stood in line for hours, braving violence, to seize the opportunity. Statistics vary, but reportedly between 60 to 70 percent of the population voted.

When we held our own elections in the United States in 2012, I was disheartened to learn that less than 60 percent of the American people voted. In contrast, Iraqi women and men were willing to face the dangers of being shot or even killed while waiting hours and hours in line for the privilege to vote. They were grateful, excited, and respected their new freedom.

Have we become complacent, forgetful of the sacrifices made, too busy or uncaring to have a high personal standard of participating in our democratic process? Are we more concerned about what our country is doing for us, rather than what we are willing to do for our country?

How would you assess your personal accountability? Be the standard for others to follow!

Leadership Principle 10
Have Courage to Act on Your Convictions

I learned that courage was not the absence of fear, but the triumph over it. The brave man is not he who does not feel afraid, but he who conquers that fear. ~President Nelson Mandela

Courage is what it takes to stand up and speak; courage is also what it takes to sit down and listen. ~Prime Minister Winston Churchill

Courage is grace under pressure. ~Ernest Hemingway

A woman authoring a book on courage recently interviewed me. The first question she asked was, "How would you define courage?" I didn't have my own definition, but I realized it was a great question and I should create a definition.

I quickly reflected on my own life experiences and the people who have influenced my life. My response was quite simple: "Courage is doing what's right even when it's hard."

I further elaborated for her, "And you can substitute the word *hard* with many other words, such as *unpopular, unfamiliar, uncomfortable,* etc." Like other leadership traits, courage has many dimensions: physical, mental, social, and spiritual.

I suspect most people presume a retired army general would focus on physical courage in wartime experiences. However, where I have had to muster the most courage has been dealing with people, making tough decisions, and doing what is right.

Perhaps you are wondering if everybody can live courageously. Absolutely! Furthermore, I believe courage can be learned. You have the ability to learn to live and lead with courage, and if you want to be an effective leader, you have a responsibility to do so.

As I thought about my definition of courage, I decided it could be shortened to, "Courage is values in action."

When I think of leaders in action, I think about how their actions reflect the traits they value. Have you ever noticed the word *courage* is also in the words en*courage* and dis*courage*? Both of those require action that is typically positive and negative, respectively.

What kind of leader are you? Do you find yourself encouraging others, or discouraging them? How are you leading yourself? Do you get discouraged and quit? Or, do you encourage yourself and others by persevering through the tough times while keeping your integrity intact?

I recognize I haven't always demonstrated the courage I should have. It is easy to rationalize it didn't matter, nobody was hurt by it, or it wouldn't have made any difference. On those occasions when I failed, I have tried to not fall into those traps. Rather, I have tried to learn from my experiences, not repeat the same mistakes, and have the courage to share my mistakes with others.

Leadership Principle 10

★ Airborne School ★

Sometimes it takes a great deal of introspection, over time, to come to grips with why we failed to have the courage to respond to situations in the way we should have when they occurred.

This is true for me when I reflect on airborne school in August of 1979. I knew at the time of the incident I should have reported it, but I was angry—so angry that I didn't care. At the time, it may not have been about courage, but it is about courage now: courage to admit my response was wrong, courage to share the story and use it to encourage others to put personal emotion aside and do what is right.

I was only twenty years old but should not have let age or maturity be an excuse.

Airborne school involves three weeks of training in Georgia. Soldiers are trained to jump out of perfectly good airplanes and parachute to the ground. I was excited about my summer training. It would be physically demanding and a welcome break from academics.

I was scheduled for airborne school, along with several of my West Point classmates, at the very end of August. The training was organized into three separate weeks: ground week, tower week, and jump week. During ground week, we learned how to properly and safely land on the ground by executing our parachute landing falls, or PLFs. To practice, we jumped from platforms of various heights into sand pits. Our instructors were male NCOs, called *Black Hats*, because they actually wore black

97

hats. They trained and tested us. To continue into week two, we had to pass all our PLFs and we had to complete all our morning physical training (PT) runs.

It was the 1970s and PT was segregated—women trained separately from men.

On the first day, the Black Hats messed with us during the morning run and caused several women to drop out of the formation. The problem was that if you dropped out of more than one run, you were recycled and pushed to the next class the following week. Unfortunately, those of us who were West Point cadets had only three weeks available because our academic year began immediately following airborne school. We had no flexibility. If we failed any part of the training, there was no time for us to be recycled.

We knew we couldn't afford to let this happen again. We held an emergency meeting in the barracks to figure out a plan. I'd been a cross-country runner in high school and knew how to pace, so I volunteered to be the corner point person of the formation. The plan was simple: I would set the pace, and they would follow me.

The good news was that we lost very few runners from that point forward. The bad news was that the Black Hats yelled and screamed at me the entire way—trying to get me to run faster. But I just kept a steady, consistent pace. I thought the worst that could happen to me was more push-ups. I sorely miscalculated.

The last afternoon of our first week of training was our final PLF test in the sawdust pits. The pit was set up with several lanes for testing. The requirement was to climb a ladder, hook up to a cable, slide down, and correctly execute a PLF as you hit the ground.

Each lane had a Black Hat who was in charge of deciding whether you successfully completed the PLF or not. As the afternoon progressed, fewer people remained in the pit, because once you passed, you were dismissed.

The Black Hat in charge of my lane approved my PLFs and dismissed me to report to the Black Hat in charge of the pit. But when I reported to the Black Hat in charge of the pit, he disagreed and sent me back to my lane for a "do-over." This happened repeatedly.

I thought to myself, *I can see what's going on here. This is a game, and I need to play the game. He's trying to teach me a lesson that he's in charge and I'm not. This is a way of getting back at me because of the morning runs.*

You see, the Black Hat in charge of the pit was the same Black Hat who ran next to me in the morning, yelling and screaming for me to pick up the pace. I was OK with this to a point, and was determined to have a positive attitude. I decided to demonstrate to him that I was not going to quit.

The temperature exceeded one hundred degrees with humidity to match, and the routine was physically exhausting: climb the ladder, slide down a cable, and repeatedly hit the ground, hit the ground, hit the ground.

When the training time expired, I was the only person in the pit. All the other trainees were outside the pit waiting to see what would happen. Once again, the Black Hat in charge of my lane passed me and told me to report one last time to the Black Hat in charge of the pit.

I was determined not to break. I moved out with a purpose and reported to the Black Hat in charge of the pit. With the strongest voice I could muster, and with the most positive attitude I could display, I reported to him that I had successfully performed my PLFs.

He disagreed. He failed me. He ordered me to report to another Black Hat at the administrative building for recycling into the next class.

My heart stopped. He was really messing with me. I thought to myself, *He must not know we have no time to be recycled. If I explain this to him, I bet he will change his mind.*

I asked permission to speak, and it was granted. I explained the situation to him. I remember his face. Not one expression. He did not care. His response was, "Somebody has to be recycled, and that somebody is you."

At that point, all I felt was disbelief and anger. I could barely think straight. I was a failure. I was going to return to West Point without my airborne wings. How would I face my classmates?

I reported to the Black Hat at the administrative building to begin my outprocessing. Within just a few hours, I was completely checked out of airborne school. During that process, I recall one person, a male whose rank I don't recall, asking me, "Do you think you were harassed?"

I clearly remember my internal response being, "Absolutely!"

However, in defiance, my response was, "No."

All I wanted was out. I wanted nothing to do with airborne school. You couldn't pay me to wear airborne wings! I was embarrassed and humiliated. I was feeling mistreated and sorry for myself. I didn't want to deal with the situation. I just wanted out.

Besides, I felt it would be my word against a seasoned sergeant's word. I was just a twenty-year-old West Point cadet. I was sure it would be interpreted that I was full of myself. I had no desire to be part of any investigation or debate. I just wanted to escape and leave it behind me. My friends were sympathetic.

What does seem odd to me now, after having spent a career of leading Soldiers and tracking training statistics, is I don't remember being asked by anybody in a leadership position at West Point about my being kicked out of airborne school after I returned.

I don't regret having the courage to set the standard for the run. It was the right decision. My regret is failing to respond properly to the harassment question. I should have done more. This realization came to me years later, when I found myself leading Soldiers and trying to understand why men and women are so reluctant to report harassment to their leaders.

Reality is that I was likely not the only airborne school candidate this Black Hat had harassed. If I had mustered the courage to report it, perhaps I could have prevented others from enduring the same mistreatment.

In this situation, I was also part of the problem, because I did not speak up. Being part of the solution requires reflection; without honest, candid reflection, we won't see ourselves as having been part of the problem. We just continue believing it was someone else's fault.

The reason I don't have airborne wings on my uniform is twofold: because of the Black Hat's actions and because of my *lack* of action. By understanding this, I learned to have the courage to respond differently in the future.

I recently incorporated my airborne school experience into a leadership keynote I gave to senior corporate leaders. An observation made by one of the leaders attending was one I had never considered but thought was encouraging and insightful: "Becky, what I take away from this story is how your actions resulted in other women having the opportunity to earn their wings!"

★ Have the Courage to Listen to Your Gut ★

Have you ever been complimented for your work and your gut sensed there were ulterior motives? How did you respond?

My first assignment in the army was in Vicenza, Italy, at a nuclear weapons storage site. When I arrived, I was a brand-new second lieutenant in my early twenties with no practical experience. Our unit was within ninety days of a critical certification inspection that determined our ability to perform our nuclear mission. You can imagine the pressure. The magnitude and responsibility was a little overwhelming.

I had been well trained at West Point for handling stressful leadership situations. It was the lack of technical knowledge and experience on my part that had me most concerned. The unit did not have a very good track record for passing these inspections, and I'd heard rumors of people being relieved.

The level of responsibility for technical inspection for our mission, including storage and transportation of nuclear weapons systems, was a whole new ball game. I had received six months of technical training before I arrived, which gave me a significant leg up on understanding the technical operations, but it was classroom knowledge and didn't involve any sort of hands-on training.

Within those initial ninety days, I had to assess how well trained my platoon was, identify shortfalls, develop a training plan, and study numerous technical manuals. I quickly developed a strong relationship with the warrant officers in my unit to teach me everything they could. In the army, warrant officers are our technical experts. The latter proved to be the beginning of many successes, understanding the huge role that developing authentic relationships plays in our lives.

The inspectors for the certification were also in the military. They were officers with many more years in the military than myself and were considered technical experts in the nuclear field. It was common, when they visited our units for inspections and training, that we scheduled time for them to see the local sites, including dinner at local restaurants and shopping at the ceramic and gold factories. The latter was popular, as many bought gold jewelry for their spouses.

The senior officer of our visiting inspection team requested I take him to the gold factory, as he wanted to buy some jewelry for his wife. I arranged to drive him out to the gold factory to spend some time selecting pieces of jewelry he thought his wife would enjoy. He asked me to try on some of the jewelry, explaining he valued my opinion as a woman and that I was about the same build as his wife. I thought nothing of it. He made his selections, and we returned to the unit.

The following day as the inspection continued, my concern grew about our performance and whether we would pass or fail the inspection. I knew we had made mistakes with some of our procedures, and in the nuclear operations arena, there is little room for error. You either get it right or you get it wrong.

At the end of the last day, we were scheduled to go to dinner as a team. I arrived at the restaurant to discover that only the senior inspector was present. I thought it was odd but didn't question it, as I was early (I've always practiced the rule that if you are not early, you are late.)

He said the others would be coming later and we should go ahead and order our meals. As we sat at the table, he reached into his pocket and pulled out a jewelry box and placed it on the table.

While initially confused, the recent events began to become clear. I was disappointed and nervous about what might happen next. He expressed his wish that I have the jewelry and told me he had a growing affection for me, and he implied I didn't need to worry about passing the inspection.

My mind raced. How do I handle this situation? Accepting the jewelry would be wrong and would send a message I didn't want to convey. But insulting him by not accepting the jewelry or his advances might result in our failed inspection. Would I be the reason the team would fail?

I could hear my parents' voices. "Right is right, and wrong is wrong, Becky." The West Point prayer lingered over me. "Choose the harder right over the easier wrong, Becky." If I accepted the jewelry, I was just as wrong as he was for offering it. I would be lowering my standards to his. Did I have the courage to take the right steps?

I told him I couldn't accept the jewelry, got up from the table, and immediately departed. I was shaken and concerned, but I knew I did what was right. My mind continued to race. So I had the courage to take the initial step, but did I have the courage to report him? Who else needed to be advised? Had I really learned from my airborne school experience?

I got in my car and drove directly to my boss's home. I informed him what happened, how it happened, and my perception of what might result. I explained I was concerned we might fail the inspection and expressed my guilt that I wasn't being loyal to my team or placing them first. I also informed my boss that I didn't believe I did anything to warrant or invite this kind of behavior.

My boss, a married man in his thirties and a major with over twelve years in the military, assured me I did nothing wrong. He confirmed that not accepting the jewelry and reporting the incident to him was the right action to take.

This incident helped me to understand that loyalty to your team and to your boss is important, but blind loyalty is dangerous. If I had convinced myself the team might fail if I didn't cooperate, that would have been blind loyalty and not the kind of teamwork that builds success. Perhaps my actions, and my courage to respond appropriately by reporting this to my superior, prevented a future incident of this sort.

We passed the inspection and did so with my character intact.

When you are confronted with right and wrong, do you demonstrate the courage to choose right? It is not always easy, and it is not always comfortable, but the best leaders display the courage they would like to see in those they lead.

As a leader, you must have the courage to do and say what is right, even when it's not the easiest thing to do. Never let your character go by the wayside by taking the easy way out.

Leadership Principle 11

Place Others before Self

> *Everybody can be great...because everybody can serve. You don't have to
> have a college degree to serve. You don't have to make your subject and verb
> agree to serve. You only need a heart full of grace. A soul generated by love.*
> *~Martin Luther King Jr.*
>
> *There can be no other definition of a successful life than that of serving
> others. ~President George Bush Sr.*

★   Service to Others   ★

Are great leaders important and necessary to our organizations? Absolutely.

Are great leaders replaceable? Of course. We are all replaceable.

Is leading about the leader? Absolutely not. Leading is about the led.

Why is understanding this important? I believe this means that in order to lead others, you must first know how to selflessly serve others. Selfless service cannot be measured. Service to others is not a goal or a destination. It is a daily journey. Selfless service springs from the inside without regard to race or gender. It is a lifestyle, not a moment of courage. It is generosity in action.

When people ask me what I miss most about my military service, the answer is not what I miss most, but *whom* I miss the most—those with whom I served, whom I led, or who led me. I stayed in service to my country for as many years as I did because of people, and people are why I do the work that I have chosen to do in retirement.

What stirs you to do what you do? Are you in service to others with your actions, with your decisions, with your goals, and with your success?

There is nothing wrong with being prosperous or popular. What matters is what you do with your success. How do you handle your success and reputation? Do you use your position for the greater good of others, or are you more self-centered?

To some people, this doesn't sound realistic or make good business sense. But let me assure you, I've seen it over and over again: people who authentically focus on others before themselves receive much more than they give—personally and professionally.

It is a lot like volunteering. Most people think they don't have enough time to volunteer. There isn't enough time in the day to do what you have to do.

Ironically, what I have discovered is that when I give of myself and my time as a volunteer, or as I make myself available to people even when I am busy, the result is almost always rewarding and even energizing. Plus, it feels good to help others, and I usually learn something new along the way.

Leaders are supposed to teach, coach, and mentor. This means investing time and energy to develop or assist others. When people approach me and share how they navigated through some rough waters because of my helping them, it just fires me up, makes me more determined, and inspires me to do even more.

Selfless leadership is about doing, not just being. Placing others before self indicates action. Consider this: being selfless means doing something for someone who can do absolutely nothing for you. How often can you say this is the case? Many times, whether consciously or subconsciously, we do for others in hopes of something coming to us in return.

I have learned to ask myself, "Why am I doing this? What are my motives? Is this all about me? Or is this about helping someone else? Am I doing this simply for my own gain? Or am I doing this to help someone?" If my motives are *selfish*, and not *selfless*, I must force myself to relook at my purpose, action and involvement.

Selfless action means taking the time to listen actively and openly to others without prejudging and being accessible to those we lead. As we move up the corporate (or any) ladder and our responsibilities become greater, it becomes easier to put up barriers between our subordinates and ourselves. There can be a variety of reasons for this, from the instinct of front-office staff to protect our time to the reality of higher-level work that requires focused attention to complete. However, this is precisely when we need to make sure we are actively paving a road from our office door that is wide enough for two-way traffic, even though our first instinct may be to dig a moat around a perceived castle.

As a leader, I had to learn to listen to that inner voice that reminded me to serve others first and check my own ego at the door.

You have to show people that it is not all about you. It is not about the general, it is about the Soldier. It is not about the teacher, it is about the student. It is not about the doctor, it is about the patient. It is not about the parent, it is about the child.

Every decision I made, every resource I approved, every action I took had to be about those I led. It was never lost on me that those I led, my Soldiers, also had the same sense of selfless service to each other.

★   Complex Attack   ★

Hard lessons are learned in combat. Chaos often reigns, there is no perfect intelligence, and the enemy always gets a vote. There is also probably no greater degree of selfless service than to give your life for your country. For all the men and women who have died in service to their nation, we owe a lifetime of gratitude and commitment to always remember their sacrifice and the sacrifice of their Families.

On my very first day of command in Iraq, I was already dealing with a significant tragedy that had actually occurred the previous day. Remember, once you are in the leadership position, you own it, regardless of what happened yesterday.

The incident was a complex attack on one of our combat logistics patrols. The enemy used every deadly measure it possessed: armor-piercing rounds, hand grenades, rocket-propelled grenades (RPGs), and improvised explosive devices (IEDs).

The unit involved was well trained, and the result of the complex attack could have been much more devastating. After every attack, our units conduct an investigation and hold an SIRB (Serious Incident Review Board). Knowing what happened, how it happened, and why it happened minimizes the potential of a repeat incident.

I had the responsibility of reviewing the entire operation, plans, and execution of the mission. If any area required changes to the way the operation was conducted, I was responsible for ensuring action was taken. My focus was on both the mission and human dimension. As we say in the army, "Mission first, people always." I had to ensure my subordinate commanders were focused on the same.

I never discuss statistics when it comes to the number of Soldiers wounded and killed in my command. Although the number was considered low, I have always reminded those who ask that when the loss is your son or daughter, your husband or wife, or your mother or father, the loss is 100 percent.

In this particular situation, one Soldier was tragically killed in the attack. His name was Sergeant Jim Witkowski, son of Barbara and Jim Witkowski. He was a brother, friend, and comrade. His story is representative of the incredible men and women serving, living, and dying on our behalf.

Sergeant Witkowski epitomized selfless service. He placed the mission and his comrades ahead of himself. First, he volunteered for the mission, because they needed more security. Second, he insisted on the position of gunner because of his experience and expertise. From the accounts of the Soldiers and leaders who knew him, he was a seasoned Soldier whom everyone respected. He was also a prankster and a lot of fun. He touched more lives than we will ever really know. Many of his comrades have named their children after him, sending a powerful message of love and friendship to his Family that he will not be forgotten.

On that fateful day, he threw himself on a grenade thrown into his gunner's hatch, saving the four men inside his vehicle. For his heroism, he was awarded the Silver Star. Sergeant Jim

Witkowski was not a statistic or data point; he was, and remains, a selfless servant to our nation and an American hero.

★ He's in a Coma and Would Not Even Know You Are There ★

Unfortunately, there have been a few times when I stood cold in my tracks and realized the action I had taken was not that of a selfless person and leader.

I have always felt this way about a situation in Iraq. I often visited the hospital at our location in Balad. I tried to be immediately available when I was notified about a wounded Soldier being flown in by helicopter. Those who worked for me understood it was a personal priority.

On one occasion, I received a call about one o'clock in the morning from my chaplain, "Ma'am, I'm sorry to call you so late. Did I wake you up?"

"No, chaplain. I was just catching up on e-mail with the boss. Just a long night."

"Ma'am, I am at the hospital. One of our Soldiers has just been medevaced in. His vehicle hit an IED that had ball bearings in it, and some have lodged in his brain. He might not make it. I'm here with the doctors. He is in a coma, and they are trying to stabilize him for a flight to Germany, but the prognosis is not good."

"Chaplain, should I come over?"

I realized almost as soon as the words left my lips that I should not have placed the burden of that decision on the chaplain. I was not being selfless and available. In asking that question, was

I hoping she would tell me I didn't need to be there, or that there was nothing I could do? And, of course that is exactly what happened. How unfair of me to place the responsibility of this decision on her.

My chaplain, of course, tried to reassure me she was just informing me and not pressuring me to head to the hospital. "No, ma'am. I am here and will monitor the situation through the night and keep you posted. He is in a coma and wouldn't even know you are here. There's nothing you can do. Get some sleep."

It was my decision to not walk over to the hospital that night. I hung up the phone, finished my work, and tried to get a few hours of sleep. Three hours later, I started my day, checked my e-mail quickly, and noticed a note from the chaplain. The Soldier had been medevaced back to Germany. As I read the e-mail, it kept plaguing me that I had made the wrong decision.

All my nights were short. That's the way it is in command and combat. Yes, sleep is important, and the chaplain was right, the Soldier probably would not have known who I was or that I was even in the room. I had rationalized that my visit could not help him. My thinking was that I had twenty thousand Soldiers in my command and could not visit the hospital every time one was evacuated from the battlefield, and I had work that needed to be done before getting even a few hours of sleep. At that moment, the decision became about me—and I failed.

Who cares if he knew I was there? This should not have been about me. The focus needed to be on him. The situation caused me to ask myself, *Becky, why do you go to the hospital? Is it all about you? If it's all about you, don't bother because you're not going to be able to touch any Soldier's life.*

Many points of view have been taken on this story. Most tell me I have beat myself up too hard, and some even feel the chaplain should not have called me. I won't attempt to argue one way or the other in this book. The fact remains that the chaplain did call me, and she did so because she knew I cared deeply about my Soldiers. I will always believe I responded incorrectly to the situation. I believe my gut caused me to immediately second-guess my decision, because it was the wrong decision.

Another very important lesson learned in this situation was that this was not just about being a leader to the individual Soldier. Since he was in a coma, I did not see the need to be present, because he would not know I was there. I made it about the Soldier being aware of me. This decision should also have been about supporting those who were trying to heal and minister to the Soldier. It should have been about the chaplain, doctors, surgeons, and nurses. It wasn't always the case, but that night I could have been there to offer some encouragement to them.

The Soldier survived the night, the flight to Germany, and was successfully transported back to a medical facility in California. He lived to hug his parents again, kiss his wife, and see his child. He even walked. Sadly, after multiple successful surgeries, to include even walking and speaking again, this Soldier died during a surgery to build a prostheses for his head. During those months of surgeries and therapy, members of his unit visited him.

Most remarkable to me, and what I call an incredible act of selfless service, was when his company commander, a young captain, used his personal leave to visit his Soldier first, before going home to visit his own Family. The captain had beautifully framed a company guidon (flag), unit coins, a combat action badge, and an award for his Soldier. He presented it to him at his bedside. In my humble opinion, the company commander demonstrated far greater selfless service than I had the night the chaplain called.

I am sharing this story with you in hopes that when these types of decisions are required of you, you will have a better perspective on this leadership aspect of serving others and that you will respond in a more thoughtful way than I did.

I learned from this situation, and changed how I responded to the many subsequent phone calls and events that occurred during the rest of my deployment. Every situation was unique, but I became a better leader—a more caring, selfless, and thoughtful leader.

As a commander for more than twenty thousand people, I understood my responsibilities were so vast that I had to carefully prioritize and measure where my time and energy were most needed. I had to trust and allow my commanders and leaders at every level to do their part, as well.

Do not lose your opportunity to be available. Be available for all the right reasons, which should include being of selfless service to others. Decide what is in it for the greater good—not what is in it for you.

Leadership Principle 12
Be Prepared

By failing to prepare, you are preparing to fail. ~Benjamin Franklin

I will prepare and someday my chance will come.
~President Abraham Lincoln

Unfortunately, there seems to be far more opportunity out there than ability... We should remember that good fortune often happens when opportunity meets with preparation. ~Thomas Edison

It's so easy to look at others as the problem and forget to look at ourselves. Each of us, however, is either part of the problem or part of the solution. To be part of the solution means we need to be in a constant state of preparation. By doing so, we will be able to seize opportunities, shape success, and provide much better responses to whatever comes our way.

★ The Power of Preparation ★

"Always be prepared" sounds great, but it's not always that easy. I remember a senior officer once telling me, "Becky, always be prepared to talk to your Soldiers. Always have a little outline on a three-by-five card either in your head or in your pocket, because those opportunities don't happen all the time."

In the business world, I believe it is referred to as the elevator speech. I believe it's even more important the higher you go, because the distance between you and those you lead becomes greater, and the opportunity for interface with individuals becomes less and less. You get many occasions to speak to the masses but not as many to connect on an individual basis.

Preparing begins with thinking and planning ahead. Most people who are professionals in the workplace are usually thinking ahead about the next promotion, the next time they might be presenting to the boss, the next project, or the next chance to excel. It is healthy to be thinking ahead, as long as you are also planning ahead. Why? You never know when an opening is going to arise.

Following retirement, I began building my new company, *STEADFAST Leadership*, with hopes of speaking on leadership to the corporate sector. I started with drafting my business and leadership model, organizing notes for outlines to potential keynote addresses, and developing material for workshops. This is always a work in progress.

In May 2010, just five months into launching *STEADFAST Leadership*, I received an important phone call. I was sitting at my dining room table, at about ten o'clock in the morning, when the phone rang. The gentleman on the other end of the line immediately took control the conversation. "Becky you don't know me, but I work for a financial institution in New York City, and I received your name from one of your West Point classmates and your phone number from your mother."

"Well, I guess you are a reliable caller and not a telemarketer!"

"I have a situation and an opportunity I would like to discuss with you. I am holding a one-day women's leadership conference for about three hundred and fifty clients of our firm. I have a keynote speaker, the secretary of energy for President Obama, who had to drop out of the conference due to her responsibilities with the oil spill in the Gulf. I was wondering if you would be willing to substitute as a keynote speaker for my leadership conference."

Imagine my shock as I sat there and weighed in my mind, *Secretary of Energy versus little Becky Halstead, STEADFAST Leadership?* It was almost enough to make me chuckle, but at the same time it almost left me speechless.

I replied, "Well, I would love the opportunity. I guess the most important question is, when?"

"Tomorrow morning at nine."

My two new emotions became anxiousness and excitement. "Well, I guess the next most important question would be where?"

"At our corporate headquarters in New York City."

Without hesitation, I told him that if he could work the logistics, then he could count me in. I felt like saying, "Send me in, Coach!" I told him I would pack my bag and look for an e-mail confirming that he could arrange a flight for me that evening.

Within an hour, I had an e-mail with all the details, and I headed off to New York City. When I landed at LaGuardia, car service was there to pick me up and take me to my hotel. It was a beautiful hotel, and I met my contact in the lobby. Now, I travel in blue jeans for comfort. There is no doubt in my mind that at first glance he had to be asking himself, *Have I made a mistake here?* He was not looking at a stereotypical general.

117

He asked me to have a seat, and we began to chat about the next day's conference. He wanted to know what I would be presenting to the audience of corporate women leaders. Fortunately, during the flight I had scratched out a quick outline. As I began to express my thoughts on leadership, I could visibly see his posture relax and his comfort level increase. "Becky, I think this is going to be perfect. Thank you."

He invited me to have dinner, but I knew I needed the time to further prepare and rehearse. I still needed to turn my outline into written remarks and rehearse to make sure my timing was appropriate. The conference was a full lineup of keynote speakers, and I knew the importance of being mindful of the time allotted. Before heading off to the conference the next morning, as I do with all my speaking engagements, I said a quick prayer and asked the good Lord to give me the right words for this group.

I pinched myself as I dragged my suitcase down Fifth Avenue and headed to the Metropolitan Club, the conference location. A whole new world and journey was opening up for me. I entered the huge ballroom and began to see the women who were in attendance, and admittedly, became a little intimidated. I had to keep reminding myself that I was going to speak to these women about the leadership principles I had been practicing for well over thirty years. I was not giving them a speech on a new subject. I was giving them my life experiences. I just needed to do so with all my heart and mind.

I made my way to my table and picked up the agenda for the day. As I read the impressive list of several CEOs from large corporations, I once again thought to myself, "I'm just a country girl from a town with no traffic lights!"

Reality is that little Becky Halstead, although extremely ordinary, has been given a lifetime of extraordinary opportunities.

The result of those experiences led me to that moment in New York City, and many similar moments since, having had the privilege to share leadership with so many others. Good fortune truly does come when opportunity meets preparation.

I've always tried to discipline myself to prepare for what is needed to accomplish the mission in front of me. Before speaking to any audience, I do my homework to understand who the audience is going to be, what is the intent and focus of the conference, and what are the mission, goals, and values of the corporation or organization. There is power in preparation.

After the presentation, a woman came up to me and said, "I noticed you did not use any notes. How long did it take you to prepare?"

My answer: "About thirty years!"

★   Details Matter   ★

Desiring to learn the details is not the same—and shouldn't be confused with—micromanaging. Leaders represent their organizations and must know what is going on. The larger the organization you lead, the more prepared you must be with systems in place to keep yourself educated, informed, and prepared.

As the commanding general in Iraq for logistics and distribution operations, I received two intensive battle updates daily. Each morning, there was a three-inch binder on my desk with executive summaries on all logistics operations from the previous twelve hours. I would review these in preparation for my first battle update in the morning. This was the same for the two-hour battle update in the evenings. My evening update was followed by a higher-level update where I would brief my three-star commander and his staff with highlights of our logistics operations.

My staff spent hours collecting, assessing, and analyzing data to present to me and to my subordinate brigade commanders, who were listening in remotely during these updates. With over two hundred different company-size units, each with specific missions—varying from transportation and maintenance to supply and medical as well as base and route security—the diversity of the data could be almost overwhelming. Regardless, I was the commander, and it was my responsibility to understand the missions and the current situations and to be actively engaged in guiding the preparation and planning of future operations.

There would be times when I did not understand what was being presented, and this would cause me to ask questions to gather more details. If my questions could not be answered easily, I would defer the answers to what I called "Saturday morning study hall." I designated Saturday mornings because this time frame happened to fit into the battle rhythm (more about battle rhythm under Leadership Principle 18). I knew I was ultimately responsible for all that my unit did and failed to do, but realistically, I also knew I wasn't the subject matter expert on all missions. I needed to be versed well enough to be able to represent my command when reporting to my three-star boss and his staff, as well as to the leaders of the units we supported. So, I designated this time for extra training in areas with which I had no previous experience and areas where we were struggling.

At first, the colonels lined up to brief me on the answers to my questions. I quickly decided, however, that this was a training opportunity at all levels. I didn't get enough visibility with the junior officers and Soldiers, so I requested they be the ones who prepared and briefed me. The result was many more people across the organization became educated and prepared. It was actually fascinating to watch.

In asking questions, I was able to assess who knew their job, who was anticipating possible changes, who was assessing the second and third levels of the effect of the changes, and who was planning ahead. I reminded them that simply collecting and reporting data aren't always helpful. For example, providing me with data that a cargo plane isn't able to fly due to unplanned maintenance needs or bad weather, but then not providing possible solutions for getting the supplies distributed, is insufficient preparation.

I have had numerous junior officers and Soldiers tell me that they were nervous about briefing me, but that it was a great learning experience for them. I even had one young intelligence staff Soldier tell me the highlight of her experience in Iraq was briefing me because she loved preparing. Her goal was to prepare in a way that she anticipated what I would ask her, and she would be prepared with all the answers. She challenged herself!

I made sure to communicate to my staff the purpose behind all the work. I emphasized to them that I represented them when I was in Baghdad at command and staff meetings. When my three-star boss asked me a question, I'd better be able to answer as the senior logistician in Iraq. I explained that my being prepared raised his confidence level that we know what we are doing. We always hear the expression "knowledge is power," but that power is not possible without preparation.

It was important for me to consider the amount of time required to gather the details and respect my staff's time, a precious commodity, especially in combat. I encouraged those who worked for me to have the intestinal fortitude to ask me why I needed details, if the reason was not obvious to them. This sort of open, collegial environment was not always possible, but I was mindful of the importance of sharing the *why* to getting the information I wanted. It is very important to remember to respect each other's time and let people do their jobs. It is a very fine line.

A key part of preparation is tracking your progress, keeping organized notes from your meetings, and following up. Details matter. Later, under Leadership Principle 20, you will read about my method of tracking details in what I call *steno pad leadership*. I have kept meticulous notes my entire life, always understanding the importance of being prepared and keeping track of details: names, numbers, dates, quantities, tasks, etc. The process helped me to hold myself accountable for getting my work completed on time. I also believe it communicated to all those who dedicated their time and energy into preparing to brief me that I was paying attention, taking notes, learning, and using what they provided to me. Those I led made me a smarter, more prepared leader, and I believe they were also better for it.

How are you preparing yourself? How are you encouraging those you lead to be prepared?

Leadership Principle 13
Shift Happens: Take
Response-ability

> *In the long run, we shape our lives, and we shape ourselves. The process never ends until we die. And the choices we make are ultimately our own responsibility. ~Eleanor Roosevelt*
>
> *The price of greatness is responsibility. ~Prime Minister Winston Churchill*
>
> *The man who complains about the way the ball bounces is likely to be the one who dropped it. ~Lou Holtz*

All of us have experienced shifts in our lives. Unfortunately, most of us focus on the shift, when we should be focused on our response. We all have the ability to choose the right response, but sometimes we don't. That's why I call this *response*-ability instead of *responsibility.*

Shift happens in our personal and professional lives—often simultaneously. So, let's discuss the personal side of the shift and our response to it before we pursue the professional. Many use different terms to describe shifts: challenges, issues, bumps in the road, and obstacles. I've used all these, but I try to quickly translate to a more positive approach. I prefer to convert the challenges, issues, bumps, and obstacles into opportunities.

When I reflect on my personal life journey and look at the highs and lows, my life is probably not that much different from many of yours. I was married and then divorced. I've had my healthy and my unhealthy years; three major surgeries in my twenties, and then chronic fibromyalgia in my forties. As I confronted those events, I was in charge of my choices and my responses.

I probably did not make all the right or best decisions, but just as good things happen to bad people, bad things happen to good people!

★ You Stand Your Tallest When You Are on Your Knees ★

My grandmother used to say, "You stand your tallest when you're on your knees." Early on, I learned that part of my response to adversity needed to include prayerful consideration of how I should respond.

When I made the decision to get married, the furthest thing from my mind was that it would not work out and that someday I would be divorced. There are usually signs that exist to help us avoid making the wrong decisions, but we often ignore them or hope we misinterpreted them. Some call this denial.

In the case of my own marriage, I thought I was being very rational about my decision. However, in a decision as huge, important, and long-lasting as marriage should be, I wish I'd had the concept of fusion of heart and mind mastered and had made it a routine part of my decision-making process.

Depending how you look at it, either he married the wrong woman, or I married the wrong man, or both. Regardless, the end result was the same: we ended up divorced. My divorce didn't cause me to hate men, or close my heart and mind to the potential of future relationships, but it did cause me to assess what mistakes I made and what I might have done differently.

★ Understanding "Not Now" Does Not Necessarily Mean "No" ★

Have you ever been promised something—a raise, promotion, new position—and then the responsible person or organization didn't deliver? Did it make you angry? Did it make you question your own ability?

In 2003, when I was selected for general officer, my boss brought me into his office and told me I was being considered for assignment as the commanding general of a Corps Support Command at Fort Bragg, North Carolina. I was ecstatic! This would be a premier job and opportunity and an awesome privilege!

I went home from work that evening, got on my computer, and researched this new command I'd be taking. The next morning, I went into work and couldn't wait to tell my boss all I'd learned about the command. Before I could get two words out of my mouth, he said, "Becky, Fort Bragg is not going to happen."

I was totally caught off guard. My head was spinning. What? Why not? Did I miss something? Should I be taking this personally? Should I be getting upset? Should I be questioning the leadership's decision on this?

"You have never been assigned to Fort Bragg and don't have the experience." In other words, he was telling me I wasn't the most qualified person for the job.

Maybe I could agree with that part of the decision, but if not me, then who? My boss explained that another officer, with Fort Bragg experience and who was on the same promotion list as I was, would be getting the job. At first I was very disappointed. I couldn't completely get on board with the rationale. I would have considered myself equally competitive, and it wasn't my fault I had never been assigned to Fort Bragg. The army had never assigned me there, but I had assignments with similar experiences in Hawaii and at Fort Drum.

What I'd learned over the years, however, was sometimes we are not privy to all the factors that play into the decisions being made on our behalf, and the end result isn't always as bad as it first appears. In this case, I came to the conclusion that the answer was not *no* as much as it was *not yet*. And that is exactly what happened.

You see, when you fast-forward my career to one year later in 2004, the army announced I was being given command of the 3rd Corps Support Command (3rd COSCOM) in Germany—the sister unit to the Fort Bragg unit. The timing and location of my selection for command, in the end, was perfect. If I'd been able to handpick the members of the 3rd COSCOM leadership staff, I could not have made better selections than the army made for me. Plus, I would be deploying the 3rd COSCOM from Germany to Iraq within my first year.

As we deployed into Iraq, the unit we replaced was our sister unit from Fort Bragg. The timing and sequence of events drew me to another lesson learned. I didn't realize it at the time, but in hindsight it was clear to me that having the additional year of experience before deploying to Iraq made me a much more prepared and responsive leader, especially as a general officer leading in combat. No doubt I needed the extra experience more than I realized.

Also, being a woman of faith, I am certain God knew this extra year was necessary, and this validated for me how important it is to trust our journey to God's direction.

When you're ready for that next promotion, do you assume you'll get it because you're next in line, because the boss likes you, or because you have all the right experience? Or do you stick your neck out and work hard to make sure your boss knows you want and deserve the opportunity to move up the ranks in your company, even if it means the possible disappointment of not receiving the position?

★   Respond the Way You Would Want Others to Respond   ★

We have a *response*-ability in our decisions and interactions to lead and take care of others the way we would want to be led and be taken care of. I can remember receiving an e-mail from a Soldier who wanted to share with me his gratitude for a decision that I'd made some five years earlier.

His e-mail began, "Ma'am, you probably don't even remember who I am. I was in your command in Germany, as we were deploying to Iraq in 2005. I was newly married, and my wife was pregnant with our first child expected within two weeks of our deployment. My chain of command at the company level disapproved my staying in Germany an additional two weeks and joining the unit later so that I could see the birth of my firstborn child. However, when this situation was brought to your attention at the general officer level, you reversed the decision and allowed me to stay in Germany and join my unit sixteen days after they deployed. Your decision changed my life forever. I will be forever grateful to you for allowing me to experience that. It was a result of your leadership that taught me to take care of my Soldiers in the same way."

I didn't have to allow this Soldier to remain in Germany. However, it was the right thing to do. My response to his situation was that I had the ability and the responsibility to change this decision and make this right for him. There would be little to no impact on his company. I used my head and my heart to make that decision and took the responsibility to correct the decisions of those below me.

I made it clear to those who worked for me that I would not judge their performance solely based on what went right or wrong. Rather, I would judge them on their response.

Do you take *response*-ability, listen to your gut, and override decisions others have made that you feel are not correct for the situation? Or, do you go with the flow and let whatever decisions have been made stand, no matter what your heart and mind are telling you?

★   Starting Over—Better, Not Bitter   ★

Following graduation from West Point, my army career included a series of eighteen moves and two or three times that many bosses. From north to south—Fort Drum, New York, to Miami, Florida, and east to west—Fort Lee, Virginia, to Fort Lewis, Washington, and Schofield, Hawaii, and across the globe—Italy, Germany, Afghanistan, and Iraq—my experiences were as diverse as the leadership styles of my all-male superior officers.

I had the great honor and privilege of leading America's sons and daughters at every level of command—from platoon leader to commanding general. Blessed with promotions recognizing my performance and potential, I moved up the chain of command on a fast track with the opportunity to continue to do so. But my life, personally and professionally, took a different turn.

My physical health had been on a downward spiral, and shortly after my promotion to general officer, I was diagnosed with chronic fibromyalgia. The result for me was that I was no longer able to reach those high standards of excellence that I had always demanded of myself. I initially convinced myself when I returned from my tour of duty in Iraq that I would be under much less stress, could get well, and would rebuild my endurance.

Unfortunately, it was not to be. The disease had a grip on me, and I eventually conceded that my health was not going to improve while on my current career track. This time my recovery couldn't include pushing myself to the next level. As a result, I made the very tough decision: the choice to respond to my situation by submitting my retirement paperwork and departing the army.

I was only forty-nine years old, but I knew I needed to leave in order to wrap my arms around this disease—instead of letting it control me.

I was approached by many leaders and subordinates and asked not to leave. Although I appreciated the vote of confidence, I still believed I needed to depart. If I couldn't perform to the standard I expected, then I couldn't justify staying. You must decide what your standard of excellence is, demand it of yourself, and be determined to hold yourself accountable and responsible.

In 2008, with a heart heavy for leaving my Soldiers and my military Family, as well as potentially disappointing those who had mentored me over the years and expected me to continue to move up the ranks, I retired from active duty.

My journey to renewed health and energy was a path I had not imagined. I attribute my wellness today—a life without prescription drugs and minimal pain—to the talented hands, minds, and hearts of doctors of chiropractic. They introduced me to routine spinal adjustments, nutrition and whole-food supplements, and massage therapy and acupuncture. As a result, I began telling my story, and I am now a passionate advocate determined to seeing chiropractic care as a fully resourced health care option for all military men and women and their Families.

In the process of telling my story about getting well, I discovered people had a great desire, especially the corporate sector, to learn more about leadership lessons from the military. Thus, I began to share my passion for leadership and stories on leadership from my military career.

Having to retire from the military was a significant shift in my life. I decided to focus on my response and make something good out of it. My *response*-ability as a leader is to look up, and look forward. When things don't go as planned, I don't allow myself to stay in a foxhole of failure or regret. My example to others by how I respond should be a source of encouragement and inspiration. I truly never want to regret my responses.

★   Minimize the Regrets   ★

If I graphically drew my life on a chart, you would see a trend line that gradually goes up with data points scattered both above and below the line. Above the line would be those remarkable, successful, meaningful, exciting moments in my life—serving our nation, successfully leading America's sons and daughters, being a faithful friend and daughter. Below the line would be my crucibles—surgeries, divorce, bad decisions, difficult bosses, deaths, early retirement because of an illness. The points for which I had momentary regret have been some of my greatest life lessons. However, the goal throughout my life's journey has been to live my life with an attitude and mentality of "no regrets."

I developed a *no regrets* litmus test and tried to consciously conduct a daily, quality control check of my attitude, actions, and decisions. As I place my head on my pillow at night, I reflect on my day and see if am I able to muster any event that happened where some other person's life is a little bit better for my having been in it. Did I do anything meaningful for someone today? Was I able to touch someone's life for the better, especially someone who can do absolutely nothing for me? It didn't even have to be anyone I know. As a matter of fact, there is more meaning in not knowing who the person was at all. If so, I can rest without regret.

My West Point Alma Mater ends with, "When my course is done, may it be said, well done, West Point for thee." As I served in the army, I would think about the day I'd depart the ranks. I never pondered much on what rank I would achieve or how long I would stay, but I did think about what would be said when I left. My desire was always that the words would at least be, "Well done, good and faithful servant." To achieve this, I think living by the notion of no regrets was quite helpful.

When it comes to my final resting place here on earth, I intend to have etched on my tombstone, "No Regrets." No dates, no titles. Why?

When passersby look at my headstone, I suspect they might think, *I wonder if this person was male or female?* The message I want them to receive is, "What difference does it make?"

They might ask themselves, *I wonder if this person was young or old?* Again, I want the message to be, "What difference does it make?!"

What is most important is that the person buried there must have tried to live life the best he or she could. The individual must have cared about character, because what really matters is what is on the inside of a person, not the outside. What really matters is how they took *response*-ability for life's curveballs.

Living each day to make a difference and minimize regret is how I choose to define my life. I hope the values shared and the compassion shown will live on in the hearts of those with whom I have come in contact throughout my journey, similar to the way great leaders have touched my life.

How are you choosing to live your life and respond to the shift that happens in it? How do you take *response*-ability for the personal and professional decisions you make every day? How can you minimize regrets for missed opportunities to make a positive difference to those around you and to yourself?

Leadership Principle 14
Embrace and Drive Change

> *Everyone thinks of changing the world, but no one thinks of changing himself.* ~Leo Tolstoy
>
> *The world as we have created it is a process of our thinking. It cannot be changed without changing our thinking.* ~Albert Einstein
>
> *Those who cannot change their minds cannot change anything.* ~George Bernard Shaw

★   Change Starts with You   ★

Do you like change? Most of us like change only if it was our idea! Fact of life: other people have great initiatives, ideas, and ways of doing things, too.

Have you spent your whole life thinking, "Someday, when I am in charge, things will be better"? It is the lifelong game of *we versus they*—*we* do it the right way, *they* don't. As I reminded those who worked for me, "Remember, someday you might be the *they*!"

During my career, the US Army went through several major transformations, but none quite as relevant to the current mission and at the same time as drastic as the changes made during

Operation Iraqi Freedom. Not only were we at war in Iraq, but we were also undergoing massive reorganization of our unit structures and missions. You can imagine the chaos and anxiety of going to war. Add to this changing the way you are organized and the way you fight, and you have a great deal of additional stress.

As a logistician in the army, responsible for the distribution of supplies and equipment across the battlefield, the radical changes in our organizations required a great deal of additional education, strategic communication, and training. We did not necessarily stay out in front of the changes as quickly and effectively as we should have, which caused even more friction and confusion.

In 2004, when I was assigned as the Commanding General of the 3rd Corps Support Command in Germany, I was given the mission to transform our units (Corps Support Groups) in Germany to the new structures (Sustainment Brigades). As the structures changed, so did their physical locations and how we performed our support operations for other units in Europe. I quickly realized that I had to personally engage and embrace the changes being mandated by the top army leaders. This meant studying and understanding the changes and reasons for them and then training my own units to grasp the transformation.

Within a few months of taking on these historic, sweeping changes, our command was notified we were headed to Iraq. We weren't relieved of any responsibility to continue to transform in Europe. Preparing for our combat mission was in *addition* to our European mission.

The combat mission upon which we would embark in Iraq was vast. The 3rd COSCOM would expand from a few thousand Soldiers to over twenty thousand. The additional forces would come from across the world, from New York to Hawaii, and from Puerto Rico to Korea.

I recognized quickly there would be a requirement for me to personally engage with the new leaders who would be working for me. They needed to know who I was, what my expectations and priorities were, and what missions they would be assigned. As their commander, I had to certify that they were trained and ready to take on their missions. Once we arrived in Iraq, there would be only two weeks to transition between departing and arriving units. Forming, storming, norming, and performing would take on a whole new meaning!

It would also be necessary for me to directly embrace the leaders of the units we would be supporting, such as the division commanders of the 101st Airborne Air Assault and the 4th Infantry Division. These two-star generals needed to be fully aware of the army transformational changes with regard to logistics operations in Iraq. A major change for them would be the loss of their senior logistics commander and headquarters (the colonel and the Division Support Command). This transformation would cause both the position and command to be reorganized under my command, the Corps Support Command, providing logistics support under one logistics umbrella.

Division commanders greatly resisted the change. My goal was to provide them reassurance that they would see no interruption in logistical support as a result of the changes. With their concerns in mind, I made the decision to personally travel to the United States and meet with the division commanders, taking along a few key leaders from my command. Our purpose was to communicate the changes and reassure the commanders and their staffs that they would not be negatively affected by the transformational changes. We even went so far as to show them how we thought operations would improve, although we were learning along with them. I had never commanded at this level before, and the new way of supporting units with logistics was new for my units and me, as well.

Choosing to use humor, I framed the change like this, "Sir, think of it like this: you are not losing a son—you are gaining a daughter-in-law. You are not losing a colonel—you are gaining a general. If you have any logistics shortfall, you can poke your finger in my chest."

Once deployed, there were many times a division commander did complain to the three-star commander, our boss, that transformation was not working and was adamant he had to have his senior logistics commander and logistics command back under his control. Those conversations would cause my boss to call me for my opinion. Each time I tried to remain calm, even though it was frustrating.

I would ask my boss, "Sir, can the division commander give you any example of a mission not being performed? If so, we must absolutely address the situation, but if not, then this is more about controlling assets than mission."

"No, Becky, there has been no mention of any specific mission not being performed."

After this happened several times, at the recommendation of my operations officer, I decided the best approach would be to take an offensive measure and build case studies on how logistics operations were working more effectively because of the transformation. This ended up being a brilliant move, because we were able to accurately and persuasively communicate how transformation was working. So, instead of always having to defend our work, we were able to present our transformation case studies to high-ranking visitors and began to use them to shape changes in our doctrine on logistics operations.

By embracing the operational and organizational changes that transformation presented, we captured new business practices, adopted new procedures in our doctrine, and more effectively accomplished our mission.

For example, an institutional process we used, called the Military Decision Making Process (MDMP), was positively impacted. By reorganizing the logistics missions under the command and control of my organization, the decision-making process was streamlined. We greatly reduced the amount of time and energy required by multiple levels of staff to develop our mission plans. We became more responsive to the constant and unpredictable changes on the battlefield, and we were able to more effectively and efficiently provide support to all coalition units. The long-term influence was adopting some of the operational changes—essentially, our best practices—into our army doctrine. By doing so, the changes we embraced, which were battle tested and proven, became our new business rules.

When change occurs in your lane, do you embrace it? Are you leading yourself first to understand what the change means and what effect it will have on those who work for you and on those you work for? Are you minimizing the angst and anxiety by communicating and encouraging others?

Our actions did not eliminate conflict, complexity, or confrontation, but those issues were minimized. As the senior logistics commander, I had to proactively lead through the storm of change, remind myself to be the calm in the chaos, and personify the change I wanted to see in others.

★   Making the Tough Decisions   ★

Most of us know when we have a leadership challenge on our hands. We are able to sense the conflict. Our gut tells us we need to address it. Some of us listen to those inner nudgings, and some of us ignore them.

Ignoring situations never makes the problems go away. Conversely, the problems get worse. Leaders must confront conflict, and they must keep people informed. When you are in the midst of organizational change, conflict and challenges only increase.

Although I believe we were quite successful at the organizational level, embracing change during army transformation and our tour-of-combat duty posed some challenges. There was one particular incident where I felt I could have done a better job of keeping open lines of communication.

One of my colonel commanders brought to my attention that his senior noncommissioned officer (NCO), the command sergeant major (CSM) for his brigade, was having inappropriate relationships with female Soldiers. Prior to deployment, his brigade had been assigned to one of the divisions in the United States. Again, under transformation they were reorganized and, upon deployment, were assigned under my command and control. By regulation, I was responsible for all they did or failed to do.

Unfortunately, in the case of this brigade, the transition of control from the division to my command was not smooth. It had been very challenging getting the division leadership to relinquish control of this brigade. During my trip to the United States to brief them, it was clear they were not embracing the changes. The division commander opposed transformation before deploying, and he carried his disdain for the new concepts with him to Iraq.

The relationship between the division commander and me was professional but not exactly friendly. We had great respect for each other's responsibilities and the mission, but we were in considerable disagreement when it came to the transformation efforts.

When the situation involving the CSM was raised to my level, as required by regulation, I directed an investigation be conducted. The investigation resulted in sufficient evidence for prosecution. After many weeks of interviews and discussions with the chain of command, I made the decision to relieve the command sergeant major of his responsibilities. Relieving a command sergeant major, especially in combat, is not a common occurrence.

After making this decision, I received a phone call at my headquarters in Balad, Iraq, from the division commander who previously had this CSM assigned to him. It was clear by the tone in his voice that he was quite irritated.

It is important to note that I had and still have a great deal of respect for the division commander and his leadership. I also had a great deal of understanding for his resistance to the major changes this transformation was causing. On one hand, I truly understood his angst. On the other hand, I felt he needed to step back and look at the greater picture—the whole army, and not just his division.

"Becky, how are you doing?"

Before I answered his question, I thought to myself, *I don't think he really cares how I'm doing, but he's being very professional to start the conversation that way.* I was also thinking this must be about logistics and his concerns over some mission.

"Sir, I'm doing fine, thank you," I responded. "How are you and how can I help you?"

"I heard you were relieving one of my command sergeant majors."

"No, sir. No, sir, I'm not relieving one of your command sergeant majors."

"Oh, my misunderstanding, Becky. I was told you were relieving Command Sergeant Major _____" (he gave me the name of the brigade command sergeant major who now reported to me).

"Oh, yes, sir, I am relieving Command Sergeant Major _____. But he's *my* command sergeant major, sir."

As I waited for him to respond, I became irritated and a bit angry about his continued reluctance to understand and accept how things had changed under transformation. This brigade CSM was not his because he was assigned to my unit. So, the responsibility fell squarely on my shoulders, and the issue was my responsibility to resolve.

Yes, I knew the CSM was originally from the division commander's home base and command. Yes, I was aware the division commander had trouble with transformation, but I never even entertained the thought of calling the division commander to inform him that I was doing the investigation, or of the outcome.

It would have been far better for me to have been more considerate and professional by informing him of the situation, especially given his opposition to transformation. I didn't purposely neglect to inform him, but in reflection, not sharing this information with the division commander was clearly a shortfall on my part. I did apologize to him for not informing him, but I didn't apologize for the disciplinary actions I took against the CSM.

Details, especially during times of change and conflict, do matter and must be communicated. Considering the second and third levels of the effects of our decisions and asking ourselves who else needs to know will minimize further conflict and facilitate smoother transitions.

Are you willing to change your thinking? Are you willing to lead yourself to make changes in your personal and professional life where change is needed? Start today to assess how you can better embrace changes that are happening in your life and encourage others to do the same.

Leadership Principle 15
Be Demanding, Not Demeaning

> *If you are going through hell, keep going.* ~Prime Minister Winston Churchill
>
> *That which doesn't kill us makes us stronger.* ~Friedrich Nietzsche
>
> *Never grow a wishbone where your backbone ought to be.*
> ~Clementine Paddleford

We have all worked for demanding bosses, and some of us are probably considered demanding bosses. Personally, I think being a leader requires being demanding—tough love. After all, you cannot *hope* people will follow the rules or perform to a standard. You must demand it.

However, there is a huge difference between being demanding and being demeaning. I don't believe there is ever room for the latter. Leaders who are demeaning can be successful, but at what cost? Just consider the extremes, such as Hitler and Saddam Hussein; their abuse of power ended with great losses. They had followers but only out of fear and blind loyalty.

The majority of my bosses were demanding, for which I am very grateful. The few who were demeaning made life miserable for everyone around. Did I learn from the demeaning bosses? Yes, I learned what I did *not* want to be like when I grew up!

As a leader I was strict—by the book, no nonsense, disciplined, and determined. I had high expectations of those who worked for me and myself. I was demanding first and foremost of myself. For leaders to be able to create an environment that is fair, respectful, productive, and desirable for people to work and invest in, it has to start with their own example.

As a demanding leader, I know it was not easy to work for me. Isn't that why it's called *work*? Some who have served with me have told me that I was their toughest boss. At the same time, and somewhat surprising to them, was that they discovered they also learned the most, developed as a leader, and found it to be the most rewarding.

My being demanding of them simply resulted in them being demanding of themselves. I didn't have to resort to being demeaning, intimidating, or controlling to achieve those results.

★ A Leader Must Know the Difference between a Pat on the Back and a Kick in the Butt ★

One of my first mentors in the army advised, "As a leader you must know the difference between a pat on the back and a kick in the butt, and you must be able to do both." He reminded me the distance between the two is only eight to ten inches, and as a leader, I better be able to deliver both—and understand the difference. He was one of the toughest bosses for whom I worked, or as we would say, "He was harder than woodpecker lips."

Although demanding, he was never demeaning. We knew what his standards were, because he published them on a small card, and we were required to carry that card with us at all times.

When asked, we had better know what his current priorities were. More important, we had better be upholding them. He had high standards and expectations, and we were a high-performing organization.

Did we have challenges? Of course. This was not about perfectionism. It was about being involved, aware, and engaged. He did not measure us only by how much went right or wrong. Rather, he graded us on how we responded to the challenges, corrected the wrongs, and established and maintained good order and discipline.

My second company command under his leadership was an ammunition unit, the only ammunition company in the Pacific Northwest. It was also one of the largest commands on post, and with it came some of the greatest challenges. Our mission was storing, securing, maintaining, and distributing ammunition. The control measures were very strict.

Every time there was an incident involving ammunition, I was one of the first ones the boss called. My fellow company commanders used to joke that they would be ready to go home at night, and I was always headed to the boss's office to address another problem. Most of those evenings were "kick in the butt" times!

Without a doubt, that company command was one of the hardest jobs I held in the army, and my boss was one of my most demanding leaders. The result was a period of significant professional development as a leader. His influence and impact were lasting. Several years later, I wrote my master's thesis on visionary leadership, citing his example and what I learned from him. When I was promoted to general officer, I requested that he officiate the ceremony, and he presented me with the stars he had worn on his uniform.

A leader must be able to praise, recognize, and reward. A leader must also have discernment, courage, and discipline to know when consequences must be delivered and how to deliver them. Knowing when, and how, to do each is equally important.

How are you developing, training, and coaching those who work for you? Do you know when to deliver a kick in the butt and when to deliver a pat on the back? Are you able to do both without being demeaning?

★   Hazed by an Upper-Class Cadet   ★

There are many times when words go through our heads as we see a situation unfold, and our emotional urge is to attack. Have you ever said something you regretted? I have often beat myself up with, "Becky, those were inside words!"

There is a wonderful book called *3 Seconds*, by Les Parrott. The premise and thesis of his book is this: if each of us paused and took just three seconds before we spoke, we would be much happier with the results. Too often we make knee-jerk responses that we wish we could take back. We reactively respond using only emotion and not intellect. Again, this emphasizes the importance of fusion of heart and mind. It will become very obvious when you are not leading with both, because the results will be either 1) you are too passive or, 2) you rip someone apart before getting all the details. As we often hear people say, you shoot the messenger.

I have witnessed people who become like the leaders whom they actually complained about or did not respect. How does that happen? Perhaps that goes back to the old saying, "If you can't beat 'em, join 'em."

During my first year as a cadet at West Point, many upper-class cadets hazed me. The majority of the readers are probably thinking that the men in the upper classes hazed the most. And you are correct, they did. However, one of the most demeaning hazing events, or "butt chewings," as we called them, was actually from a female cadet, a member of the first class of women. I remember being surprised, and then disappointed, by her words and actions.

I had gone to morning classes and carried my rain gear, because it was the uniform of the day. By the time classes ended, it had begun to rain. I put the plastic cover over my wool cap, donned my gray plastic raincoat, and then pulled my gray rubber galoshes over my black leather low-quarter shoes. As I pulled the back of the rubber up over the heel of my shoe, the rubber split in half! No matter how I tried, I could not get it to stay on my shoe. This was a problem, because I would be out of uniform without my galoshes on.

I placed the galoshes on top of my pile of books, tucked them into my chest, and tried to obscure myself in the middle of the pack of students racing back to the barracks. As we passed by the upperclassmen (we were required to walk faster, since we were first-year cadets), we were obligated to shout, "Good morning, sir. Good morning, ma'am."

I was about halfway to the barracks when I heard a loud and thunderous, "Miss, halt!" I wasn't the only *Miss* out there, and even though I had a pretty good sense they were talking to me, I kept pinging (slang for moving out at 120 paces a minute) toward the barracks.

Again, I heard from behind me, "Miss, halt!" I decided this was only going to get worse. I'd better stop.

I stopped and executed a perfect about-face. Much to my surprise, standing in front of me was an upper-class woman! At first I thought, *Phew, a woman, she will understand.*

She got right into my face and wanted to know why I was out of uniform and not wearing my galoshes. I asked permission to explain, and she granted it. I showed her my ripped galoshes. Again, to my surprise, she began reprimanding me in a very loud voice. From her perspective I was a loser, a disgrace to the women, and inept, because I failed to maintain my uniform.

Of course, I could not say what was going through my head, such as, *Are you kidding me? Do you think I wanted to tear my galoshes and be out of uniform?* As I watched this unfold, I realized she was proving herself to all the male cadets passing by. She became immensely demeaning and was performing at my expense, which made me even angrier.

I went from thinking I was going to get one of my easiest corrections to receiving one of the harshest I ever received. Granted, showing me favoritism because I was a woman would have been equally wrong.

As I reflect on that day and think about my own experiences coming up through the ranks and trying to prove myself worthy, I realize there are requirements to becoming accepted. Often, there is a strong tendency to behave like the demeaning leaders who preside over us. That's exactly what this cadet did. She wanted to fit in, prove she was not showing favoritism toward women, and demonstrate she was just as tough as the men.

Although I understand why she acted that way, I didn't agree with it. The lesson for me, and I hope for you, is not to allow yourself to fall into the trap of repeating the bad leadership behaviors of those whom you do not respect.

In contrast, when a demanding leader has led you, you have great appreciation for the responsibility that leaders have and the way they hold themselves accountable for making sure the mission is accomplished. You also have a great appreciation for how horrible that experience is when a demeaning boss has bullied you. As a leader, you have a choice. Choose to be demanding, not demeaning.

It is very difficult to deal with toxic leaders, especially when they are your bosses, as I shared with you under Leadership Principle 3. The greatest advantage of having been immersed in that type of horrible command environment was that I was able to recognize when I had subordinate leaders who were creating the same negative, horrible environment. As I discovered, equally as challenging as toxic bosses are toxic leaders who work for you.

★   Toxic Leaders Who Work for You   ★

I was blessed to have incredible leaders of character work for me throughout my career. Occasionally, you find some who are not meeting the standards. There are varying degrees of not meeting expectations. For me, the most challenging were those who were demeaning and controlling. They also seemed to be the ones who were experts at showing the boss one face while mistreating others when the boss wasn't around.

One of the most demeaning leaders within my command in Iraq had great finesse at appearing completely professional when higher-level leaders were around but then controlling and disrespectful when they were not.

As I investigated this leader's behavior, I likened it to the abused-spouse syndrome: knowing when and where to punch, twisting words, hiding the bruises, and controlling in a threatening way so no one dared come forward to report. I knew in my gut things were not right, but even after directing investigations, nothing specific was substantiated.

People who abuse are not stupid. They choose their victims carefully, and they choose how and when they abuse, so they remain in control. They measure their words and actions and ride a thin line of disrespect. Toxic leaders have a way of threatening a person's career, so they won't pursue or report. When called out, they will immediately turn it around as your misinterpretation of their intent.

Ironically, the way we measure success in most organizations actually facilitates toxic leaders getting away with their behavior. They are smart enough to get the mission done, meet the performance objectives, and sometimes even exceed goals. However, at what expense?

This particular leader said to me condescendingly, "Ma'am, you cannot rate me poorly, because I am the only commander who accomplished the mission with no Soldiers killed during our tenure in Iraq."

At first, this comment stopped me in my tracks. My initial thought was, *How bold.*

Then I thought, *Good point? Factually correct? Perhaps, but what about the daily lives of those who worked in that toxic environment?* There is nothing we should value more than the lives of our men and women.

As I thought through this, I kept thinking about what it must be like to work every day under the threat of this leader. In reality, how many lives were adversely affected? How many people did we lose because they decided to leave the army as a result of this person's toxic leadership? Equally troubling, how many leaders adopted the same leadership style in order to survive, and then subsequently ruined other people's lives?

I thought about the mission, too. Was the mission just to deliver supplies on the battlefield? No. The mission also encompassed training, educating, and developing people and leaving a legacy of knowledgeable, seasoned, trustworthy leaders—leaders who would lead the next generation of men and women honorably. Had this part of the mission been accomplished? No.

After a few moments of collecting my thoughts, I responded, "Well, I agree you had no Soldier killed by enemy combatants. I would submit to you, however, that you personally *killed* a few careers because of your poor leadership and you destroyed morale."

When people have to work and operate in a demeaning environment, they will leave that environment as soon as possible.

I always listened to my gut, and when necessary, investigated my notions. Just because the investigations turned up empty-handed did not mean there was not a problem. My gut still told me there was a problem. I caution leaders not to throw up your arms in despair. Continue to monitor and follow your instincts and keep the pressure on the individual in question. Eventually, the person's demise will come. I might not have had enough evidence to fire the commander, but I had enough influence to ensure there would be no promotions in the individual's future.

Have you ever worked for a leader who was always angry? Did you wonder how the leader could have possibly achieved the level at which the person was? I had a subordinate leader who was a bitter, angry person. He was quite senior, and when we began working together, I was dumbfounded as to how he could have been promoted to his current level. I doubt he liked any boss he ever worked for during his career.

I knew I had to address the situation, since everyone walked on eggshells, fearing they might set him off. I began by counseling him on his anger issues, to which he was not very receptive, but I felt I had to do something.

At first, he was defensive and let me know in no uncertain terms, "Ma'am, you are the only person to ever tell me I have a problem." I have thought about his comment many times. Perhaps I was the only one to express this criticism. It wouldn't be surprising, as I often had people tell me I was the first leader to ever counsel them, even though the army requires it by regulation. All too often, I saw leaders who did not invest time and energy into personnel situations because they did not like to deal with confrontation. No leader *likes* to deal with conflict, but we must. Not dealing with a problem allows it to get worse.

It became evident he had anger issues beyond my capability to help him resolve. Fortunately, we have wonderful resources in the military to support and assist the commander. My next step was sending him to anger management classes.

He wasn't too pleased about this, but initially it seemed to help.

After a few sessions, he even thanked me for sending him. He conducted himself more professionally at first, but after a few weeks, he defaulted to his old behavior.

Although the result of my counseling many people over the years was usually successful, this individual was never able to live up to and lead to the standard expected of him in his senior position. I had to remove him, and he retired. In the short-term, you might say this was a failure. But, in the long-term, the effort of helping him was a success. His marriage, which had been on the rocks, survived, and his anger eventually became more controlled.

I don't want to leave the impression that I believe there is no hope for helping a toxic leader, because that's not the case. It is a much greater leadership challenge to try to change the behavior of a toxic leader than to develop someone with fire in the gut to learn and grow as a leader.

Do you work to develop your subordinates in a positive way, or do you use bullying and intimidation to get the job done? Do your team members enjoy working with you, or do they jump at the first opportunity to work somewhere else? Do you take the time to counsel employees who are not living up to the expected standards?

Be demanding without being demeaning. Others will respect and follow you. You will build trust and loyalty. You and your team will move from good to great.

Childhood Days – My Leader DNA
(top) Family photo, 5 years old, 1964
(bottom left) Bucky Becky, 8 years old, 1967
(bottom center) Rancher of the week, 12 years old, 1971
(bottom right) Senior photo, 18 years old, 1977

West Point Years–Don't Quit
(top left) BEAST barracks, 1977
(top right) Plebe year, I love a parade, 1977
(bottom left) Completing RECONDO training, Mom cheering, 1978
(bottom right) Firstie year, full dress over white, 1980

Attitude – Never Forget Where You Started
(top) Second Lieutenant, with Mom and Dad before
leaving for first assignment in Italy, 1981
(bottom) Captain, company command in Fort Lewis, Washington, 1985

Commit Yourself Daily
(top left) Major, 101st Airborne (Air Assault)
Division, Fort Campbell, Kentucky, 1994
(top right) Lieutenant Colonel, Battalion Commander,
25th Infantry Division, Hawaii, 1997
(bottom) Colonel, re-enlisting a 10th Mountain
Division Soldier, Afghanistan, 2002

Leave a Legacy
(top left) Lieutenant Colonel, Aunt Becky with
nephew and legacy Soldier, 2000
(top right) Brigadier General, with namesake, Rebecca, 2007
(bottom) Colonel, serving Thanksgiving dinner
to the Soldiers, Germany, 2003

Battle Buddies for Life–Relationships Matter
(top) Lifetime friendships, success is a team sport, 2004
(bottom) Sister Soldiers: Deputy Commander, Commanding
General, and Chief of Staff, 3rd COSCOM, Balad, Iraq, 2005

Trust the Differences
(top) The Commanding Generals, Baghdad, Iraq, 2006
(bottom left) Receiving the Iraqi flag, southeastern Iraq, 2006
(bottom right) Sending Soldiers home after year-long
deployment, thank you and well done, 2006

Create Hope and Shape Success
(top) Saluting Iraqi Soldiers, respect has no
language barriers, Taji, Iraq, 2006
(bottom) Working with Iraqi commander and his team, Mosul, Iraq, 2006

Unconditional Love – Define Your Success by
How You Make Others Successful
(top) Mom and Dad, celebrating West Point graduation, 1981
(bottom) Mom and Dad, enjoying last military formal, 2008

You Have a Purpose in This World
(top) Last Army change of command ceremony, Ordnance
Center and Schools, Aberdeen, Maryland, 2008
(bottom) New journey as inspirational speaker, Network
of Executive Women, Cincinnati, 2012

Leadership Principle 16
Be the Calm in the Chaos

> *As a leader, you must be a good bad-news taker.*
> *~General Leon Salomon, Ret.*
>
> *Be like a duck. Calm on the surface, but always paddling like the dickens underneath. ~Michael Caine*

I think true leadership is determined by how a leader responds during chaos. In the military we refer to this as being "battle tested." Uncertainty, unplanned events, unknown outcomes, unexpected failures, and unfamiliar surroundings individually or collectively can result in chaos.

Reflect for a moment. How do you respond to these things? Are you a calming force, or do you immediately react, inflicting more chaos? Are you able to control your reaction, listen instead of speak, quickly assess the situation, and then calmly give guidance and direction? When someone comes to you with a crisis or bad news, are you a good bad-news taker? Do you pray for the storm or crisis to go away, or do you pray to get through the storm?

A calming attitude in a storm of activity eases the situation for all involved. It leads to a higher level of productivity by helping people to work through the challenge, rather than letting them run in circles trying to figure out what to do. A calm response to chaos results in the best solutions being developed in a professional, responsive manner. But it doesn't just happen. It must start with you, as the leader, being the calm in the chaos.

I've worked for a few bosses who couldn't take bad news, some of them to such a degree that if you had bad news, they didn't want you to tell them. I had one boss tell me, "Becky, the way I operate is like this: if you bring a problem to me that means you cannot handle it at your level."

I thought to myself, *Is he serious?*

Think about that statement. Think about how difficult it would be to keep a boss like that informed. It took me months to figure out his tactic. It allowed him to deny knowing about any problems below him. It was a horrible work environment.

What sort of environment are you creating? Are people afraid to approach you? I did not want people bringing me every problem to solve, but I wanted to stay informed. How else would I be able to guide them? Besides, bad news doesn't get better with time. Problems don't go away just because we don't talk about them—and they don't disappear just because you have a positive attitude. You have to be open to discussion and be willing to address situations.

Overcoming chaos starts with you, the leader, providing the thoughtful calm.

★   Organized Chaos—Treating the Wounded   ★

When I arrived in Iraq in October 2005, one of the first tasks I set for myself was visiting the combat support hospital. I wanted to meet the commander and staff, as I believe they had one of the most important missions on the battlefield: keeping our wounded alive.

As the incoming commander, I needed to be knowledge-able about their work and wanted them to know they had my full support. They knew I was visiting, and they had prepared a briefing and tour of the hospital.

Just as we approached the hospital area, we could hear the sounds of helicopters, and it seemed everyone was in motion. "Wounded inbound!" was being shouted as people moved out with purpose to their assigned locations. Later that night I wrote in my journal:

> As I approached the main entrance, I could clearly see organized chaos. I was met by several people, all very apol-ogetic that they had to delay the briefing and tour because of inbound, severely injured Soldiers from an IED attack. I told them to not focus on me; do what they needed for these Soldiers. As we walked by the emergency room, the scene before me was one I had never experienced. There was blood everywhere. The surgeon was holding a Soldier's right leg in his hands. His eyes said it all, "I can't save his leg, but I can save his life." I told him to focus, do what he is trained to do, and I turned around and walked out.

I did not want the doctors wasting one more minute paying attention to the new boss. I was not the priority. In this case, my staying would not have provided calm. There was plenty of time for a return visit, presentations, statistics, and education. At this moment, the mission of saving lives was at hand. I was able to provide calm by knowing it was better to leave than to stay.

Do you know when to get out of the way and let your team members do their job?

★   Black Hawk Down   ★

A few months later, on January 12, 2006, there was a knock at the door of my hooch (the place where I slept and showered). I opened the door to see the ashen faces of three of my senior officers. Immediately I knew there was bad news and motioned for them to come in.

The operations officer started the conversation, "Ma'am, a helicopter has crashed in northern Iraq. We believe we have one, maybe two personnel who were manifested out of Baghdad on that flight. There is still a lot of chaos and uncertainty, but we wanted to let you know right away."

I knew better than to start drilling them with questions. Doing so would just aggravate them, and enough negative emotions were already in the room. I also knew they were doing their best to maintain their own composures, to mentally and emotionally process what was happening, and to remain calm for me as I did the same for them. The loss of a Soldier begins a strict and stressful process of notifications, reports, leader huddles, investigations, and memorial services. It is a gut-wrenching and sad time, especially for the Family members and battle buddies of our fallen.

I did ask if they knew the identity of two Soldiers, and they gave me their names, ranks, and units. Their uncertainty came from the fact that the individuals in question had been on standby for the flight, and, at the last minute, several people were bumped and replaced by other personnel.

As the hours passed, more details became available to us. Twelve people were killed on the aircraft, and one was an officer from our command.

Do you know when to press your staff for additional details and when it is best to reduce or minimize anxiety by allowing events to play out before gathering all the details?

★ Seconds of Chaos, Lifetime of Changes ★

Before deploying to Iraq, one of my mentors told me, "Becky, watch your Soldiers carefully. In combat there are days, even weeks of boredom, but there are moments of intense chaos. You have to be the calm."

Early on the morning of January 16, 2006, I was working out in a small tent facility where we had a few treadmills, bikes, and weight machines. About thirty minutes into my workout, I heard the sirens sound, and I knew the base had been hit with mortars and possibly rockets. It was not an uncommon occurrence because of our location.

I immediately ran to my headquarters a few hundred feet away to find out what part of the base had been hit and receive a damage assessment. My number one concern was loss of life or people wounded. My operations officer informed me that they received an initial report of possible Soldiers injured, and one senior Soldier was at the hospital in critical condition.

The command sergeant major and I headed to the hospital. As we entered the Soldier's room, the doctor pulled me aside. I could see and hear the words of encouragement from the Soldier's first-line leaders and fellow battle buddies. The doctor gave me a status on his situation. It wasn't good news. The doctor assured me that he would live but would lose both of his eyes. Shrapnel had gone into one eye and ricocheted out the other. Miraculously, he suffered no brain damage.

Every time we visited our Soldiers, I had a Purple Heart ready to present at the bedside. As I held the Purple Heart in my hand, I realized he would never see this ribbon. I placed it into his hand, described it to him, and had him feel the shape of the heart. I reminded him how grateful we were for his tremendous service to our country. I asked him to feel the shape of the heart and told him he had the heart of a Soldier—character, competence, and compassion.

As I spoke to him, he could feel my hand, my sweaty palm, and sensed my sadness. At that moment he began to console me—telling me not to worry, not to feel sorry for him, and not to be discouraged. He told me he was grateful, because he was going home, would still be able to hug his wife, and would walk his daughter down the aisle one day. He knew so many others didn't get that second chance.

He knew he couldn't return to his team, and that saddened him. But he told me, "Ma'am, I may never *see* my team again, but I will be there when they redeploy [return home], and I will know them by their voices."

I thought about his words and how powerful they were coming from a person in his position. Powerful. In the moments of chaos that took his eyesight forever, he became a man who saw his world and his future more clearly than most of us with twenty/twenty vision. He was leading up and providing us with calm in the chaos.

The battalion commander, who reached out and touched my arm, quickly interrupted my thoughts. He said, "Ma'am, may we have your approval to send the lieutenant as an escort on the medical flight to be his eyes as we return him home?"

I unhesitatingly responded, "Absolutely. Absolutely."

Upon agreeing to allow that to happen, the energy in the room visibly changed. It was almost a shift from chaos to peacefulness, knowing that with the lieutenant's presence, they were being allowed to fully embrace their comrade and escort him home.

For me, the thought of being blinded was suffocating. Providing an escort to be his eyes until he could be reunited with his Family and properly integrated into the health care system was a brilliant idea on the part of the battalion commander. If it had been me, I would have wanted the same consideration.

That evening as I lay down for a couple of hours of sleep, I was suddenly very anxious and very awake. I began to question my authority to make that decision. Within minutes, confidence overcame anxiety as I reassured myself that I had made the right decision. My litmus test for leading myself and making decisions had always been this: if I had to stand in front of my commander in chief, the president of the United States, and defend any action or decision I made, I would be able to do so. I was confident I would be able to do so in this case.

The young lieutenant was gone for only a few days, and I doubt there was any noticeable degradation of mission on our end in Iraq. I do know for certain that approving the request to send the lieutenant affected the wounded sergeant's life and those of his battalion. No doubt he will forever remember the graciousness, compassion, and sacrifice of his unit to send a valuable asset with him to be his eyes as he made his way home. In this way we were able to provide him a bit of calm in the midst of his chaos.

When your team chooses to make a sacrifice for the good of one of their members, do you support their efforts, or do you consider only the work that needs to be done? Do you lead with calm and compassion in moments of chaos, or do you join in the chaos?

Leadership Principle 17
Create Hope and Shape Success

> *A leader is a dealer in hope.* ~Napoleon Bonaparte
>
> *No man that does not see visions will ever realize any high hope or undertake any high enterprise.* ~President Woodrow Wilson

Do the people around you know what your expectations are? Do you use your leadership role and responsibility to establish priorities, goals, missions, and vision? Most important, do you enforce these standards?

Why are these things important? I believe we have a responsibility to create an environment of good order and discipline. Doing so creates hope and shapes success for the individuals within our organization and the organization at large. It begins with you as a leader. You must set the stage.

Early in my career, I learned the importance of developing two personal documents: my leader philosophy and my priorities card. The leader philosophy was a two- or three-page document concisely outlining who I was and what was important to me. The priorities card was the size of a credit card, so it could be carried at all times, and it highlighted the values and goals most important to me.

I provided these to all who worked for me as well as my bosses. They were a quick and consistent way of letting people know who I was and articulated my standards and vision. The leader philosophy was an informal, written contract. In many ways, it helped me hold myself accountable to the same expectations I had for those who worked for me. I think it minimized surprises and managed expectations, as well. The priorities card was convenient and easy to carry, and it served as a constant reminder of what was important to every person I was responsible for. No surprises.

Regardless of whether I was a leader within an organization or the top leader, it was important for me to also know and understand the vision, mission, and goals of the organization. If these were not already developed and published, we created them.

People must know whom they work for, what the priorities are, what the mission is, and what is expected of them. A team operates much more efficiently and effectively when this sort of structure is provided. The leader shapes success for the team.

It's not good enough, however, just to have the structure in place. It must also be enforced, which is what creates hope in an organization. This becomes critical during times of transition and sweeping change. I found this to be particularly true as we prepared for our deployment to Iraq and as our team grew from a few thousand Soldiers to over twenty thousand, and as we executed our wartime mission.

★   Building the Bridge As We Crossed Over It   ★

As I've mentioned in earlier days, during our deployment to Iraq, we were also an army going through transformation. We were reorganizing, realigning, and temporarily redesignating our units. You can imagine the chaos and discontent, especially given that the army is steeped in rich history and tradition.

For instance, we traditionally had thirteen branches in the army, and I was commissioned into the ordnance branch. When you are part of a branch you are part of its history, including the insignia, mottos, legacy, and pride in the mission, much like being part of a professional sport and the rivalry associated with it.

We were several years into the war in Iraq. After multiple deployments, there were significant shortages in the transportation branch of the army, and the mission required more truck drivers than we had in our army inventory. This meant redesignating artillery Soldiers to become transporters, as the demand for artillery had decreased significantly.

Over the years, I had served directly with the artillery, and I knew how proud they were of their history—from their artillery red to their crossed cannon insignia to the way they were still called batteries instead of companies. All of these were symbols of their rich history and identity. My command sergeant major and I decided to visit the home of the Field Artillery in Fort Sill, Oklahoma, to smooth the transition as the leaders were working to meet the requirement of becoming truck companies.

We initially met with the commanding general for the Corps Artillery as well as his brigade and battalion commanders. They provided us with briefings on the status of their training and certification and confidently reassured us that their units would be prepared for their new wartime mission. I also wanted to assure my fellow commanding general that we would embrace his Soldiers, integrate them into the team, perform the mission proudly, and bring them home. We provided them with the wartime mission and goals, and I provided them with my leader philosophy and priority card.

I believed it was important to show them we were proud to have them as part of our team, and I requested a morning PT run with the units. As we began our run, my command sergeant major and I would run side by side with each battery commander and first sergeant. We would talk as we ran, learning who they were, how long they had been in command, and what were their greatest concerns about the mission at hand. After we finished with one battery team, we would drop back in formation to the next and talk with those leaders. Cadence was being shouted, morale was high, and it was energizing.

During the run, one of the battery commanders mentioned to me that he hated having to give up his battery guidon (military flag) for a company guidon while deployed. It sounded like a minor concern, but I understood the history and esprit de corps runs very deep. I thought about his concerns, and when the run was finished and we were all together, I made an announcement to the formation and the leadership, "I know you are concerned about losing your rich history as artillerymen. So, instead of being transportation companies, we will make you transportation *batteries*! You can display your field artillery battery guidons and maintain your artillery pride!" The response was thunderous.

I believe the higher morale and motivation contributed directly to their incredible success and the pride with which they performed their mission in Iraq. To this day I remain in touch with some of these leaders. As leaders, my CSM and I set expectations and embraced our new team members. We created hope. We shaped success.

★   Creating Hope and Success One Person at a Time   ★

Part of my leader philosophy addressed providing discipline, setting standards, and operating with respect. As far as I am concerned, few things are worse than the mistreatment of Soldiers who have volunteered to potentially give their life for their country.

I was a realistic leader, and I recognized that people would violate the rules and each other. I also knew, however, that if mistreatment of Soldiers happened under my watch, consequences would be delivered. Without consequences, there was no hope; and without hope, there was no victory.

While in Iraq, one of my commanders brought a case involving a male major who was a chaplain and a female NCO. The chaplain broke army regulations and attempted to fraternize and develop a personal, sexual relationship with the NCO.

The NCO had been struggling, and she sought out the chaplain to receive counsel, which is why we have chaplains. They function as the military version of civilian employee assistance programs. In her sworn statements, she talked about how chapel services really helped her get through some hard times. However, as she began to frequent the chapel, the chaplain became more informal and friendlier toward her. She was smart and mature enough to figure out what was going on. In no uncertain terms, she let the chaplain know she was not interested in him and what he was doing was wrong. He apologized and suggested he was not trying to send any sort of sexual message.

We train our men and women to be their own first line of defense and make sure they understand it is all right for them to attempt to stop unsolicited advances. We do so because sometimes the advance truly is a perception, not a reality, and the concept is that by dealing with doubts about someone's intentions directly with them in the early stages, you may stop an inappropriate advance before it starts.

It wasn't very long before he made advances again, but this time by expressing his feelings in an e-mail to her. He stated he was very attracted to her. She took action again by elevating the situation to her supervisors; obviously, he did not heed her direct attempt to correct him. After that, he appeared to back off and not pursue her.

After her two-week, mid-deployment-year-tour, rest-and-relaxation (R&R) leave, the chaplain saw her and told her how much he missed her stopping by the chapel. He also sent her another e-mail. Again, she took it to her chain of command, and this time they decided to fully investigate and pursue discipline under the Uniform Code of Military Justice (UCMJ). The chaplain was clearly *not* getting the message.

Since the chaplain was an officer, it was necessary to bring this disciplinary action to my level since I was the first general officer in his supervisory chain. I read through every detail of the investigation packet and made a decision to go with an Article 15 under the UCMJ. In short, an Article 15 requires the person receiving the punishment to come to the general's office with the individual's boss and lawyer.

As I explained under Leadership Principle 2, the procedure I used was to always ask whoever was standing in front of my desk, "Why are you here today?" I wanted the individual to tell me in his or her own words. It gave me a good idea whether or not the chain of command had properly informed and counseled the person and if legal counsel had been given, and I could assess if the person was taking ownership of his or her mistakes or was in denial, argumentative, or pleading ignorant.

To help set the stage, visualize the fact that this was a major, a chaplain, standing in front of my desk at attention the entire time. There was no looking around the room to see how I had it decorated. I set the stage up front and did not proceed until he was looking me straight in the eye. I wanted his undivided attention the entire time he was in my office.

The chaplain expressed to me that he was in front of me for *allegedly* trying to have a relationship with the female NCO. I read the Article 15 word for word to the chaplain. During the reading of an Article 15, the person receiving the disciplinary action has to make a decision. The accused has the right to proceed with the Article 15, or the person can, if desired, demand a trial by court-martial.

Some will actually choose a court-martial. They do so when they are adamant that they are innocent, believe there is not enough evidence to prove the charges against them, or are just arrogant and stubborn. The lawyers also play a significant role in guiding and recommending to those accused what they should do.

I asked him, "Chaplain, do you choose to proceed with an Article 15 or demand trial by court-martial?"

He chose trial by court-martial. This wasn't a problem for me. Why not? You see, as a commander, I never took disciplinary action to that level unless I was sure I had a solid case. My theory was to be prepared for the person to choose trial by court-martial and be prepared to win if it came to that. If I didn't believe I could win a trial by court-martial, I would never offer the Article 15. I don't play games. I knew in my leader heart and mind that he had violated the rules and had potentially diminished a Soldier's hope that she would be treated with respect and dignity.

I slammed the cover to the investigation, looked him straight in the eye, and said, "Chaplain, I suspect you believe in prayer. I recommend you start praying, because you are going to need it. We will proceed with trial by court-martial. You are dismissed." With that he saluted, executed an about-face, and marched out of my office.

It was quite dramatic. There are times to be dramatic and show a little anger. There are times to raise your voice. There are times to be very direct and stern. This was certainly one of those times.

The next day, I found the lawyer and the chaplain standing outside my office requesting to see me. I allowed them to enter and the lawyer spoke for the chaplain, "Ma'am, my client has changed his mind. He wishes to withdraw the request for trial by court-martial and wishes to proceed with the Article 15."

I hesitated long enough to make them think I was considering denying his request. Sweat a little. I could have easily denied the request, continued with trial by court-martial, and won.

"I'm not surprised. Your request is accepted and approved. Get on my calendar for the Article 15 proceeding. Dismissed."

The only reason I didn't proceed directly to trial by court-martial from the beginning was because the relationship never happened. The female NCO, by doing what was right, kept it from going too far. However, had she been *willing*, he would have seized the opportunity.

Since there was no actual relationship, there were several leaders who thought my punishment of the chaplain was too tough. Some argued I should not even proceed with an Article

15. What kind of message would I be sending if I took no action? Do they think he was going to stop trying to have inappropriate relationships just because this sharp, disciplined NCO said no? I reminded those who questioned my actions that the *only* reason there was not a relationship was because of the right actions taken by the NCO!

Not punishing him would have sent a message that his actions were acceptable. That would result in the female NCO, and others who find themselves in similar situations, not bothering to report these incidences. That would breed mediocrity where standards of conduct are concerned. I found that totally unacceptable.

We scheduled the proceeding to determine the level of punishment. He was given seven days to prepare himself and present his case. The next time he came into my office, I again asked him to state clearly for the record why he was there. Once again, he said for "allegedly" trying to have a relationship with a Soldier.

So, I said to the chaplain, "Chaplain, you use the term *allegedly*, which leads me to believe you still don't believe you did anything wrong, and you are trying to convince me that was never your intent. Is that correct?"

He said, "Yes, ma'am, that is correct. I never intended or attempted to have a relationship."

I said, "OK. You and I clearly do not see this the same way. It appears we are at a standstill here. You believe one thing, and I believe the other. I think we need a tiebreaker. We need someone else to look at this and give us their assessment and recommendation based on the facts discovered during the investigation. Here is what I suggest we do. I have highlighted and read every word of every e-mail in the investigation. I am going to call someone and read them some of those highlights."

I picked up the phone receiver, and as I began dialing, I said to him, "Chaplain, I am calling your wife and I am going to read to her the following sentence in one of your e-mails to the NCO: 'I have finally met the woman of my dreams after thirty-four years.'"

He instantaneously said, "No, ma'am. No, ma'am, don't call her."

"You don't want me to call your wife?"

"No, ma'am, I understand. I understand what you are saying. I understand why you think I wanted to have a relationship."

"Oh, you do? Oh, OK, so *now* you get it?"

"Yes, ma'am."

"OL, so we are on the same sheet of music?"

"Yes, ma'am."

I hung up the phone and delivered the appropriate consequences. I kept in mind that throughout this process, there had already been consequences. His unit had returned home while I held him back until the Article 15 was completed. Anybody who has ever been away from home for a long period, not necessarily for a yearlong deployment but maybe a long business trip, understands there is no greater feeling than coming home. There is such joy in having your Family throwing their arms around your neck, telling you how much they love you and how much they missed you. You can imagine how even more powerful that is after being gone to war for a year. He missed that. He missed going home with his unit. He missed hearing the band and the Families cheer, hearing the laughter and seeing the smiles, and getting hugged. He missed all that because of his own selfish desires and lack of discipline. That was the first consequence.

The remainder of the punishment was a pretty steep monetary fine and filing the Article 15 with a general officer letter of reprimand in his official file to be seen by promotion boards. The severity of these consequences resulted in his being forced to retire. I intentionally delivered those consequences. Leading is an honor and a privilege. You have to earn the right to lead. He lost that right. He violated the trust between officer and Soldier, and he violated the trust between himself and his spouse. He lost the respect and confidence of his superiors.

My responsibility as the commanding general of this unit was to enforce the policies and regulations across my command. Doing so created hope for those Soldiers being mistreated, because once I was made aware, I took action. My actions reinforced to leaders at all levels that I expected them to do the same. Our actions together shaped the success of the command at large.

I didn't enjoy punishing people. It was my responsibility to do so when the situation warranted. I reminded myself that those who violated the rules made the choices to do so. There is a tendency to be lenient and rationalize that the actions were a result of combat stress, separation from home, anxiety, and exhaustion. None of those reasons ever justify taking advantage of your leadership position to threaten, violate, or attempt to control another person.

The chaplain's actions violated the trust he was there to instill. He abused his leadership position. He destroyed morale and robbed Soldiers of their hope for a corner of solace and peace. My leadership heart broke for the Soldier who was let down by a man of the cloth.

My actions were the first steps toward restoring the hope he stole.

How do you instill hope across your organization and ensure that those who report to you are treated fairly, and that standards are enforced, regardless of the position held?

Leadership Principle 18

Find your PBR—Personal Battle Rhythm

> *Most people are about as happy as they make up their minds to be.*
> *~President Abraham Lincoln*
>
> *The way I see it, if you want the rainbow, you have to put up with some rain.*
> *~Dolly Parton*

Are you in search of work-life balance? Do you constantly struggle with having more on your to-do list than you have enough time to accomplish? Are you killing yourself in an effort to have it all? Some people refer to juggling all the balls in your life as having work-life balance. I call it finding my Personal Battle Rhythm, or PBR. There are as many opinions about how we should live life as there are people doing it. Leadership Principle 18 is not about how to achieve success or find happiness. It is about helping you think differently about how you live each day and orchestrate your activities.

You see, most of us are focused on managing our time so we can get it all done and please all people, but we intuitively know there isn't enough time to do so. What we should be paying attention to is managing our energy. We can have all the time in the world, but if we don't have energy, the time is of no value to us.

What do I mean by managing energy? To start, I separate my life into three categories: Physical, Mental and Spiritual (PMS). Instead of trying to balance each of these, I consciously recognize there are spikes, like a heartbeat on a cardiogram, in each of these areas, depending on what is happening in my life. By visualizing this, I begin to pay more attention to how I prioritize the events in my daily life.

Please note I did not include "happy." Being happy is great, but it's a temporary emotion versus an intentional, determined state of being. Some of the most rewarding times in my life have had nothing to do with being happy.

★ There Is No Such Thing as "Work-Life Balance" ★

I used to talk about having balance in my life. I don't anymore. I discarded the concept a few years ago when my doctor of chiropractic said to me, "Becky, when you think of balance"— she raised her hands even with each other as if she were balancing something on a scale—"notice there is no motion. None of us is ever in a state of no motion." The lights went on for me. This made perfect sense, but if it wasn't work-life balance, what was it?

I began to think about my year in Iraq from 2005 to 2006. Hands down, it was the toughest year of my life. How did I do it? My responsibilities were massive, my health was shaky, and there was little time for sleep. My daily physical training was altered significantly, because I was confined to working out at a gym and not running the normal long distances I enjoyed. Yet, I managed to keep myself going because I took deliberate steps to make sure I was paying attention to all aspects of my life—physical, mental, and spiritual.

Before I deployed, I created twelve monthly Excel spreadsheets to help me track my Personal Battle Rhythm; one sheet for each month deployed. I knew it would be important to keep track of some of my daily activities in order to maintain the harsh pace for a year. Vertically down the left side of the spreadsheet was simply 1 to 31, representing the day of the month. Horizontally across the top were twelve items important to maintaining my PBR: call mom and dad, read my daily devotional, write thank-you notes to spouses, run on the treadmill, etc.

I simply placed an X in the box to show I completed the task on that day. At a quick glance I could track how I was doing. When some columns had a lot of blanks, I reigned myself in, recalibrated, and reminded myself to pay more attention to the priorities I'd been neglecting.

In Iraq we operated twenty-four hours a day, seven days a week; we worked two or three times more than normal. To do so efficiently and effectively, we developed systems to follow. We published an operational battle rhythm to keep everyone on the team synchronized. It was an all-encompassing calendar with daily, weekly, monthly events and meetings.

The beauty of establishing an operational battle rhythm was our ability to respond quickly and appropriately, make adjustments, and reprioritize our work and focus, especially when unpredictable events occurred—such as bad weather, enemy activity, maintenance problems, etc. It was an incredibly effective tool for managing our time and assets. I figured if this *concept* works for an organization, then it can work for individuals, and developing a Personal Battle Rhythm made much more sense to me than work-life balance.

Life is a constant rhythm. When we have a good rhythm, we are able to oscillate between events, activities, and people. In the process we can achieve a much healthier and purposeful life style.

Are you surging when you need to surge, resting when you need to rest, and doing so in the areas that most need your attention?

What's important to you? If you created a monthly matrix for yourself, what would be the items you would place across the top of your page?

★   Have a WIN—What's Important Now—Mentality!   ★

When I was in command and preparing to take my unit to combat in Iraq, it seemed as if everything was coming at me faster than I could digest it. There would be moments when it was overpowering for me to think about the mission facing me, and the people and lives I would be responsible for—twenty thousand Soldiers and five thousand civilians located in fifty different places in Iraq. It was huge.

Sometimes when you look at the big picture of everything you need to deal with, you can feel anxious and overwhelmed, almost paralyzed into circular inaction, like a dog chasing its own tail. What should I do next? What should I do first? What's more important? Your mind can really start to play games with you. When that happens, you physically start to get stressed, and it can turn into a vicious cycle.

During the preparatory phase of our deployment, I remember calling one of my mentors and expressing to him my concerns, frustrations, challenges, and the fact that I wasn't sure I was the calm in the chaos. My concern was that if I wasn't able to remain calm, cool, and collected as we were preparing to deploy, what was it going to be like for me when we were physically in combat?

My mentor's advice came from his own combat experience. "Becky, when I was going into Desert Storm in 1991, I found myself tagged by my general to be responsible for a mission that candidly I had never really dealt with before. There was another colonel working with me. The two of us were directed to take on this mission and be the lead for our general. We just sat down and looked at each other and decided we had to figure this out and determine what was most important."

He told me it was at that moment when they came up with what they called the WIN concept—What's Important Now. This was perfect guidance for me. From that point forward, and to this day, when I start to feel overwhelmed, I pause and ask myself, "What's important now?" It's a simple but brilliant litmus test to help me maintain my personal battle rhythm.

How do you determine where you should be spending your time when you feel pulled in multiple directions and overwhelmed?

★   Are You Working Hard, or Are You Working Smart?   ★

I don't know about you, but as my career progressed I found myself with increasing responsibility, growing demands on my time, and everybody wanting a piece of me. Often I felt there just wasn't enough of me to go around. I believed in selfless service, and I knew I needed to make myself available and approachable, but I struggled to know where to draw the line.

I often discovered that many people associated being busy with being important and needed. I worked hard, but I wanted that translated as being selfless, determined, and dedicated. In some measure those were true, but I was blaming my busyness on everyone except me. In reality, I wasn't being as smart as I could have been about my time and energy. I began to recognize being busy does not necessarily mean you're getting the right things accomplished or for the right reasons.

When I speak in the corporate sector, I ask people, "How many of you are working hard?" Consistently, across the room hands will go up in the air.

Then I say, "I am not surprised by your response. Now, let me ask you this: How many of you are working smart?" You can visibly see the change in their facial expressions as they think about this, and fewer hands are raised, and most go up slowly.

There is an important distinction between working hard and working smart. Working smart combines the concepts of PMS (Physical, Mental, Spiritual), PBR (Personal Battle Rhythm), and WIN (What's Important Now). The natural tendency is to keep very busy and equate being busy with being important. You might even give yourself credit for being better than those you consider lazy, but who are actually working smarter.

How are you doing? Are you working hard or smart? Do you query yourself on a regular basis to make sure your personal battle rhythm is in sync with your current priorities as well as your overall values?

★ Empty Tank—Diagnosis, Chronic Fibromyalgia ★

My physical tank went on empty while I was still serving in the military. It was the reason I reluctantly, and sadly, retired in 2008. I wish it could have been different. I loved the military, and from all indications I had great potential for more promotions and responsibilities. I do know and accept that I could have, and I should have, paid more attention to the physical aspect of my PMS and taken action earlier than I did.

No doubt the military mentality of "gutting it out, this doesn't hurt, don't be a wimp, you can do it, keep going, and people are depending on you" was what I listened to instead of getting help. I just kept going, and I did it to the point of tapping out my physical energy tank, which affected my mental energy.

While we were training and preparing to deploy to Iraq, I finally sought medical care and received the diagnosis of chronic fibromyalgia, a musculoskeletal disease. I did my research and quickly learned a couple of key things. The disease was not going to kill me, but I would be in constant pain. The military's solution to keep me going was a host of prescription pills for sleep, pain, and depression. I took the prescriptions during the months leading up to our deployment but then made a conscious decision to cease taking them during the deployment. I wanted no doubt in my mind, or anyone else's, that my decisions were made with a clear mind and sound judgment.

After one year in Iraq, our mission completed, my body was in bad shape. I returned to the United States and took command of another organization, the Army's Ordnance Center and Schools. This was another huge mission with a great deal of responsibility (ordnance being the second largest branch in the army). I spent the next twenty months continuing to lead Soldiers while trying to regroup and get well. Although not in combat, the pace never slowed, and the fibromyalgia continued to spin out of control.

It became obvious to me that I had to change paths in order to wrap my arms around this disease. I loved the army but could no longer lead in the manner I believed my Soldiers deserved. I was only forty-nine years old but had to make the tough decision to retire. I had to start working on the physical aspect of my PMS concept of wellness.

Over the preceding years, I had become aware of chiropractic care, but it wasn't available to me in the military. When visiting home, I would occasionally visit my dad's chiropractor, and every time I walked out of his office I felt so much better. I knew there was hope.

During my R&R (rest and relaxation) leave from Iraq, I was a guest speaker at West Point for the thirty-year celebration of women being allowed to attend the military academy. In the process of the visit, my mother met a very passionate chiropractor who was the sister of one of my West Point classmates. My mom told her about my challenges with fibromyalgia, and she immediately went into motion.

She hunted me down, poked her finger in my chest, and said, "You do not have to live in chronic pain."

That introduction began our friendship. Two years later, when I retired from the army, I began my journey to wellness under her supervision, coaching, and care. I had been prescribed over fifteen different medications for pain, sleep, and depression over my last five years in the army. The doctor who first diagnosed me with fibromyalgia in 2005 had given me a host of prescriptions, and two were for depression. I immediately called him. "Doc, I think you must have confused my prescription with someone else's. You prescribed me medicine for depression. I'm not depressed. Do you think I am depressed?"

"No, General, but you will be!" I was shocked. This was not the preventative fitness program I endorsed. In hindsight, he was almost spot-on (army talk for dead right).

With the help of my chiropractor, I educated myself on chiropractic care and nutrition. I am convinced that when we have a mentality of learning every day, we become mentally tougher and more prepared. As a leader, I trained my people to become subject-matter experts. I had to lead myself to do the same as I embraced the disease of fibromyalgia. I had to change my thinking, my routine and battle rhythm, and break old habits and develop new ones. With routine chiropractic care, I began to again enjoy a higher quality of life.

In the military, we are physically fit: we do twelve- to twenty-mile foot marches with full rucksacks, we jump out of planes and rappel out of helicopters, climb the mountains of Afghanistan and patrol the streets of Baghdad. We are physically fit, but we are not necessarily healthy.

Today I am healthy. I take no medications. I routinely see my chiropractor for an adjustment of my spine. The adjustment restores functionality to my nervous system, and I don't live in chronic pain. Adding chiropractic to my PBR was life changing for me. It wasn't a miracle—it was education. I wanted to share my story and educate others. As a result, I became an advocate and spokesperson for the Foundation for Chiropractic Progress.

Instead of medications, I take whole-food supplements to boost my immune system and provide what I lack nutritionally—as the result of a long history of surgeries and digestive challenges. I discovered I was literally feeding my disease. There is a lot of truth to the saying "We are what we eat." I had to conduct a major overhaul of my eating habits to improve my PBR and get my health on track.

I still have fibromyalgia, but it is not chronic. I have learned to listen to my body, take better care of it so it can heal itself, and be disciplined with my decisions and actions. I am the healthiest now that I have been in a long time. The "P" in my PMS state is now a capital "P"—and life is good and getting better.

How would you rate your wellness? What changes could or should you be making? You don't have to struggle or take the journey alone; you have choices and resources.

★ Mental and Spiritual Fitness—Pressing toward the Goal ★

As a young girl, I often heard my grandmother speak about keeping focused on the goal and always pressing toward victory. Being, and staying, focused required mental toughness and spiritual fitness.

What are you pressing toward? Do you have an ultimate goal for your life? Are you mentally determined and spiritually grounded in a way that provides you with the courage to press on when you aren't sure you can?

Remember Leadership Principle 6, when I wrote about daily commitment and my dog tags and shield of faith? The act of committing daily to something greater than myself is part of what I consider mental toughness and spiritual fitness. It is very personal. I know what works for me and why I practice what I believe. You must determine this for yourself.

For me, spiritual fitness is tied to Family, friends, and faith. I practice a Christian faith. I believe God created me in His image. I'm not perfect, and I never will be. When I mess up, I ask God's forgiveness. I believe that when I die, I'm going to heaven—not because I earned my way and not because I tried to do good, but because God created that opportunity for all of us through His son. This belief prevails no matter how we have chosen to live our lives. Jesus died and rose again for me, for all of us. My spiritual fitness sustains and strengthens me. That's what I center and focus my life on every day. It takes discipline to feed my soul, to continue to grow spiritually, and to be strong in my example.

My Family and the friends I have chosen are integral in maintaining a strong spiritual fitness. I cannot imagine the journey without their prayers, coaching, and support. My mental and spiritual battle rhythm encompasses daily quiet time, reading a devotional and my Bible, prayer, attending church, and doing my best to do what is right. These things help keep me humble and real.

As a military leader, I believed chaplains were instrumental to our preparedness and readiness. I fully integrated them as staff officers into our planning and execution. They added value to the team and to me personally as I faced the challenges of leading my teams in wartime.

In Iraq, I personally met once a week with my chaplain. It was a time of personal sharing, prayer, and focus. The chaplain also provided me with valuable feedback from a different set of eyes and ears, and we would share ideas from both the personal and professional perspective. I treasured those minutes together because I felt restored, encouraged, and grounded, as if for a few brief moments combat did not exist.

Are you enjoying the peacefulness that spiritual fitness can provide, or is life overwhelming you? Lead yourself to discovering the joy and peace you may be missing.

Leadership Principle 19

You Must Circulate, Communicate, and Connect

Communication—the human connection—is the key to personal and career success. ~Paul J. Meyer

The single-biggest problem with communication is the illusion that it has taken place. ~George Bernard Shaw

A man's character may be learned from the adjectives which he habitually uses in conversation. ~Mark Twain

Communicating doesn't mean simply talking and hoping people are listening and comprehending. It is also about *your* ability to listen. Communicating is supposed to be about connecting. It is based not only on your words, but also on your tone and body language. Equally important is precise communication, meaning that what you say is, in fact, what you want people to hear.

Very few people effectively connect from behind their desk. Communicating and connecting with people requires circulation. You must make it personal by looking people in the eye, paying attention, and caring about how and what is being said.

I used to tell my Soldiers that when I looked them in the eye I could see what was in their hearts. I could sense what they were thinking and how they were feeling. I could pick up on competence and confidence levels.

How many times has someone asked you how you are doing, but then kept walking down the hallway without paying any attention at all to your response? Or have you greeted someone and they totally ignored you? Have you ever worked with, or for, someone who never looked at you while speaking to you?

One form of communication people struggle with, and often avoid, is correcting or disciplining. The reason many people are uncomfortable with confrontation is because it's difficult to look people in the eye and tell it like it is. Let me reassure you that those who do are the most effective communicators.

As with anything, it takes practice. What better way to rehearse than by looking straight into your *own* eyes? I know this may sound corny, but try it. Start your day by looking straight into the mirror. Part of my morning routine, when draping my dog tags over my head, was to look myself straight in the eye. Think about it—if you can't look yourself in the eye, then you can't look others in the eye.

To be effective and truly connect, you must choose your words wisely and be aware of your tone and mannerisms. As in precision target shooting, with precise communication, if you're off target, you don't score.

When you connect with people and precisely communicate, you will have a much greater chance of getting what you want *versus* what you asked for—and there can be a huge difference between the two.

★   Precise Communication: Two Plain Cheeseburgers   ★

When you got what you asked for, but it wasn't what you wanted, did you ever consider that maybe it was your own poor communication that was the cause?

On one occasion, my driver was scheduled to take me to the airport and was running out to get lunch before we departed. "Ma'am, I'm going to Burger King to get lunch. Can I pick you up anything?"

"Yes, I would like two plain cheeseburgers. Thanks."

"Ma'am, are you sure? Just two plain cheeseburgers?"

"Yes, that's it, two plain cheeseburgers."

With a questioning look and tone, he asked me one more time, "Ma'am, are you sure?!"

"Yes, thanks. Go. *Just* get me two plain cheeseburgers!"

When he returned, I climbed into the backseat of the car, per army protocol. On the seat was my lunch from Burger King. We headed off toward the airport, and I dug out my cheeseburgers from the bag.

I was hungry. With my driver warily watching in the rear-view mirror, I unwrapped my first cheeseburger and took a big bite. It was nasty. I took off the top of the bun, and there was *nothing* on the cheeseburger. It was just a piece of meat and a slice of cheese.

I looked up into the rearview mirror and saw that my driver's eyes were getting bigger and bigger. He could see I wasn't happy. I put that cheeseburger aside and opened the other one. I didn't bother to bite into it; I just inspected it. Same nasty-looking cheeseburger: a piece of meat and a slice of cheese. Nothing else.

I looked up and my driver's eyes caught mine in the rearview mirror, and I said, "There is nothing on these cheeseburgers!"

Without a moment's hesitation, and with a bit of frustration, he said, "Ma'am, I asked you two times, just two plain cheeseburgers? And you said yes!"

We were looking eye to eye, neither of us giving ground, and both frustrated. Can you imagine the thoughts going through his head?

Then I broke the silence. "You were going to Burger King. I did not want a Whopper or Junior, or King or Queen, but I at least wanted condiments, dude!"

After a pregnant pause, I admitted, "You know, you gave me exactly what I asked for!"

I cracked a smile, as did he, but I quickly said, "Not so fast. I'm still not happy with what I got!" We both laughed.

I could have responded differently. I could have taken the attitude that I was the boss, and I didn't get what I wanted, so he was wrong, not me. What would have been the impact? Do you think he would want to keep driving for me? I don't think so.

Fast-forward five years. I received a call from him. "Ma'am, I heard you need a driver. My wife and the kids want to move to Germany, and I would like to be your driver again."

I knew he had just returned to Italy from Afghanistan, and I was about to deploy to Iraq. "I need a driver, but I can't do that to you and your Family. I know you just returned from Afghanistan."

"I want to go to Iraq with you. The wife says no problem."

Now, the cheeseburger story may seem silly, but do you think he would have been as eager to drive for me in a war zone if I had responded differently that day? I admitted my fault instead of blaming him. I did select him to be my driver, and he deployed to Iraq with me.

What would you have done? Are you getting what you want, or are you getting what you asked for?

Your words matter and your actions count. How many people are you cutting off at the knees by the way you converse with them? If you don't care about connecting with people, then continue to talk *at* them instead of with them. If you want to lead them, you must connect with them.

★ Battlefield Circulation ★

A popular show on television is *Undercover Boss*, where the boss becomes one of the workers to experience what the employees' work life is really like. While you don't need to go undercover, you do need to make yourself available and approachable. By watching, learning, and listening, you can understand your employees' points of view, ask them what they think or what they would do, and listen and implement their ideas. This often means parking your ego at the door.

At all levels of leadership, I was constantly out and about checking on Soldiers, training, and missions, and even spending time with Soldiers' Families. In the army, we call it battlefield circulation. As a leader, you have to see and hear what is going on with your own eyes and ears. This personal investment of time and energy helps you make better assessments of your organization.

When I was a captain with only five years of service and assigned as a company commander, my boss two levels up (a full colonel and brigade commander) was a demanding, no-nonsense officer who often showed up at our formations and training sites. He invested time in us and inspired dedication, discipline, and standards of excellence. He shared his experiences with us—from leading in combat in the Vietnam War, to the importance of being ready in peacetime for any potential scenario that may unfold. He taught me the importance of circulating and being present with my Soldiers. His style of leadership profoundly impacted my approach to leadership.

Nowhere was circulation among the Soldiers more important than in combat. While serving in both Afghanistan and Iraq, I spent a great deal of time visiting units. I needed to see firsthand how they were doing, including living conditions, morale, and the overall leadership environment. I enjoyed strategizing with leaders and talking with Soldiers. It allowed me an opportunity to see if standards were being followed, if appropriate policies were in place, and how I could better resource and lead them.

★   It Is Better to Have Emotions Than Be Emotional   ★

When I was counseled in the army—and only a few bosses actually made the effort—most of the sessions were quite positive. The only negative comment I remember was simple but powerful: "Becky, you are too defensive."

When I heard those words from my boss, I immediately leaned forward and in a rather deep but possibly harsh tone asked, "Too defensive?! What do you mean too defensive, sir?"

"Go think about it, Becky."

I left his office steaming on the inside, thinking to myself, "Grrrrrr. Too defensive? I'm not too defensive! I'm passionate!"

Well, maybe that's what I thought I was, but that obviously wasn't his perception. Given the high level of respect I had for my boss, I knew I had to make an adjustment. I didn't want to be viewed as a defensive leader. Something was clearly wrong in my delivery.

I quickly realized a few things. There is a difference between being emotional and being passionate. I started to think about how I responded when he asked questions about my organization. My answers were emotional instead of being stated *with* emotion. Unfortunately, emotional is quickly translated as defensive.

When you sound defensive, do you know what happens? People don't hear what you're saying. They shut down. They mentally place their hands over their ears and say to themselves, *La, la, la, la, la!*

I will stereotype here and allow that it is even worse if you are a female leader. First of all, I think our natural tendency as women is to get excited about our work when we are passionate. Our speech becomes more rapid, louder, and higher pitched. The cumulative effect of those three qualities can be off-putting. What's the impact? They are no longer listening to you. They are wishing they had never asked you the question. You lost their attention. You have just been rendered less effective. No leader, male or female, wants to lose the vote of a boss or coworkers when communicating passionately.

Although I was definitely affronted by my boss's assessment, it was great counsel. I consciously needed to think about the way I communicated. I needed to connect effectively with my boss and make sure he remained engaged when I spoke. It wasn't a difficult change, but it was a necessary one in my communication style. I disciplined myself to pause before answering, speak more slowly and clearly, and soften my tone.

The counseling experience with my boss was valuable. It also helped me identify the same challenges among those I led, both men and women. As a result I was more prepared to coach and mentor them and help them improve their communication skills to be more effective leaders.

★   Social Media—Are You Really Communicating?   ★

Technology certainly has played a huge role in the field of communications. I tend to embrace technology and encourage others to do the same. My recommendation, however, is to thoughtfully define your purpose in using each of the different social media modes. In other words, don't hide behind it, but at the same time, don't fool yourself into thinking you are actually communicating and connecting with people!

For instance, having a few hundred friends on Facebook or Twitter doesn't mean you really have friends or that they care about you in the same way a true friend does. Nor does sending an e-mail to all your employees mean they understand and are now in sync with you—any more than sending an e-mail to someone and carbon copying (cc) your boss means that your boss has been informed!

I was very clear with the people who worked for me that if they wanted me engaged in the conversation on e-mail, then they better place me on the "to" line. Likewise, I told them to not abuse the "reply all" option, or think it equates to everyone being informed.

Social media can be of great value for informing the masses, marketing, and providing quick snapshots and updates. These forms of communication do not and should not replace the human connection achieved with a face-to-face meeting, personal phone call, or the occasional handwritten note.

It is very difficult to accurately convey emotions when you take away the human contact. Without meaning to do so, we communicate messages that we never intended, and some backfire. Don't we all laugh at the litany of autocorrect phrases that have been sent? I found I could easily become offended, depending on the subject and the sender. It takes only a few missed punctuation marks and all lowercase words to send the wrong message when communicating by text, or by using all uppercase words in the case of an e-mail.

The purpose of communicating ought to be that the message sent was the message received, and only to the person or persons who need to receive the message. Before using the different types of social media available, ask yourself what level of effectiveness you want to achieve. Is it informing the larger audience or personal, urgent or just nice to know, sensitive in nature or routine dialogue? Having some sort of filter guides us to use the right medium, increases our probability of being effective, and results in actually communicating and connecting.

I remember flying in a small military aircraft, a C12, with my boss and one other officer. The flight was a few hours long. I sat next to my boss, and the other officer sat in the seat across and facing me. Hardly a word was said the entire flight. My boss was a quiet man and much more comfortable working on his computer than carrying on a conversation, and he did so the entire flight.

When we got off the plane, we each hopped into different vehicles and went back to our office locations. As I turned on my Blackberry to check e-mail, the first dozen e-mails that hit my inbox were all from my boss. He had written all of them on the plane as I was sitting right next to him!

Some of the e-mails from him had questions about projects that I was working on. For me, that was too much. We could have discussed these on the plane. We could have had a real conversation!

A leader must consider the message that needs to be conveyed and the most effective method to do so. Are you communicating effectively and connecting?

★   Profanity Is Not Professional   ★

Verbal communication requires choosing the right words. I completely agree with Mark Twain that a person's character can be quickly discovered by the adjectives they use. I became so frustrated with the frequent and routine use of profanity by my Soldiers that I decided to make some innovative changes.

Since profanity was not illegal or against the regulations, I knew I had to address the subject from a different perspective. I decided to attack it from the viewpoint that I considered profanity unprofessional, and since I rate my people on their professionalism it grabbed their attention.

I wanted to do more than get their attention, though. I wanted the behavior to change, and I wanted them to see the value in changing their words and actions. I decided to integrate the concept "profanity is not professional" into our leader development programs. During my initial counseling sessions and my briefings for new personnel, I discussed the subject, and I even wrote and published a one-page memo that I used in Iraq.

Are you professionally communicating and demanding the same of others? If not, today is a great day to start!

Leadership Principle 20
Make Time for Reflection

Wisdom comes from reflection. ~Deborah Day

Learning without reflection is a waste. Reflection without learning is dangerous. ~Confucius

In our busy lives, it's important and healthy to pause from our hectic schedules and take time for reflection. It doesn't have to be every day or a rigid process. There are many ways to make reflection part of your life, and you must find what works best for you. How you do it is not nearly as important as making sure you do!

For instance, I have a variety of ways to reflect. Running provides me with wonderful thinking time. I carry a pencil and a three-by-five card and jot down a word or two as different tasks and ideas come to me. When I drive, I use a small digital recorder to think out loud and document my thoughts. I have a pad and pen (love the pens with the lights) next to my bed for those moments in the middle of the night when I need to capture a creative idea that wakes me up.

The beauty of reflecting is that it begins to feed into your vision for what lies ahead, and how you want to influence your journey forward. In reflection, you think about how events unfolded, what you learned, and what you might have done differently. It is then you begin to shape your thoughts and actions for the future.

The military uses a formal process of reflection called the After Action Review, or the AAR. We simply review an event and critically assess what went right, what went wrong, and what can be learned. These AARs lead to higher standards, better quality, better performance, and better return on investment of time, money, and energy.

To do an AAR right, it is best to be candid and critical; you need to have tough skin and a sense of humor. The AAR process is simple but powerful—so much so, I informally use it in many aspects of my life. I carried three-by-five cards and jotted down my ups (what went right), downs (what went wrong), and LL (lessons learned). Along with my three-by-five cards, I always carried a steno pad, as well. I used these tools to review, reflect, and focus my future efforts.

Recently, a good friend of mine spoke on the subject of reflection and used the analogy of the car windshield and rearview mirror. There is a reason our vehicles have both and why there is a difference in their sizes. Our greater focus needs to be forward through the large glass windshield and toward the landscape that lies ahead of us. Occasionally, however, we need to glance in the rearview mirror and assess what lies behind us or what we just experienced.

★   Blackout   ★

The military must conduct field-training exercises to prepare for war. Our training had to be tough and realistic, and I instilled in my people a "go to war" mentality. After each exercise we held AARs. Anything we could improve upon while training would reduce our risks in combat.

As a commander, I led an operations center where my staff worked 24/7. It was the central nervous system for tracking all missions and facilitated rapid response to shifts in the fight. When I wasn't circulating around the battlefield, I took my battle updates from my operations center. Everything in the operations center depended on effective communication, which meant radios, computers, and generators had to always be functioning.

If you and your staff couldn't communicate with other commanders and their staffs or track current operations, the result would be degradation in your ability to visualize the battlefield and support combat missions. This connectivity between commands is called lines of communications. When they were severed, it was as if someone shut off the lights on the battlefield. You couldn't wait for the lights to go off to figure out the fact you needed a backup plan. You couldn't afford to lose connectivity with the man or woman out front in the fight.

As a commander, if you wanted to see me lose it, I mean really get irate, you would give me a *blackout* situation in the operations center that could have been prevented.

Realistically, the enemy gets a vote and has the potential to wreak havoc. That's why we did everything in our power to minimize those opportunities. However, when we failed to do our jobs correctly and we caused the chaos—what I called having the enemy inside the wire—it was extremely disheartening, because the problem was preventable.

We were only weeks into our yearlong deployment in Iraq when the lights went out. No power in the operations center. Blackout—no backup plan. The generators stopped running.

Why? Had someone cut the lines? Had someone failed to maintain the generators or check the fuel levels? No. The generators were under a civilian contract, and the contract had expired!

We had incorporated contractors on the battlefield in our exercise training, but, in reflection, we never peeled the onion back quite far enough. Contractors were being integrated on the battlefield faster than commands were keeping track of who they were, when the contracts started, how much they cost, etc. Immediately we figured out the problem for the blackout. The fix, however, would be a much longer discussion and project.

As we investigated the situation, we discovered we had no idea how many contractors or contracts were associated with our missions. That was completely unacceptable. As the commander, I had to know those details in order to allocate the right monies, decide if there were still valid requirements for the services, and assess whether or not the terms of the contracts were being met.

For the next year we looked through the battlefield "windshield," collected data, made assessments, and ended and renewed contracts. At the same time, we kept glancing into the rearview mirror, remembering what we learned from our blackout and sharing it with the unit that followed us. We facilitated and improved their predeployment training and handed them the status of all their contracts. Doing so prevented them from having to relearn the same lessons.

In no way do I blame the team that preceded us. In combat, there is a great deal of uncertainty and change. With army transformation in full swing while we simultaneously were prosecuting a war, we were building the bridge as we crossed it. Remember, once you are in charge, you own it. *Reflect* back to shape success, not to cast blame.

★ Steno Pad Leadership ★

Leaders absolutely must pay attention to detail. The only way I've learned to be able pay attention to detail has been to listen hard, take good notes, define task and purpose, assign responsibility, and track actions to completion by assigning proposed completion dates.

To successfully do this, I became an avid note taker and carried a steno pad with me at all times. The steno pad was organized with dates, times, subjects, and names of people I was to meet or talk with by phone. I routinely reflected on my notes to assess what was completed or still open, who was the lead person, and what follow-up actions were required. I often referred to this process as my "steno pad leadership."

One evening a young company commander came by my office to talk to me about personnel actions he was dealing with. I was his boss and he was looking for guidance. I welcomed him into my office to discuss his concerns.

As he laid out his situation, I listened and jotted down his major points in my steno pad, prompting my own thoughts for guiding him. I wrote down my ideas so I would remember them, mindful not to interrupt him while he was speaking. Interrupting people was a bad habit that I had to be careful of as a leader.

When he was done, I shared with him some options to consider for handling the situation. I noticed he didn't take any notes. I told him he must be brilliant, because I wouldn't be able to remember all the things we discussed or the suggestions that were made. I recommended he might want to consider carrying a leader's notebook with him and certainly when he came to see his boss.

I decided to take advantage of his visit by discussing a few things on my list with him. This was a typical way for me to operate. I didn't want to peck to death those who worked for me—you know, send an e-mail every time I had a question, or pick up the phone to discuss every idea that popped into my head. I preferred to maintain my random thoughts, questions, and ideas in my notebook. I placed the associated individual's name in the margin next to the note. Later, when an opportunity arose to personally engage with the individual, I maximized the interaction by pulling out my notes. I found that note taking was a very effective and efficient use of time and energy.

"Well, while you're here, let me ask you, Commander, how are you doing on getting the operations plan together that was due to me *last* week?"

His demeanor changed immediately. "I'm still working on that, ma'am. How did you remember it was due last week?"

"Well, because I write these things down. Perhaps, you might want to try doing the same!"

Fifteen years later that young company commander is now a colonel and a brigade commander mentoring his own company commanders. I am quite certain they are being mentored about carrying leaders' notebooks. How do I know this? In 2012, he blessed me with the honor of promoting him to colonel. During his promotion ceremony, he mentioned this story to those in attendance. He told them how he learned from me the importance of paying attention to detail, following up on actions, tracking projects, and taking notes.

As he began speaking, I was embarrassed and wondered to myself if I had been a little overboard on my attention to detail and guidance to him. However, as he continued, he spoke with such deep regard for me as his mentor that I lit up with a sense of fulfillment and pride—the way I imagine a parent must feel.

As I reflected on my own leadership style, I recognized that I was a detailed and demanding boss. However, the product of my leadership was now standing in front of me—a successful officer, husband, father, and friend—a mature, caring, successful, strategic leader who is creating his own leadership legacy. To have played even a small role in his professional journey was gratifying and gave purpose to my own journey.

There are many simple but powerful ways to organize yourself as a leader, reflect on what has to be completed, and be more effective. As you reflect on those you have led, and are leading, are you able to experience the same sense of satisfaction?

★ Reflect, Regroup, and Reengage ★

Having been a woman in a traditionally male-dominated profession for twenty-seven years, I thought I knew what diversity was all about. To a degree, I did; but I definitely had some shortfalls in my perspective.

I recognized that diversity was about male and female, and different races, backgrounds, and cultures. It wasn't until after I retired from the military and served as a commissioner on President Obama's Military Leadership Diversity Commission (MLDC) that I placed much more weight and consideration on diversity being about differences in the way we think, lead, and respond to situations.

After fifteen months of serving on the MLDC and much reflection, I realized I had not always fully stood my ground when the discussion of women in combat and women serving in combat branches surfaced. As a member of this commission, I had the opportunity to reflect, regroup, and reengage.

Recently, there has been much discussion about the military "lifting" the policy regarding the ban on women "in combat." This issue always struck a very strong chord for me, but I never took action on my convictions until serving on the commission. My motivation was the fact that the news was communicated as if women were not already in combat. This was completely misleading and wrong.

Speaking up became integrity and leadership issues for me. Women have been in combat for a long time, serving in every war since the Civil War, where they disguised themselves as men. Women represented over 15 percent of my command in Iraq. Women have been wounded and have died in combat. They are already integrated on the battlefield, serving side by side with their male counterparts. They are commanding and leading men, and as in my case in Iraq, even have Infantry Brigade Combat Teams assigned to their commands.

The issue at hand is a Department of Defense policy regarding the assignment of women to combat units, not women serving in combat. We technically haven't been allowed to serve in some of the combat arms branches, such as infantry and armor, or to be assigned to those types of units. Women and men are already serving together on missions below the brigade level, but the women are only *attached* not *assigned* to these units. In other words, women are *with* the team, but not *on* the team.

Lifting the ban reflects reality, as it was in our recent war in Iraq and as it is in our current situation in Afghanistan. It brings greater credibility, appreciation, and respect for what women are already contributing in the military. Women are assets, not liabilities, for our military, and to quote one of my bosses (a male, four-star, infantry, Vietnam veteran), "Our military is more professional because of women, not in spite of them."

The more women are integrated across the force, the more professional our military will become. As my time unfolded as a commissioner, I began to regroup and reengage on the policy of women in combat. Since I had never wanted to be infantry or armor, I never officially engaged in the argument while I was on active duty. While commanding in Iraq, I didn't want my gender to be a distraction to the larger mission. I recognize now, upon reflection, that I wasn't bold enough, and I regret not having taken a stronger position on the subject before retiring from the military.

Serving on the MLDC gave me a second chance to make a difference in this area.

When I reflect on the women who disguised themselves as men in the Civil War, I am inspired by their deep-rooted convictions. I can't help but believe that we must do everything possible to ensure that those qualified and willing to serve are allowed to do so in the capacity they choose. As a woman, my personal desire to serve my country was not greater than a man's, but it certainly was not less!

Do you understand how important it is for you to take time to reflect, regroup, and reengage? Think about simple ways you could incorporate these practices into your personal and professional life.

Leadership Principle 21

Lead for the Betterment of the Team

Alone we can do so little; together we can do so much. ~Helen Keller

The achievements of an organization are the results of the combined effort of each individual. ~Vince Lombardi

No one has ever become poor by giving. ~Anne Frank

Leaders must understand the importance of being part of a team and caring about the greater good of the team over their own personal gain. I believe this means you must define your success by how you help others be successful. Decisions shift from me to we, and it is up to you to make sure you are vested and invested in the team.

For example, sending a team member to a training conference that you would really like to attend or asking them to lead a pet project will go a long way toward their growth as well as yours. Sharing the wealth, so to speak, will contribute rather than consume the energy of those on your team.

You must be willing to learn and promote continued learning as an essential element of being part of your team. The personal growth of your team members will only add value to the team and the organization. Encouraging continuous learning empowers the people reporting to you. One way I encouraged my rising leaders to grow was by giving them books that had influenced my leadership thinking, such as John Maxwell's *The Winning Attitude* and *Good to Great* by Jim Collins.

Promoting the concept of the betterment of others requires allowing collegial dialogue among the team without judgment. This creates an innovative environment where diversity of thought is respected and sharing ideas is the norm. The success and buy-in of an idea are more likely to occur when individuals across an organization believe these have been well thought out and presented as a concept to be reviewed, rather than an order to be followed.

When upper leadership presents a final outcome or challenge, such as a new system or a budget reduction, the end result will be more palatable to the people affected by the change when they have been an integral part of the process. Why? Because when people actively participate in change, they are more likely to take ownership in execution and outcome. Remaining open to a collegial exchange of varied ideas goes a long way toward building bridges and tearing down walls.

A routine I practiced on weekends to give myself some personal downtime was staying away from my work e-mail until Sunday nights. Then I'd go through my in-box and forward notes to the people who worked for me. I was focused on what worked best for jump-starting *my* workweek. Little did I know while this was great for me, my staff felt defeated, behind the power curve, and exhausted before their week had even begun.

A subordinate had the intestinal fortitude to bring this to my attention during his quarterly counseling session. (I always felt as if those sessions did as much for me as they did for those I counseled!) I asked him at the end of the session, "How can I be a better commander for you?"

I did not expect his answer. "Ma'am, honestly, when I come into work on Monday mornings, I already feel behind. I turn on my computer and the e-mails start dumping in, one after the other, from Halstead, Halstead, Halstead. It kills me and I feel like I'll never catch up."

I hated to admit it, but his comments were spot on. How would I feel if my boss bombarded me that way? Well, I knew exactly how I'd feel because it had happened and I hated it! Why treat my people the same way?

So, I changed the way I handled e-mail based on his suggestions. Oddly, all I really needed to do was handle my e-mail in-box the same way I handled the physical in-box on my desk. During my entire career I had prided myself in making sure no action stayed on my desk or in my in-box for more than twenty-four hours, and if it did, I notified the sender I was working or thinking on it.

I listened and I changed my routine. Doing so created positive change for everyone on the team. Listening, encouraging others to think outside the box, and allowing others to share their thoughts have always been my priorities as a leader. If they had not been, I probably would have continued to do business the same way, eroding the morale of my team.

A leader who is truly interested in the betterment of others understands the importance of allowing open dialogue and recognizes that disagreement does not have to equal disrespect. When you are making decisions, developing plans, and creating a vision for your organization, you must keep foremost in your mind what is best for the team. It sounds simple, but it's easy to default to "what's in it for me?" if you're not careful.

There are times when situations develop quickly and you respond the best way possible. Then, upon reflection, you realize you were either self-serving or that you did not think of the team first. It boils down to doing what is right, paying attention to your heart and mind, and making the best decisions you can with the information you have at the time.

Warning: many times I have had to make decisions without all the information, as is probably the case for you. As more information became available, I occasionally modified or reversed a decision. Don't be afraid to do so. Too many people think changing a decision is a sign of weakness and don't want others to know they made a mistake. I disagree. Being able to admit that a decision may not have been the best is a sign of strength. You must have the courage to change it and do what is best for the team. Perhaps this is where the saying "Two wrongs don't make a right" came from!

The bottom line is this: always do what is right for the team. In some cases, it may be years before you realize the significance or the impact of your actions. I found this to be true when I thought back to my second summer at West Point, when we learned survival training at Camp Buckner.

★ Don't Chicken Out ★

Camp Buckner is a training area outside the main gate of West Point, designated for rising second-year cadets and their summer training. We spent several weeks learning about all the different branches in the army. One particular week was called

Recondo (**Recon**naissance and Comman**do**), during which the Special Forces cadre provided survival training.

Survival training included learning what we could and couldn't eat. To simulate hunting animals, they trained us on how to kill and prepare chickens for one of our meals. Imagine, one day you're eating a good meal in the mess hall, and the next day you're out in the woods learning how to kill chickens to survive.

Each squad was given two chickens to kill and prepare for our evening meal. I was the only woman in my squad of ten cadets. We formed up in a line to march in front of the Special Forces Green Beret who was handing out the chickens. Since I was the shortest and always at the end of the line, I peeked ahead to the right of the formation to monitor him handing out the two chickens. As we moved forward, one cadet at a time, I saw him give only one away, and he held strong to the second one. I could see my destiny unfolding. It became clear to me that the second chicken was headed my way.

Remember, my claim to fame is, "I'm just a country girl from a town with no traffic lights." Although he might have intended to push my limits, he didn't realize he'd chosen a country girl to do the task. Although I had never killed a chicken, it was not a big deal to kill and prepare the chickens for dinner.

As our chicken was cooking over the open fire, the Special Forces NCO came over to us with a disgusted look on his face. He began to yell, "I can't believe you cadets are so wasteful!"

He reached into our garbage bag and began to pull out things he claimed to be edible, continuing his lecture on our wastefulness and how we would need these if we were trying to survive in the wilderness. He aggressively moved toward me. He had the chicken heart in one hand and the liver in the other. Looking me squarely in the eye, he barked, "Which is it going to be, Halstead? The heart or the liver?"

Now, while killing the chicken was no big deal, eating the raw heart or liver was unacceptable. To make matters worse, despite being a country girl, I was an extremely picky eater and had never entertained the thought of consuming anything raw, let alone chicken innards. I thought to myself, *Which is it going to be? Are you kidding me? Neither!*

After quickly determining that what he was asking me to do was not illegal or immoral, I had to figure out what to do. Trying to keep my composure, I looked at the heart and then the liver. The heart had yellow fat on it, but I could probably swallow it whole. The liver was flat and too large; I would have to bite into it. I chose the heart.

I grabbed it from his hand, threw it in my mouth, and tried to swallow, but my gag reflex caused me to spit it out. I looked at the Special Forces NCO, and his face said it all: "Don't even think about it, Halstead." I threw it back in my mouth, massaged my neck, and swallowed, swallowed, swallowed. It may not have been immoral or illegal, but it sure was disgusting!

My squad mates were standing behind me. When they realized the vile task had been completed, they let out a victory roar. Of course! That was one less chicken heart any of them would have to eat!

At the time, my focus was not on a positive side of the situation. But in reflection over the years, I recognized the favor gained with my male squad mates. Had I not been up to the task, I am quite certain I would have heard about it for the rest of the summer. Fortunately for all involved, it became an unintended, early leadership opportunity.

Perhaps your reaction to this story is that I failed to stand up for myself or should have refused the disgusting task. Before you are quick to judge, not just in this but in any case, always put yourself in the other person's shoes (or boots). Keep the right context and perspective.

This was a demanding, tough training environment designed specifically to make us stronger, push ourselves, and discover our limits. There is a time and place for discussion and collegial dialogue, and there is a time and place for giving and taking orders, and then action has to be taken. I was at the beginning of my career, learning to follow, as well as lead, and training myself to be disciplined and obedient so I could train and lead others.

Maybe I could have said no, or simply, "I quit this training. You cannot make me eat that chicken heart." I decided I wasn't going to quit. In that moment, I didn't consciously do this to gain any sort of appreciation from my male squad mates. However, that was a result of my action.

I may not have gained complete acceptance, but by "taking one for the team," I was at least not alienated from the squad. Somebody was going to have to do it, and my refusing to do so wouldn't have solved the problem.

Are you willing to "eat the chicken heart" for your team, or do you pass the less "savory" parts of projects off to others?

★ For the Greater Good of the Team, But It Was Killing Me ★

As a general officer, one of the most critical leadership positions on my staff was the G3, the senior operations officer for my organization. My G3 in Iraq was a talented officer who had worked for me the previous year in Germany prior to our deployment. In the corporate sector, the G3 would be equivalent to the COO.

The relationship between a commander and the G3 is extremely tight, not unlike a CEO and a COO. There were many times while receiving my two hour-long, daily battle updates that I would hear or see something that wasn't quite right. I would turn around, look straight at my G3, and without a word being said, he and I connected. We respected each other, we depended on each other, and I cannot imagine having commanded in combat without him as one of my right-hand leaders.

About two-thirds of the way through our one-year deployment, we received wonderful news: the army released the Army War College list and announced my G3 as one of the officers selected for attendance. Going to the war college was one of the steps for being selected for brigade command, the next stepping-stone for potential selection as a general officer in the army.

Again, I found myself struggling between heart and mind. My heart was thrilled about his selection because it indicated the army thought he had the potential to serve at the highest levels of our army as a strategic leader. But my mind struggled with the thought of letting him return to the United States to attend before our deployment was over.

I couldn't imagine not having him there as one of my top confidants, following up on critical details and operations. He was a great listener and incredibly proactive, which always raised my confidence that we were on top of issues. He was instrumental to the success of our team.

While I was struggling with the thought of him departing or not, I knew he was doing the same. He was the type of leader who was completely selfless. No way did he want to leave the team and go to school. I knew if it were up to him to decide, he would never choose attending school over staying in combat. He would put his personal advancement second to the team, and I had great respect for that fact.

I knew that was exactly how he felt, which was why I knew I couldn't leave the choice up to him. I had to be the one who made this decision. If I had given him the opportunity to make that decision on his own, it would have been extremely unfair. Many other commanders did leave the decision up to the individual officers, and doing so placed them in a catch-22 position.

This is an important point. Too often leaders don't want to make the tough decisions. They defer to someone else. As a leader, my responsibility was to look at the bigger picture and make decisions that were best for the greater team. In this case the greater team was not my command. The greater team was the army. I knew I had to let him go to school. Even beyond "letting," I was going to have to direct him to go.

Just as I thought he would, he begged me not to make that decision. It was a difficult but necessary decision, and it was for the betterment of the larger team, the army. Today, he is serving as a general officer. It is possible that may not have happened if he had been delayed from attending the war college.

In reality, I've always known that pulling one person out of a position will never collapse the whole team. As a young lieutenant, my boss explained to me that we are all replaceable, "Becky, it is like putting your hand into a bucket of water and then pulling it out. It's still a bucket of water. There's no hole."

Yes, my G3 was replaceable and, yes, we continued to successfully carry out our mission. Making the right decision wasn't easy. I was sad the day we held his departure ceremony as I pinned a Bronze Star Medal on his chest. I missed his sense of humor, intuition, problem-solving ability, and friendship. You see, I was a better leader because of my G3, and we were a better team because of him. But, by allowing him to advance, the greater army became the beneficiary of his talents.

Are you making the tough decisions for the betterment of the team?

Leadership Principle 22

Trust the Differences

It is never too late to give up your prejudices. ~Henry David Thoreau

Strength lies in differences, not in similarities. ~Stephen R. Covey

No culture can live, if it attempts to be exclusive. ~Mahatma Gandhi

When I reflect on my time in Iraq and the commanding generals with whom I served, the diversity of our team was amazing. We were short, tall; male, female (I was the only woman); combat arms, logistician; army, marine corps, and air force; and we represented different countries—Korea, Britain, and Poland. Our complexity and diversity encompassed different experiences, cultures, languages, and knowledge.

We were brought together as a coalition to jointly accomplish a mission. How did we do it? We trusted the differences.

Isn't that what diversity is all about: trusting and empowering people who are different from ourselves? I believe it was our diversity of thought—our thinking differently—that was our greatest strength. The result? Everyone on the team was meaningful, all were included, and fulfilling the mission depended on our complete integration.

I think the best solutions come from the bottom up, from the people who actually do the work. Unfortunately, too many leaders think they are fully capable of coming up with all the answers, or they are driven by a need to control the entire process.

The first step in creating a functionally diverse environment is purposefully bringing together individuals with varied backgrounds and perspectives. The second step is creating ways to positively leverage the differences. This requires leaders who are comfortable in their own skin and allow collegial dialogue, especially during the problem-solving process. The next important aspect is inviting the right people to the table. To do so you can't surround yourself with people who think the same way you do.

★ Don't Surround Yourself with Little Becky Halsteads ★

Prior to my departure from battalion command in Hawaii, I received tremendous, but unusual, guidance from my boss during my final counseling session. My boss was the two-star, commanding general for the 25th Infantry Division. He was one of my favorite leaders in the army; I admired his leadership style, loved his character, and considered him one of my top mentors. However, his comment during my last counseling session left me a bit perplexed.

He invited me into his office, and we briefly chatted. It was a short counseling and started out well. "There is very little I would tell you to change, Becky. You're one of my best." Those words made me feel great.

Then he said, "As you rise up through the ranks and become a colonel, command your brigade, and become a general—and you will be a general someday, Becky—I want to advise you on one thing. Do not surround yourself with little Becky Halsteads."

It was like the air coming out of a balloon! He didn't say it in a demeaning way. He was thoughtful and matter-of-fact. I knew there was a purpose behind his words, and he expected me to figure it out.

I left his office and walked back across the base to my office. The weather was beautiful. Palm trees were swaying in the wind. I was feeling great but struggled with his comment. What did he mean? Why did he say that to me?

I had just been selected for promotion to colonel—two years early—as well as for brigade command. Without his top ratings of my performance and potential, those advancements would have been impossible. He identified me as being one of the very best, so why would he recommend not surrounding myself with people like me?

Then came the "aha" moment for me. When you surround yourself only with people who think like you, act like you, and maybe even look like you, then you don't create an environment of thinking differently. You fail to leverage diversity to become the best, strongest, and most effective team possible. Let's face it—leading people who look, act, and think like you is easier, but leadership wasn't meant to be easy—it was meant to be effective!

That's what he wanted me to understand. Diversity is an organizational strength. When you have the opportunity to select the people you place around yourself, pick people who differ in thought, experience, knowledge, training, education, race, gender, culture, Family structure. You want to surround yourself with people who are willing to challenge your thinking, who have different opinions, and who see the problem and solution from different perspectives. You will build a team equipped to think more creatively and come up with the best solutions, with the added benefit of sharpening your leadership skills in the process.

I acknowledged the wisdom of his guidance and practiced it the rest of my career. I constantly sought new ways to diversify and leverage the differences on my teams.

Are you willing to surround yourself with people who think differently? Are you trusting those differences and creating the best team to accomplish the mission?

★ Thinking Differently Moves You from Good to Great ★

Operations in Iraq improved each year, as units rotated in and out of the country. We train our Soldiers to have a mentality of always improving their foxholes.

My command, the 3rd Corps Support Command, replaced a successful organization, but I knew there were areas where we would be able to improve. After all, we provided a fresh set of eyes, we were rested and energized, and the combination of our experiences was different from those we replaced.

The motto we had chosen for our deployment, "Good to Great," motivated us to seek new ways to conduct our operations. We didn't want to be satisfied with "good" or become complacent. I recognized, however, that we needed to take measured steps, be deliberate in our thinking, and be careful in how we implemented changes.

Why was this important? As we arrived in Iraq, only two weeks were authorized for the transition between all units. This isn't much time to fully grasp your routine and missions. With this in mind, I decided to establish three phases for our yearlong deployment: the first ninety days, the middle six months, and the last ninety days.

My rationale for the three phases was my observation that some leaders made so many changes when they first hit the ground that they created chaos. I believed it was better to first understand and execute the missions transferred to us before making any sweeping changes.

I also saw leaders make decisions and changes in the last ninety days of their deployments that they didn't have time to execute. In my mind they were transferring the risk to those who followed, potentially not setting them up for success. If they couldn't practice the new procedures themselves, then it wasn't fair to lateral them to the incoming leaders. My units were directed not to make *major* changes in operations in the first or last ninety days of our deployment.

Our focus became the middle six months. This was where we would and could affect the way we operated, move from good to great, and shape success for those who followed us. Deliberate thinking and planning was needed to make this phasing work. How could I bring people together and take our operations to the next level?

The best approach seemed to be regular hour-long meetings targeting a specific mission within one of our Lines of Operation (LOO). Military LOOs would be similar to what most organizations refer to as their core competencies. For instance, distribution of logistics was one line of operation for my command. We called the meeting our LOO. The people invited would receive the agenda ahead of time with task and purpose identified. They were expected to come prepared to discuss and develop better ways of conducting our missions.

My operations officer and planner were the lead agents for me. They collected topics that surfaced across our command and presented me with options to prioritize for the LOOs.

For example, the task and purpose of the first LOO was to minimize the movement of empty trucks on road networks to reduce the risk of losing Soldiers who were driving them. Why was this a priority? The thought of having one of our Soldiers killed by the enemy while driving an empty truck was more than I wanted to accept. Yet, based on the distribution plan, I knew Soldiers were driving empty trucks. Convoys of supplies moved to locations, off-loaded, and returned to their original locations. Realistically, it was impossible not to have any empty vehicles on the road, but I knew we could do a more effective job of minimizing them.

As I entered the room for the first LOO, I looked around and discovered the room was full of colonels. As they took their seats, I began the meeting by saying, "This meeting is over."

You could hear a pin drop. Can you imagine the looks on these senior officers' faces as they heard those words? They shifted in their seats and looked at each other as if to say, "What did we do wrong?"

I asked the group, "How many of you drive trucks?" Of course, not one hand went up.

"How many of you give safety briefings to the convoys or put the mission plan together?"

You could see the lights turning on inside their heads. I explained to them that the LOO would be most beneficial with the right players at the table. How could we possibly come up with the best solutions for minimizing empty vehicles being driven around the battlefield if we didn't invite the people who did the work? We needed the Soldiers who drove the vehicles, were in charge of the convoys, conducted the rehearsals, put the plans together, and wrote the mission orders—the people who made it happen and lived where the rubber met the road. They began to see my point. Those who were intimately involved with the operations were the ones who needed to be at the table to reach the best solutions.

The LOO became my favorite meeting. It was exciting to see and hear the variety of opinions and different experiences. It was fascinating to watch such a diverse group work together and begin to trust the value of their different viewpoints. More rewarding was what happened after they left the meetings.

They began to go back to their units and consciously look for new ways of conducting operations. They shared with other Soldiers how they had the opportunity to give opinions that were listened to by the leadership.

Do you know how excited people become when they discover they are being given credit for a creative idea that's put into practice for others to use? That energy is contagious and moves an organization from good to great. People on the team begin to look forward to collectively and collegially discussing how to solve problems and to participate in the move into greatness as a team.

The LOO became our think tank. I was the moderator and the mediator who enforced the rules of engagement during the meetings. One important rule was to park your ego at the door. Equally important was remembering that disagreement does not have to equal disrespect. When the meeting started, we were equals, intellectually and collegially discussing a critical problem we wanted solved. If a private who was a truck driver was speaking, and someone senior interrupted, I made the appropriate adjustments and allowed the private to continue to speak. I wanted unfiltered ideas, their innovativeness, and everyone to know they were instrumental to the success of our team.

The time spent in our LOO ended up being some of the most worthwhile hours of the week. We came up with many of the best solutions for improving our ability to execute missions. We developed new ways to provide logistics on the battlefield, which were later adopted into army doctrine. That was one of the greatest compliments to our teamwork!

I believe I would have been a stronger leader earlier in my career if I'd been more open to the ideas of those around me. But I also discovered it's never too late to adopt a new concept!

Sometimes the danger of being a very structured person or organization is the resulting lack of creativity, innovation, and trust of those who think differently than we do. Everyone understands the importance of the structure within which the military must operate, as we are asking men and women to serve in a capacity that may require the ultimate sacrifice of losing their lives. However, I don't think we should lose track of the benefits we can achieve by allowing more latitude to question procedures, taking risk in proposing or trying out new ideas, and learning from our mistakes. There is a time and place for providing these opportunities, and leaders must make that determination.

In the military we have a chain of command that is equivalent to a supervisory chain in the civilian sector. Everyone is expected to respect and work within the chain of command. Where I've found failure in the system has not been with the system per se but with the leaders within the system. Leaders who looked at the chain of command as being one directional, and that direction always being down, tended to be the ones who failed or who were not as effective. Just as in communication, the chain of command must flow in multiple directions in order to achieve trust and engagement—up, down, and across an organization.

Diversity is about inclusiveness, respect, and trusting our differences. I'm not sure you ever fully reach a point where you have no biases—or at least I haven't reached that point. So, I work very hard to consciously remind myself to trust the differences. I encourage you to do the same.

Are you inviting the right people to be at your meetings, and embracing their diversity of thought and experience? Are you allowing collegial dialogue that advances your organization to a greater level of performance? Are you surrounding yourself with the right people on your team and trusting the differences?

Take the next thirty days and look around the room before you begin every meeting. If the right people aren't present, don't waste your time or that of your team members.

Leadership Principle 23
Be Impactful: Build Bridges, Not Walls

A life is not important except in the impact it has on other lives.
~Jackie Robinson

And in the end, it's not the years in your life that count. It's the life in your years. ~President Abraham Lincoln

I'm a people watcher. I enjoy observing people's behaviors and what is going on around me. I also want to experience life, participate not simply spectate. I look for opportunities to help people and be impactful, although I know my job isn't to solve every problem.

My style varies depending on the situation, but the majority of the time I choose a teaching style over an authoritative one to bring home a lesson. I encourage people to confront difficult or less favorable situations with a mind-set of building bridges and not walls. Extend yourself to others, share, listen, influence, and even be willing to address the fact you are not always right. Be impactful!

★ Gentlemen, Stand By! ★

The military abides by strict protocols and long-standing traditions of etiquette in the way we speak to each other, present ourselves to others, and prepare for senior leaders to enter a room.

One afternoon when I was stationed at Fort Drum, New York, with the 10th Mountain Division, all the battalion and brigade commanders had assembled at the division headquarters for a meeting with the commanding general. As a colonel and brigade commander, I was one of the senior officers in the division. My assigned seat was in the front row with four other colonels and two one-star generals. The room began to fill quickly as the time of the meeting neared, and with all the commanders and division staff present, there were well over seventy-five people.

Protocol for these meetings was to find our seats and remain standing until the commanding general (CG) arrived. A young major was positioned at the conference room door; he was the secretary of the general staff (the SGS). His responsibility was to stand at the door, await the arrival of the CG, and announce to the rest of us when the CG was about to enter the room.

The announcement, by protocol, is a two-part command—a preparatory command and an execution command. On this day, the preparation command given by the major was, "Gentlemen, stand by!"

Hearing his command, the room became quiet and people positioned themselves in front of their seats in anticipation of the CG. I did the same but was irritated and thought to myself (inside words!), *Gentlemen? Can he not see me? I'm in the front row! I'm the only female commander! How hard is it to adjust? Enough already!*

At this point I had been in the army almost twenty years. Yes, I was used to being the only woman on the team, or the only woman commander, or many times, the only woman in the room. Today there was at least one other female colonel in the room, our lawyer for the division. What was different this time was I had reached my limit for accepting it.

As I stewed, the young major bellowed, "Gentlemen, the commanding general!"

With the execution command, we all snapped to attention as the CG entered. After a few steps into the room, the CG stated, "Take your seats." You could hear the shuffling of people and notebooks as we all took our seats.

Meanwhile, I kept stewing. I even thought to myself, *Maybe I will just stay standing.* It didn't take long to come to my senses and realize that approach would only gain me negative attention, not correct the situation.

But as I sat there, I continued to fume. I couldn't shake it off this time. It wasn't a crisis, it wasn't life threatening, but neither was it right or respectful. I was one of the top six officers on the installation, and yet, no real attempt at proper recognition was made.

You may be reading this and thinking, *What's the big deal?* Maybe you are even telling me to build a bridge and get over it.

At the same time there are others of you reading this who can relate to this story, maybe even remember a similar situation, and now your blood pressure is also rising. You might be thinking what I was thinking that day: *When are they ever going to understand? How would they feel if they were blatantly ignored as part of the team?*

For the entire meeting, I played out in my head the possible actions I could take. I had to do something. I had to practice what I preached: "Be the standard, don't walk by a mistake, but also be a bridge and correct in a way that will be impactful and not taken defensively." My actions had to be positive and focused on changing the behavior—the bad habit.

At the conclusion of the meeting, I approached the SGS. "Major, do you have a minute?"

"Yes, ma'am."

"Great, let's walk over here. I want to discuss something with you quickly." We walked away from the hustle of people so we could chat.

"Do you remember what you said to all of us in the room just before the CG entered?"

The major gave me a very odd and bewildered look, trying to figure out where I was going with this conversation. "Ma'am, I'm not sure what you are talking about."

"Do you remember the command you gave when the CG was almost to the conference room?"

"Yes, ma'am, of course." (I'm sure he was thinking, *The one I always give, Colonel!*). "I do remember. I said, 'Gentlemen, stand by.'"

"Exactly. That's what you said. You don't see anything wrong with that?"

He became visibly frustrated with me. "Ma'am, I'm not getting the point. I don't understand."

"Well, that's the point! It's such an old habit—and a bad habit—you don't even see it. Do I look like a gentleman to you?"

"Oh, no, ma'am. Of course not. I meant nothing by it. I'm sorry. I wasn't trying to be disrespectful."

"I know you weren't trying to be disrespectful, but in reality you were. Think about it. How would you feel?"

At this point his body language had become more powerful than his words, and I could almost hear his thoughts. *I can't believe she's correcting me for this. I meant nothing at all. It's just what we say. It's the command we give.*

"Major, bear with me for one moment. It's obvious you don't think this is a big deal at all. And candidly, it's not a big deal, but it is a bad habit. For just a moment, let's do a role reversal. If I stood at the door and gave the preparation command of, 'Ladies, stand by,' how would that make you feel? Do you think for one second that the men in the room would have allowed me to continue? I don't think so. They would have immediately corrected me, and it would have been a one-sided conversation!"

The major changed his demeanor and a small smile surfaced. "Ma'am, I get it and I am sorry."

"Major, you also realize that if I had immediately corrected you in front of everyone what the impact would have been?"

"Ma'am, I'm not sure."

"Let me help you. The impression would have been that I am the one with the problem. Intuitively all those men would have known I was right and that they should have corrected you, too. But most would have shrugged it off as I'm a female with a problem. So, I opted to correct the situation and correct you this way. My goal is for you to break the old habit, be more aware of your surroundings, and recognize and respect everyone in the room. It's simple: treat others the way you would want to be treated."

"Thank you, ma'am. I will do better next time."

I wanted to make an impactful learning point for this major. I understood he was not deliberately being disrespectful. He was just blindly practicing old, bad habits.

As leaders we have a full-time responsibility to correct, to facilitate change, and to be impactful—twenty-four hours a day, seven days a week. To be impactful, the response must be made in a meaningful way.

★ Do Not Judge a Book by Its Cover ★

I recognize there are times when I have been either the source of a problem or created a problem that didn't even exist because of my own faulty thinking. Remember Truth #4: leaders identify their strengths and manage their weaknesses. Since I know being quick to judge is a weakness of mine, I have to pay closer attention to my own habits, biases, and judgments. Unfortunately, I don't always get it right even though I'm paying attention.

Once I realize I've failed, I do my best to correct the situation and prevent a repeat performance or decision. Most of the time my shortcomings are a result of not consistently practicing Leadership Principle 22 of trusting the differences. On the positive side, once I catch myself, I typically have the courage and discipline to address and correct the situation. The good side of genuinely admitting a wrong, especially to those who work for you, is that trust and respect are strengthened and you can have a tremendous impact.

Most of us are probably guilty of being judgmental to some extent. Having a bias is natural, but we need to be disciplined and suppress our tendency to judge—catch and train ourselves to think and respond differently. This takes being aware of how your mind works and engaging your heart to remind yourself not to be so quick to judge or speak. Ironically, sometimes we judge in the same way we disliked others judging us.

For example, I spent an entire military career teaching and training leaders that leadership is about what's on the inside, heart and mind, character and competence—not what's on the outside, such as titles, gender, or size. I wanted people to see me as a leader of character, and I disliked being categorized as a petite woman. To me that translated as weak or less capable and not impactful.

Even after all the years of personally struggling with, and resenting, being immediately characterized by what people first saw when they met me, I fell into the trap myself. The incident weighed so heavily on me that I went to the Soldiers I judged and asked their forgiveness.

It was 2007 and I was the designated general officer representative for a Soldier's funeral. When a Soldier dies in combat, our army sends a general officer to represent the military and support the Family of our fallen comrade. I had been notified that the honor guard—the team of Soldiers who were designated to conduct the military funeral—would be from the 10th Mountain Division, Fort Drum, New York. I had served with the 10th Mountain Division and was thrilled the team was from there. I knew they would be well trained, physically fit, sharp, and professional.

The Soldier who was killed was a large young man, a solid country boy who grew up in the farm country of upstate New York. On the day of calling hours, I met with the honor guard at the hometown church. I was immediately dismayed, because the sergeant in charge of the honor guard was a female about my size, and two other Soldiers were also women, not much larger than me. I made a quick judgment call to myself that this could be very problematic.

The funeral was being held on a bitterly cold winter day, and over six inches of ice and snow was on the ground. My mind went crazy. *What if they are not strong enough to carry the casket, especially with the poor weather conditions? The uneven ground with ice and snow in the cemetery, along with the weight of the casket, could be catastrophic.*

As I began to speak with the Soldiers, I could feel their determination, compassion, and heart's desire to perfectly perform their duties in honor of their fallen comrade and in support of his Family. My confidence rose much higher. As we shared the details of what would unfold for calling hours and the funeral, a few key specifics arose.

First, the Family and local funeral home director decided that after calling hours, the casket would remain at the church. The Honor Guard did not like the idea of their fallen comrade being alone at the church, and they independently decided to take shifts all night to stand watch. I was moved to tears by their compassion.

Secondly, when we left the church to go to the cemetery to rehearse the graveside ceremony, I discovered the Soldiers had not brought any heavy winter clothing. They brought their green, class A uniforms, equivalent to a polyester suit. They had not brought their long, black overcoats. Their headgear was the black beret—no earmuffs or scarves. Their gloves were the ceremonial white cotton; they were not authorized to wear black leather gloves. My concern began to rise again. The graveside ceremony had to be conducted with precision and as a team.

Since they didn't have their overcoats, I wasn't able to wear mine. We had to be in the same uniform. No exceptions. I thought to myself, *We are going to freeze. Someone is certain to collapse from the cold or drop a weapon or slip. What can I do to focus them?*

I decided to lead them the way I knew I was going to have to lead myself and keep myself from freezing or slipping. I huddled them together for a pep talk. I didn't want to convey specific concerns or question their ability in any way. I didn't want to create any doubt in their minds. I decided my approach needed to focus on how confident I was in their ability. "Tomorrow is a very important day for the Family of our fallen comrade. We are not going to fail. We are going to perform the ceremony with honor and respect, precision and professionalism, in remembrance of our comrade and in honor of his Family."

They were paying attention to my every word and possibly trying hard to convince themselves. I continued. "Here's what I want each of you to do. Every time your thoughts start to wander about how cold you are, I want you to divert those thoughts. Think only of our fallen comrade and his Family. I want you to start focusing with your heart, instead of with your mind. Here's why: when you use your heart, it begins to beat faster, and the blood pumps faster. Your heart will push warmth to your extremities, and I guarantee you, you will not freeze. This will help keep your mind off yourself. We are honoring a Soldier for his tremendous service to our nation and the ultimate sacrifice he gave with his life. We are also honoring his Family for their sacrifices. We can do this."

The following day, as we took our positions at the graveside, I prayed silently for each of the Soldiers in the Honor Guard. We stood at attention in freezing temperatures. Only the crunching of the snow and ice as the townspeople gathered for a final farewell to one of their hometown boys broke the silence in the cemetery. I watched every movement of the Honor Guard as they received the hearse, saluted, and then carried the casket to the plot under the awning.

Every movement was executed with precision and loving care. I could feel their measured and calculated steps as they fought not to slip on the ice and snow. I don't think I took a breath as I stood at attention observing them. They did not miss a beat. They laid our comrade to rest with honor and dignity.

They rendered their final salutes, ceremoniously folded the flag, and passed it to me.

With meticulous facing movements I turned and walked over to the parents seated under the awning. With every step you could hear the ice crunching in perfect rhythm under my feet. I stopped, stood at attention, and then got down on bended knee. With warm tears flowing down my frozen cheeks, I presented the flag to his parents. "This flag is presented on behalf of a grateful nation and the United States Army, as a token of our appreciation for your loved one's honorable and faithful service."

As the ceremony ended, and people departed, the Honor Guard jumped into their van. I went over and jumped into the van with them. They were rubbing their hands together. Some had their shoes off and were rubbing their feet, and the driver had the heater fan on as high as it would go.

These ceremonies are unbelievably moving, and everyone in attendance becomes consumed with emotions. For the Honor Guard, the emotions tend to come after the ceremony when they can let down their guard.

My personal emotions were all over the map. I was feeling sadness for losing a fellow Soldier, loneliness for the Family who had such a void to deal with, and great pride for how the Soldiers honored their comrade. I was also feeling a heavy weight of guilt that I tried not to acknowledge, lumping it in with the emotions of the day. But it welled inside me. *How could I have doubted them? Why did I allow myself to doubt them? How could I question the competence and capability of the woman sergeant, especially when I had spent a lifetime trying to keep people from doubting me?*

I began by commending them for an incredible job well done, praising them, "You did it! None of you fell out of the formation.

None of you have frostbite. You can move all your fingers and toes! I'm very proud of you."

As I praised them, I was filled with conviction and felt compelled to share with them the doubt I had and how I misjudged their ability. "I want to share something with all of you." My voice cracked as I spoke.

"All my life all I wanted was to be respected for who I was—determined, compassionate, professional, and someone who was appreciated as value added to the team, someone who could be depended upon because of my character and competence. I hated being judged strictly for being a woman." I had to slow my words, swallow, and suppress the emotions welling up inside.

"Yesterday when I met you all for the first time, I made a poor judgment call. I saw a woman in charge, no bigger than myself, and then two women, not much larger, and I doubted your ability. I want, and I need, to ask your forgiveness. Somehow I allowed myself to become like those I have tried so hard to prove myself to."

They were visibly surprised, and I could tell they were convinced of my sincerity and authenticity. I doubt that a general officer had ever apologized to them, let alone asked for their forgiveness.

Did I have to share how I felt with them? Did I have to apologize or ask forgiveness? Of course not. So, why did I? First of all, sharing both the good and the bad is important for learning and professional development, yours and those you lead. Sharing your mistakes may also prevent others from having to endure the same sort of mistakes later in their own lives and careers.

Leaders must understand the importance of lifelong learning, always improving their foxhole, and certainly always working on leading themselves to ensure they remain humble and authentic. Recognizing and admitting your shortfalls only makes you stronger. These are skills that will make you a more impactful leader.

Leadership Principle 24

Define Your Success by How You Make Others Successful

> *Talent wins games, but teamwork and intelligence wins championships.*
> *~Michael Jordan*
>
> *To me, teamwork is the beauty of our sport, where you have five acting as one. You become selfless. ~Mike Krzyzewski*

Success is a team sport. I can think of very few successes, if any, I have had in my life that I achieved all on my own. No matter the accomplishment, big or small, someone else was always involved—parents, friends, teachers, coaches, bosses, peers, those who worked for me, and sometimes, even complete strangers.

★   You Don't Even Have to Run   ★

When I was in high school in the 1970s, women's sports were barely acknowledged. Thank goodness for Title IX being passed in 1972, giving women a greater opportunity to participate in athletics! I played several sports and earned nine varsity letters. But please don't be too impressed. Remember, I'm just a country girl from a town with no traffic lights. All I had to do in some cases was show up.

As a matter of fact, one of my best friends who played with me on the volleyball, basketball, and softball teams approached me one day about running cross-country. "Beck, we are going to start up a cross-country running team. You need to join the team."

My idea of running at that point was short sprints up and down the basketball court, maybe around all four bases if I hit a home run, or away from a bull in the pasture! "What do you mean by 'running'? What is the distance we would have to run?"

"The courses are four miles long, but we just need you to join so we can form a team. We need five girls to be eligible to compete against other schools. You don't even have to run. You can walk across the finish line if you want!"

It sounded good to me. I joined. As we began to practice, it became immediately obvious that running long distance was quite different from sprinting up and down court. I stopped and walked about every fifty feet. On the first night of training, my friend said, "Halstead, you can't stop. You can slow down, but never stop and walk, or you will never win a race."

I thought to myself, *Win a race? What is she talking about? I'm out here only so that we have a team for our school. I can't run four miles without walking.*

"Hey, you said all I had to do was walk across the finish line!"

She knew what buttons to push, and she pushed every one of them. "I know you are more disciplined than that, Halstead!"

At every turn she challenged me. By the end of the season, I was running eight-mile training runs and placed third in our division to compete at state finals, although only the first- and second-place winners were sent to compete.

Although the cross-country experience involved an individual sport, it taught me more about teamwork than so many other sports activities. My coach taught me how to lengthen my stride, relax my hands, and meter my breathing. My friend taught me that one of the hardest muscles in the body to train was the one between my ears. Without disciplining my mind, I would have never been able to run eight miles without stopping. My parents managed to place themselves at multiple corners of every race and cheer me on, preventing me from walking, because there was no way I was going to let them see me walking.

At the time, I had no idea how this experience was also preparing me for my future. First of all, if you don't like to or cannot run, the army is probably not the place for you. In the army, we run every day!

The experience also helped me to be a better team player. During my four years at West Point, I had a few friends who were like me in high school. They loved team sports such as basketball and softball but hated running. I was able to help them. I coached them the way that I had been coached. I encouraged them to keep their feet moving and to keep their minds focused and disciplined to finish the mandatory two-mile runs in combat boots.

The stakes were much higher at West Point and in the army. If you didn't run two miles in the required time for your age, you failed. You could be a top performer academically and a great athlete, but if you failed the two-mile run test, it was grounds for separation.

Over my career, I was thrilled to be able to help my friends become better runners and, subsequently, my Soldiers. I received more joy out of seeing them succeed than I did from my own success. These were certainly unintended consequences of joining the cross-country team in high school, but running cross-country gave me such an appreciation for teamwork and the fact that success is truly a team sport.

When we get together, my friend and I still laugh about this experience. But it prepared me for army life and helped shape my success and the success of those I led.

★   A Real Dose of Humility   ★

Along the way, I also had to accept that the role I played on some teams might end up being quite different from what I expected. In high school, I lived in the gym and dreamed of playing collegiate-level sports with the hopes of becoming a physical education teacher. When I went to West Point, sports took on a whole new dimension. I received a real dose of humility.

In high school, my favorite sport was basketball. I was short, but I was fast. I could steal the ball and be down the court in a flash. But the first year I played in high school, I could not hit a layup shot to save my life. My coach had me spend hours practicing layup shots until I was good at them. Being small, I was also good at drawing out fouls, especially when I was crazy enough to try to rebound under the net with the tall girls. I took more than one knee to the face! My coach had me spend hours at the foul line so I would make every possible free shot that I could for the team.

None of us on the team was concerned about who had the most points individually, as long as we had the most points as a team and won. Our coach drilled into us the importance to play and win as a team. If you hogged the ball or took all the shots, you found yourself on the bench. Her philosophy was that success was a team sport, and you better learn it and practice it. Little did I know she was providing me great leadership skills that I would later apply in the military.

At West Point, I was told not to bother trying out for basketball because I was too short. I was crushed. In hindsight, I should have tried out anyway. Instead I became the manager for the women's team during my second year. If I couldn't play, but I still wanted to be part of the team. It was the most humbling position I "played" on any athletic team. To be on the receiving end of dirty towels and empty water bottles was not where I expected to find myself.

In the process of being manager, I learned a lot about myself. I certainly had to adjust my attitude and be service oriented toward the rest of the team. I knew all the women on the team because my roommates were players and our room was the meeting place for many of the players during study hours and weekends.

As a plebe (freshman), it was rough not being on the team because I knew all the women, but I was not allowed to socialize with them or call the upper-class women by their first names. It was particularly hard when they would drop by our room with pizza. Everyone would be having a good time, and I was stuck calling them "ma'am" and feeling guilty even accepting a piece of pizza. I was also required to stand at attention while speaking to them. They backed off that requirement and let me relax, but I never felt comfortable. Joining the team the following year as a manager was a step up, albeit a small step up, but nonetheless an improvement!

Both of my roommates were star basketball players during all four years. In my opinion, they were incredibly humble about their talent. I loved to watch them on the court. They were team players to the nth degree, as we would say as cadets when referring to limitless. Both could have easily earned more individual records when it came to scoring and rebounds. I know, because as manager I helped to keep all the players' statistics! Their winning mind-set was about team, not personal records. What good would it do to achieve a personal high-scoring game if the team lost? I learned a great deal by watching them in action.

How do you make sure you are doing the best you can for your team? What talents do you bring, and how are you adding value? You have to know, and you must act upon them.

Serving as a manager may have been one of the most valuable training events for developing me as a leader, especially a servant leader. It was humbling to go from being on the starting varsity teams in high school to sitting the bench in college. It was even harder to be a manager, but it reinforced the fact that everyone on the team is value-added and integral to the team's success.

★   One Team, One Fight!   ★

I learned quickly at West Point about the value of our motto "Cooperate and graduate." Success definitely was a team sport, or as we learned, "One team, one fight."

Success happens when you realize and accept that it is a 360-degree effort. It cannot just be about pleasing the boss. Success must also be about working well with your peers and making sure everyone on your team is included.

Competition is healthy and wonderful, as long as it's tempered with not worrying about who gets the credit. As I stated in Leadership Principle 21, I have always encouraged people to define their success by how they make others successful.

As a logistician in the army, I was responsible for making sure that the people in my unit delivered the right supplies to the right place, at the right time, and for the right people. We defined our success in terms of making the units we supported successful. This shouldn't be translated that those we supported were more important than our own people, but they were not less important either. I reminded those who worked for me, "Without them, we would not have a mission. However, without us, they cannot successfully perform their mission."

I remember arriving in Bagram, Afghanistan, in the spring of 2002. The base was in the early stages of being established for coalition operations. There was unexploded ordnance everywhere you looked. Forces were coming in almost faster than we could accept them. There was no real road network and very few building structures, and the runway was littered with deteriorated Russian equipment as far as the eye could see.

My mission was to assist in organizing and establishing the logistics operations and housing (tent cities). The only way to accomplish this was to circulate at least twice a day and visit every supply point for fuel, ammunition, water, and food operations. I had to see with my own eyes what was in place, how the Soldiers were doing, where changes or more resources were needed, and how the distribution plan was being developed and improved.

One morning I stopped at the fuel point on the airfield where we had thousands of gallons of fuel stored in large canvas bags. I met a young Soldier, who by the expression on his face was quite dissatisfied and unmotivated. I asked the Soldier, "What is your job here?"

The Soldier replied, "I'm a Ninety-Two Lima."

"Great. What are you responsible for doing?"

"I test the fuel we store for the aircraft."

I asked, "Do you think your job is important?"

Again, the less than motivated attitude was obvious as the Soldier shrugged and responded, "I'm not sure, ma'am."

Although the Soldier seemed proud to be serving his country, I could tell he was miserable about being in Afghanistan. He was young, inexperienced, a long way from home, and working in a very dangerous location. He was struggling to see his value to the mission or even the value of the mission at large. All he really wanted to know was how long we were going to be there.

I wanted to get his mind and emotions off himself and onto the team. It had been my experience when people were able to grasp how important they were to the mission, that they wasted less time thinking about how miserable they were. I began to ask him more specific questions about his job.

"So, a Ninety-Two Lima tests fuel. Why is testing the fuel important?"

"We have to make sure we don't have any bad fuel, ma'am."

"OK, that makes sense. What happens if we have bad fuel and you fail to detect it?"

"Well, ma'am" he said, "the aircraft would not work properly and bad fuel could damage the engines."

"That's serious. What happens if the helicopters and planes break down?"

He thought for a moment. "The units won't be able to transport their Soldiers or receive supplies."

"That's right. The mission does not get accomplished! Are you beginning to see why your job of testing the fuel is so important?"

"Yes, ma'am, definitely."

"If the helicopters are not operational because of bad fuel, we cannot get the job done. Other people and units are depending on you. We need you to successfully do your work so they can do theirs. Do you see how the success of all of us requires each of us? Every person on this team is value added and important to our being successful as a team. Without you, we cannot accomplish the mission and go home!"

As we discussed the details of his job, the team, and the mission at hand, he began to see how he fit in and how he, personally, added value. There was a visible change in his stance and an audible change as he more confidently answered my questions.

Are you ensuring that all the people on your team know that they are value added?

★   Take STOCK in Your Customers   ★

When I was a battalion commander in Hawaii, I had a small unit with a very large mission. My two hundred-plus unit provided supply, maintenance, and medical support to a two-thousand-person infantry brigade combat team. It could be quite frustrating to explain and defend why some of our work took as long as it did. I realized that part of the problem was that those we supported didn't really understand how much smaller our unit was or how we operated. Without that understanding, they were unable to comprehend why work needed to be scheduled the way we requested or why work orders could not be fulfilled as quickly as they expected.

I decided we needed a program to train and educate them on who we were, how we operated, our organizational structure, and how we brought value to the bigger team. To accomplish this, my staff and I developed what we called the STOCK program.

The acronym STOCK stood for Support and Train Our Customers through Knowledge. We developed a round-robin system whereby we invited key members of the infantry brigade to our work area and introduced them to the people who performed the work for them. This training and education created awareness for them about the complexity of our work and the constrained resources we had to perform the work. This personal introduction made our work much more real for them since we put faces on the workload.

The result was a much better understanding of who we were and what we did. This changed the dynamics of our collective team. There was less frustration, less angst, and more consideration when the workload became very heavy. It helped us manage expectations, but most important, it created a much greater appreciation for everyone on the team.

★   You Either Contribute or Consume   ★

As I mentioned at the beginning, I truly believe everything in my life that has meaning is because other people were intimately involved. There is a popular quote that says, "There is no 'I' in the word team."

The premise of that quote is excellent—team should be about we, not me. However, we must not forget the important role each of us plays. We have to lead ourselves to be the best we can be on the team, for the team. In other words, I have to do more than just show up and walk across the finish line!

I must lead myself to be and do my best, be disciplined, and contribute to the greater team. I must be an active participant.

When people came into my office to attend meetings, I could sense whether or not they were there to contribute to the team or consume our oxygen. I did not hesitate to share my observation with them in order to motivate the consumers to become contributors.

So there may not be an "I" in teamwork, but we cannot have a team without individuals. A successful team is not possible until all the individuals grasp on to the concept of "TEAM"—Together Everyone Achieves More.

Success is a team sport. Are you contributing or consuming?

Leadership Principle 25

Accomplish the Mission Effectively by Focusing on the Human Dimension

Efficiency is doing things right; effectiveness is doing the right things.
~Peter Drucker

While you can think in terms of efficiency in dealing with time, a principle-centered person thinks in terms of effectiveness in dealing with people.
~Stephen R. Covey

Character may almost be called the most effective means of persuasion.
~Aristotle

Each of us has a mission, personally and professionally. We were created and designed for a purpose, and accomplishing our life's purpose is important. The key word in the title, though, is the word *effectively.*

Most of us tend to think in terms of efficiently instead of effectively. Right? Faster! Cheaper! Bigger! Better!

I don't deny that being efficient is important, but when we shift from being efficient to being effective, we incorporate the human dimension. This is one of the major differences between managers and leaders. Managers focus on *things*, and leaders focus on *people*.

Being effective means choosing the right people, at the right time, and for the right mission. When we are effective, we put faces on the data and celebrate the outcome. I firmly believe if more leaders put faces on the data, there would be less greed, corruption, and catastrophic failures.

★   Put Faces on the Data   ★

When you look at data, do you see faces or just numbers? When you analyze and assess numbers, are you able to visualize the lives affected by those numbers? I believe we should never forget the human dimension in everything that we do.

Have you ever been in a Family home where they have pictures of the Family at all stages of their lives hanging on the walls? Their pictures grace a hallway, stairwell, living room, or Family room, giving you a sense of togetherness, love, comfort, and care for each other. What about when you go into a home without them? It's not quite the same feeling.

When you go into the workplace and see displayed on the wall the faces of the people that you support, the faces of your customer, or the faces of the people who work there, there is a sense that the corporate headquarters cares. It gives you a sense they realize that although technology is wonderful, it's the *people* who operate the technology who make the difference. Technology may make us more efficient, but the people who operate it make us more effective.

When I deliver keynote speeches on leadership in the corporate sector, I ask the audience at large, "Do you place faces on your data?"

Immediately, you can hear a pin drop in the room. I explain to them that if all of us were to put faces on the data we are assessing, analyzing, estimating, and projecting, then we would do our work with much more attention to detail. If we would see the data as someone's retirement, education, or new home, we would be far more likely to practice the Golden Rule: treating others the way we would want someone to treat us.

This concept became very meaningful to me while commanding in Iraq. Every day, I received battle updates in the morning and evening. The updates were designed to provide me with a macro view of the battlefield. A tremendous amount of data was presented.

Remember, I was responsible for twenty thousand people in my organization, supporting 250,000 people across Iraq. We conducted our mission twenty-four hours a day, out of fifty-five different locations, by ground and by air. We moved millions of gallons of fuel and water each day, distributed tens of thousands of rounds of ammunition, ordered and tracked thousands of parts for fixing vehicles, and the list goes on and on. Suffice it to say, if you ate it, used it, wore it, shot it, or drove it, then the units in my command were involved in getting it to you. Our Soldiers were in constant danger of the enemy. We had Soldiers wounded and killed by improvised explosive devices (IEDs), mortars, rocket-propelled grenades (RPGs), and rockets.

The data I received on a daily basis was almost overwhelming. I had several hundred people on my staff whose primary duty was to track all the data, prepare for the briefings, and provide charts, trends, and analyses to me.

Within the first few weeks of receiving daily updates, I began to notice the staff was very much focused on getting through their briefing slides and hoping I would not ask too many questions. Trust me, I did not hesitate to ask questions, but I did try to suppress my appetite for more details during the actual briefing. I understood the need to keep the briefing moving because all areas of the operation were important and needed to be covered within the two hours. Plus, there was a lot of work to be done in the twelve hours between updates.

As I listened carefully to what they were presenting, however, it became obvious to me they were briefing data. They were already beginning to lose touch with the human dimension. To me they were failing to connect with the people on the ground who were doing the work or experiencing the conflict, chaos, and tragedy.

It hit me square between the eyes during a morning update. "Ma'am, at 0315 hours this morning there was a complex attack on one of our convoys."

The briefer proceeded to provide me with a very *efficient* update by giving me the unit, the type of attack, number of vehicles involved, and number of people wounded. Without even coming up for air or missing a beat, he said, "Next slide."

I slammed my hand on the desk and said, "Stop. What do you mean 'next slide'? Are you forgetting what the leadership on the ground must be dealing with based on this attack? For the wounded, lives are changed forever. Can you imagine the chaos that had to ensue while this was happening? How can we help the leaders dealing with this?"

There was silence in the operations center. My head was spinning. It wasn't that I had problems with the data—it was thorough. There was something missing in the delivery. My heart was feeling it, and my head was catching up. What was I sensing that was wrong?

It was another "aha" moment for me. They were not putting faces on the data. I sensed no emotion. I detected no grasp for what was emotionally at stake.

I immediately thought to myself, *I need to make this real to them. I need them to feel the emotion, the complexity, and the urgency of what that data represented.* They were just briefing as if it was an event recorded in the computer versus people on the ground wounded, scared, and trying to respond to the chaos around them.

I wanted them to think about what else the Soldier or leader had to be dealing with, and how they could be of greater assistance to them. They needed to be thinking about what other support was needed on the battlefield. Does the unit need more medical support, ammunition, or recovery assistance? Has there been anybody critically hurt? Our staff, operating in the safety and relative calm of the operations center, should be a lifeline to the unit dealing with the enemy.

I said, "You just told me about an attack on a convoy, on a certain route outside of Baghdad, where we had vehicles hit and people wounded. You made it sound so matter-of-fact. I feel as if you have forgotten there are real, live people involved here—a young company commander or a first sergeant, or a young NCO or lieutenant. They are out there dealing with all the chaos of that moment."

I turned to my command sergeant major seated on my right side, "Command Sergeant Major, I want a digital photo of every commander—company, battalion, and brigade—and every first sergeant and command sergeant major. I want those photos hung on the walls of this operations center!"

Now, that is a lot of photos. We had over two hundred company size units, twenty-seven battalions, and sixteen brigade-level headquarters in the command, nearly five hundred photos.

Every command had a digital camera, and over the next few weeks, the pictures began appearing one by one on the wall. There was almost a feeling of cohesiveness that began to occur as the faces were placed on the walls.

My charge to the staff was simple: "When a battle-loss report comes in from a unit, I want you to go to the wall and look at the leaders who are dealing with the situation."

After we hung their photos, there was a much greater sense of the whole team being in the room. You could feel the human dimension. The photos brought life and breath to the events occurring on the battlefield.

The staff began putting faces on the data. They were incorporating the human dimension into their briefings and more effectively presenting the battle updates to the entire group and me.

Personally, the display of photos on the wall helped me better connect to the enormity of the command, my responsibilities, and the magnitude of our mission. Seeing their faces reminded me of how important it is, no matter how big the organization, to make sure I connect on an individual level and help others to connect.

In this era of social media, I think many of us fail to remember the human dimension. It is easy to forget there are real people, lives, and emotions behind the names, the messages, and the data.

Are you surrounding yourself with the faces of the people who are important to you? Your Family? Your employees? Your clients? Are you effectively performing your mission?

★ Heroes of the Month ★

Another effective way to motivate and inspire your people to accomplish the mission is to recognize and reward them. Many leaders do this internally, but extending the recognition beyond your organizational borders can be powerful and effective.

Do you ever observe what is going on around you and wonder who is involved? What makes it all work? I do. All the time. What about your own team? Do you know what they all do to create the overall success?

When I was leading at the tactical level as a platoon leader and company commander, it was expected that I knew all my people and fully understood their skill sets. I had to be technically competent on all the weapons systems and licensed on all the equipment, from machine guns to twenty-ton cranes. As I was promoted and my responsibilities increased, the size of the organizations I led grew exponentially.

It became more and more difficult, actually impossible, to be a technical expert on every aspect of my unit, but that did not relieve me of being responsible for everything we did or didn't do. Of course, this is why staff meetings and updates, in-progress reviews, and quarterly reports were all developed and designed.

I don't know about you, but I wanted more than figures and briefings. I wanted to know the people and understand who they were and what they did. Over the years, I tried to find creative ways to make sure everyone on the team knew they were integral to our effectively accomplishing the mission.

I wanted to do the same in Iraq, but the magnitude of my responsibility and the mission seemed too daunting. For instance, in Balad alone over thirty thousand people lived and worked on the base, and only two thousand were assigned to my organization. However, I was the base commander and responsible for the safety and force protection of everyone. In other words, I was responsible for keeping them protected from the enemy.

Balad was the largest logistics base in Iraq, and it was the most attacked by the enemy with rockets and mortars. I was familiar with base defense at a much smaller level from my previous experiences. What I had to do was to build on the success of the commanders who preceded me in Balad. I reviewed the programs they had in place and continued to shape them and further develop our base defense plans.

A Friday evening dinner, which we called the force protection dinner, was already established when we arrived. The attendees were the senior leaders from all the tenant units and organizations. It was an excellent forum to network and understand the base defense capabilities of all the units at Balad. As a result, we made great strides in several different areas related to force protection.

It was during our force protection dinners that I kept getting a sense that something was still missing. People didn't seem to fully appreciate the incredible complexity and competencies that all the units brought to the fight. So I decided to start a monthly program whereby we would recognize our *heroes of the month*.

Each month we held a one-hour ceremony where each commander at Balad, from about thirty different organizations, recognized one hero from his or her command. The beauty of the ceremony was that each commander would introduce the chosen hero to the rest of the commanders and then give a brief explanation about that person's talent and how the individual had made a difference for the team. As the senior commander, I would follow them by presenting the award recipient with a general officer note and commander's coin for excellence.

The ceremony was uplifting. After all the recipients had been recognized, they lined up and everyone went through the line and congratulated them. It was magnificent to watch the interaction, pride, morale, and relationships formed out of this simple, one-hour ceremony.

Morale, respect, and knowledge of unit capabilities expanded significantly. The more everyone across an organization understands what everybody brings to the team, the more effective the team becomes and the more effectively the mission gets accomplished.

Do you know and appreciate the full spectrum of talent and skills of the people across your organization? Do you appropriately and adequately recognize those talents and share them with everybody on the team?

If not, take a few moments today and jot down some ways in which you could do a better job of making sure the people on your team are appreciated and acknowledged and that their contributions are understood by the entire team. When you've done this, you will be effectively accomplishing your mission and strengthening the relationships across your team.

Leadership Principle 26
Invest in People by Building Relationships

One loyal friend is worth ten thousand relatives. ~Euripides

In life you'll realize there is a purpose for everyone you meet. Some will test you, some will use you, and some will teach you. But most importantly, some will bring out the best in you. ~Angel Chernoff

Associate yourself with men of good quality if you esteem your own reputation. It is better to be alone than in bad company.
~President George Washington

I am often asked what I miss most since retiring from the army. My answer is always, "I miss the people." There is no place where you receive a greater return on investment than on your investment in the human dimension. There were many people who "invested" in me during the course of my career and life. I truly believe those relationships—mentorships, partnerships, and, most important, friendships—were the greatest reward I received.

★ Your Best Investment! ★

The best place for me to start when talking about relationships is with my Family and friends. We don't get to choose our Families—they happen. We are born into them, married into them, and sometimes divorced out of them. But Family ties have an awful lot to do with the subject of relationships. I was blessed, as I have mentioned before, to have a strong, loving, values-based, Christian Family. I witnessed solid marital relationships between my grandparents, parents, and great-aunts and -uncles. Those same Family members also had faithful, prayerful relationships with God as part of their daily lives.

I enjoyed tremendous friendships at school and church. My teachers and coaches were attentive, disciplined, caring, and available. Growing up in a small town with no traffic lights translated for me into discipline, respect, and taking care of each other. Home and community expectations were that you'd do well in school, finish what you started, be hardworking, reliable, and God-fearing, and always place others before yourself.

When you invest in people, and they invest in you, it's all about being responsible *to* each other. Building relationships and networking are very important in business and in life. I think faith, as in being dependable and reliable, is an integral part of relationships. If you have faith in me as your daughter or faith in me as your friend, or sister, or coworker, then that means you know you can rely upon me. I will be there when you need me to be. I will provide a listening ear, a shoulder to comfort, a critical mind to help you improve. I will be helpful. I won't be judgmental, but I will give you my opinion.

Doesn't it give you a great deal of assurance and comfort when you know you can rely upon others, and they can also depend on you? When people have faith in each other, I liken it to my spiritual faith and the comfort I receive in knowing God is ever present—my rock and shield. I have faith in God, and I rely upon my relationship with God in all situations. I have a similar faith with my human relationships.

Consider this: Have you ever truly achieved anything in your life entirely by yourself? I know that I haven't. Remember, developing relationships requires investing in others, and it is a two-way street. I am a better person because of the people who have entered my life. My hope is that I have also had the same effect on others.

As a leader, you also have a responsibility to figure out how and if you fit in, and to help others to do the same.

★   Relationships—Fitting In Starts with You   ★

People are surprised when I tell them that I have not always fit in. My title, retired brigadier general, leads people to believe I was always popular and successful. It's easy to forget that in life, we all have our crucibles to bear.

I doubt few people look at me and think, *I wonder if the general was ever bullied?* Reality was, I was often bullied. I had buckteeth, talked funny, and was a scrawny kid. At the beginning of a new school year or when we moved to a new school, I was always the last to be picked for a team, such as kickball. After they saw how hard I played, however, that changed. Throughout my army career I was often the only woman on the team or in the room. I have spent a lifetime figuring out how to fit in, which relationships were smart and healthy, and which ones were best left alone.

I learned a lot over the years about building relationships simply due to the fact that while I was growing up, we moved a half dozen times. Then I moved eighteen times in twenty-seven years during my military career and had to integrate onto new teams, as well as to navigate different cultures. The most important learning point has been the fact that "fitting in" started with me. If I wanted to enjoy successful personal and professional relationships, I had to accept that I played a vital role requiring an investment of my time and energy.

People matter. Relationships are the rainbows in our life. When I reflect over my life, most prominent are the images of the faces of people who have influenced and impacted my life. I learned from the tough relationships, as well as the collegial.

★   My First Leadership Position—I Had Three Strikes against Me   ★

When I reported to my first duty assignment in Italy, my greatest anxiety was how to earn the trust and respect of my platoon sergeant, my right-hand man. We were taught at West Point to allow the first thirty days to unfold—watch, listen, learn, and take charge. The relationship with my platoon sergeant was the most important one for me. After all, he had been with the platoon, knew all the Soldiers, and had a firm grasp of our mission—the storage and issue of nuclear weapon systems.

The platoon sergeant was over six feet tall and towered over my five-foot, one-and-a-half-inch frame. He was a skinny, somewhat expressionless man with more years in the army than I had on earth. A Vietnam veteran, seasoned and tough, he was not thrilled about training another new lieutenant.

I joined the unit at a difficult time. We were only ninety days away from a high-level nuclear inspection. The track record of the unit was not very good, and failing meant being decertified for our mission. So, I had greater concern than might have been normal as I navigated through the first thirty days. It was a rough time.

In addition to the pressure, there seemed to be something else not quite right between us. He rarely smiled and there was no small talk. It was as if he was avoiding me or embarrassed to call me his lieutenant. I didn't get it. I'd studied all the regulations and memorized all the inspection points for transporting and storing our nuclear weapons. I had taken all the tests to certify as an emergency action officer, should we be required to conduct an emergency destruction of the warheads. I was working hard.

So, what was the problem? I had to figure it out and resolve the situation. Our Soldiers were depending on us to function as a team and accomplish the mission. They trusted us to lead them through this major inspection.

Our unit was located at a small, remote base in the countryside of Italy. Formations were held in the parking lot in front of our headquarters building. The sidewalk had a curb consisting of rocks, which the Soldiers painted white. After the morning formation, I dismissed the platoon to the mess hall for breakfast. I then signaled to my platoon sergeant to stand by so I could talk with him. We were at the end of my first thirty days, and I knew it was time for me to confront him with my perceptions of what was wrong.

I asked him to walk with me. As we approached the end of the sidewalk where we had some privacy, I stopped and said, "We need to talk. Clearly there is a problem preventing us from working together the way we need to for our platoon. I have been thinking about this for the past few weeks. I think I've had three strikes against me from the beginning."

He quietly listened without any expression on his face.

"The first strike against me is that I'm another new second lieutenant whom you have to train." There was still no expression from him.

"The second strike is that I am a West Point lieutenant." There was only a slight change in his expression. He was probably in agreement, because West Pointer grads had horrible reputations for being know-it-alls. He made no comment.

"The third strike against me"—and as I spoke I stood up on one of the painted rocks so I could look him in the eye—"is that I am short!" At that moment his face exploded with a huge smile! He laughed. We both laughed!

Was he likely expecting the third strike would be something else? Surely. He had never worked for a woman, and probably never had a female Soldier in any of his platoons. Women represented only about 3 percent of the army in the early '80s, and they could serve only in certain areas. Only three women were in our entire unit of over two hundred people. This was new territory for him.

It was a significant breakthrough in our relationship. I used humor to move the relationship off the dime and earn his trust. I found the courage to confront him and address the friction between us. We needed a bridge where a wall had been slowly going up for the past thirty days. He learned that he could have a professional relationship with a woman leader, one that was built on trust and confidence. We went on to be a very tight team and passed our inspection. Furthermore, we were both selected for higher levels of responsibility in the unit.

★ Going from Peer to Boss, but Still a Friend ★

Leaders must be very careful not to show favoritism. It's easy, right? Not really! Aren't there some people you connect with more naturally and enjoy being around more than others?

I had the great fortune of going to war with friends I had known and served with in the army for many years. At one point we had been peers, but then I was promoted and became their boss. I had to think long and hard about how I would handle these relationships. As the boss, it was my responsibility. It can be awkward when you are the boss and your friends are your subordinates—you don't want to lose them as your friends. However, you also want to make sure to maintain a professional relationship at work. It's not only expected, it's also required in order to maintain a solidly functioning organization.

My top two senior leaders in Iraq, my deputy and my chief of staff, had been my friends for over twenty years as well as my peers for the majority of this time. We knew each other's Families very well. My chief of staff and I had been cadets together at West Point, and as captains, all three of us had been company commanders in the same battalion. My chief of staff's parents honored a longstanding tradition of passing rank insignia on to others by presenting me with Silver Stars that had been worn by my chief of staff's grandfather, a 1928 West Point graduate himself. We were tight; we were life-long battle buddies.

As our professional relationship changed, we had to figure out how we could adjust and interact with each other in order to maintain professionalism but still enjoy being friends. Protocol and chain of command must be honored, but our friendship was also important.

Given the fact we were such good friends, I decided it would be important to talk about this and brainstorm a few *what-if* drills before we deployed to Iraq. For instance, the army rules are quite clear and strict regarding notification of next of kin when a Soldier is killed in combat. We are not allowed to call from Iraq or Afghanistan back to the States to notify the Families of even our closest friends over the phone. Notification must be done in person. The military sends a casualty assistance officer from the local area to personally engage and embrace the Family, face-to-face at their home.

My concern was making sure we agreed with what actions we were going to take as friends if any one of us was killed. In my heart, I knew they would want to be the ones to notify each other's Families, including mine, should the situation require it. My mind knew I had to address it with them.

So I brought them together. "Look, we need to discuss what we are going to do if one of us gets killed. For instance, if I am killed, how will my parents be notified?"

My chief of staff responded, "Well, I think if something happens to you, ma'am, I've known you the longest and I know your parents the best. I think I need to be the one who tells your parents."

I looked at my deputy commander. "What do you think?"

"Yes, I agree, ma'am."

"OK, both of you are wrong. I know that's what you would want to do, but that is not what we are going to do. If something happened to either of you, I would want to call your Families, too. They would expect me to do so because I have known you for over twenty years. But, if I do that, I'm breaking the rules. If I break the rules, what's to keep our Soldiers from breaking the rules? If we break the rules, we've just created a new standard, and it will be lower. If we don't follow the rules, it gives them permission to not follow the rules. We are not going to do that."

So I said, "No, the answer is this. We will let the army notify and inform our Families, the same way our Soldiers' Families would be notified and informed. That's the way it has to be."

My chief of staff emotionally disagreed and expressed concerned. "Ma'am, if something happens to you, your parents will never understand why I did not personally notify them."

"Great point. I think you are right. My mother would never forgive you. I think the same would be true if something happened to you and I didn't call your parents. They would never forgive me. That's why before we deploy we must tell them what the rules are and how this will unfold if something happens. We need to make sure our Families understand. So, call your Family, tell them that if anything happens, they are not going to be hearing from any of us. They are going to be hearing from the army. We have to make sure this is perfectly clear. We are the leaders of this organization. We have to be the standard of what is right. Right starts with us."

So, that is what we did. It would have been easy to place our relationships over the rules. It also would have been wrong. Instead, we used the strength of our relationships to do what was right. I believe this resulted in increased loyalty and our being better examples for those who worked for us, strengthening those relationships, as well.

How are you using your relationships? Do your friendships, including those at work, strengthen you as a person?

★   I've Got Your Six   ★

Friends have always been integral to my life. Unlike Family, we get to choose our friends. When speaking on leadership to youth, I encourage them to choose their friends wisely. Choose people you trust, who are decent and kindhearted, and be the same to them. As a friend, be understanding and forgiving, because none of us is perfect.

I love this quote: "A friend is someone you know and still like." We see the bumps and bruises, blemishes and warts, and dings in each other's armor, but we can still be friends as long as there is trust, honesty, and loyalty.

I won the lotto when it comes to my friends. I have grade-school friends I still get together with two or three times annually. For years, when I visited my Family on leave, we reserved one night for girls' night out. We even invited our retired schoolteachers. The year I was deployed to Iraq they had a birthday party for me and videotaped it. It was hilarious! They ate all my favorite foods, played games, had my photo taped to the end of Popsicle sticks to honor my absence, and spent an afternoon laughing and reminiscing. They mailed me the DVD, and I played it over and over again. Listening to their laughter after some very long days was healing.

My West Point and army friends are battle buddies for life. We pride ourselves in saying the army is a Family because of our friendships, our strong bonds of camaraderie, and willingness to take care of each other. We are willing to die for each other, but more important, we are willing to live for each other. As we say to each other in the army, when we want to assure our buddies that they can rely upon us, "I've got your six." In other words, I have your back. You can depend on me.

Sometimes it takes relationships to get things done. We can be more effective by picking up the phone and calling a buddy, one who has the ability to help you get things moving a little bit faster in the right direction. That is an amazing asset.

Trusted relationships are important because you must have people you can speak to in confidence. You have to have people you can share your thoughts with, and get honest, candid feedback.

Who is your inner circle of confidants and trusted agents? Who are those people in your life? Are you a trusted agent to anybody else? If you're not, you might ask yourself why not? Is it because people are afraid that when they tell you something, you won't keep it in confidence? Do you listen openly and nonjudgmentally when others are confiding in you?

Leadership Principle 27

Show Them How Much You Care

> *We will never know how much just a simple smile will do.* ~Mother Teresa
>
> *There is no pit so deep, that God's love is not deeper still.* ~Corrie ten Boom
>
> *People don't care how much you know, until they know how much you care.*
> ~John C. Maxwell

How do you show people that you care about them? When someone has shown you that they cared about you, how did it make you feel? It is said that the greatest form of flattery is to mimic another person's good behavior, so show that person that his or her caring attitude is appreciated by paying it forward.

I learned about caring for others from the incredible examples of compassion and encouragement I saw in my parents, grandparents, church, community, and school role models. Not everyone is blessed with such a firm foundation, but we all have access to powerful and influential role models through history and reading the stories of others.

As a young girl, my life was hugely impacted by the story of Corrie ten Boom, *The Hiding Place*. She and her Family were Dutch Christians from Holland, and during the Nazi Holocaust in WWII, they helped hide Jewish Families. In 1944, Corrie's neighbors turned her Family in to the authorities; her entire Family died in concentration camps. She was released on a technicality only days before all women her age were killed. Corrie shared her story of caring for others and God's grace in her life until she died at age 91.

While stationed in Germany in 2004, I traveled to Holland to visit Corrie's home and see where her Family provided refuge to Jewish Families. I've often wondered if I would have cared as deeply or had the same courage.

During my last year in the army, I had a unique opportunity to visit Israel and meet with my counterpart, the chief of ordnance for the Israeli Defense Force. Our visit included going to the Israeli Holocaust Museum in Jerusalem. I had the honor to place a wreath on the eternal flame in memory of all who had been killed. It was one of the most solemn moments of my life.

Our guides also took us to a beautiful garden where trees had been planted in memory of courageous human beings, such as Oskar Schindler. I asked if there was a tree for Corrie ten Boom, and they took our group to her tree. They didn't know her story, so I shared it with them. There wasn't a dry eye among us.

I know Corrie ten Boom impacted my life, and I learned how to care more about others through her story.

★ The Power of a Handwritten Note ★

You don't have to write a book or have a movie produced about your life to impact others with your caring. I learned from my mother the power of a simple, handwritten note.

Being the pack rat that I am, I still have most of her notes. When I decorate for Christmas, I pull them out of ornament boxes from 1982, my first Christmas away from home in Italy. Some of her letters were corrective in nature, as an effort to change some of my rebellious behavior, especially in high school. I earned every one of her pieces of guidance.

Whether I was facing challenges or enjoying little victories, mom always seemed to find the most appropriate, meaningful words for the occasion. Each was well thought out and heartfelt and often sprinkled with the reinforcement of scripture.

Remember my story in Leadership Principle 6 about going to air assault school? I'd shared with my mom how concerned I was about getting through the rigor and how important it was for me to earn my air assault badge. She immediately noted dates on the calendar and started to work on a plan to encourage me. She has always cared deeply, and her actions reflected her caring spirit.

Understanding my turmoil and anxiety, she wrote the most wonderful letter to me before I started the air assault course in Kentucky. Included in her letter were very specific Bible verses to encourage me—for example, "I can do all things through Christ who strengthens me."

It was so hot in August that they would cool us down during training with fire hoses, so I kept her folded letter protected by a zip-lock baggie in my cargo pants pocket. We were given breaks, and while sitting in the bleachers, I would pull out her letters. Knowing she cared for me and her reminder that God cared for me was all I needed to keep pushing myself. If she believed in me, I could believe in me.

I have found the power of a handwritten note to be one of the most effective ways of encouraging, connecting, and showing people I care about them. When you are in the army, receiving letters from home is a great morale boost. There is nothing more depressing than standing at mail call every day and never hearing your name. Recalling how some of my friends seemed to be so discouraged by not receiving mail, I suspect this shaped in my mind the importance and power of personal notes, especially in this era of texting, e-mail, Facebook, and Twitter.

It makes sense that there is such power in a handwritten note or personal call. After all, doing so requires an investment of your time and energy. So much more than simply communicating with others, a personal note or call opens the door to new relationships through a higher level of caring.

As a commander, I selected specific key events to reach out to those who worked for me: anniversaries, birthdays, births of children, Eagle Scout accomplishments, and Christmas.

In 2000, as a brigade commander responsible for over two thousand Soldiers, I created a Christmas card on my home computer, printed copies, and then signed them all. One of my battalions, about three hundred Soldiers, was deployed to Kosovo. So those cards were boxed up and mailed to Kosovo.

Much to my surprise, I received an e-mail from a young Soldier telling me the *only* card he received in Kosovo was from me. Although that made me sad and wish for a better support group for that Soldier, it validated my actions as a leader. At least my efforts made a difference for that one Soldier. Not getting feedback from 1,999 others who received cards from me didn't matter, because at least one Soldier's life was better for my having taken the time to care.

There seem to be too few leaders who extend themselves in this way, and I believe they are the ones who lose. It's humbling, but rewarding, to visit one of your subordinate's workplace and see a note that you have written to that person hanging on the office wall.

Leaders who fail to understand the power of a handwritten note as a way of showing their people how much they care are losing out on a simple way to touch someone's life. When people know they are appreciated and cared for, they will work harder. Their dedication and loyalty increases, they seek out more responsibility, and they are proud to be part of the team. The greater benefit is knowing how that personal letter made them feel. The positive impact is that many will begin the practice of sending their own.

★   Extend Your Care beyond Those Who Directly Work for You   ★

As a general, I had the privilege of being authorized a personal staff to support me. I could dedicate another book to the contributions made by my drivers, secretaries, protocol specialists, executive officers, and aide-de-camps. In previous pages I have mentioned the selection process for choosing my aide-de-camps (aide).

Knowing how demanding the aide position was, I wanted to extend a note of congratulations to their spouse or parents. It was my way of reinforcing the dedication and long hours that would be required, but it was also my way of sharing with them that I cared about their loved one, and the Family should be proud of their selection for the position.

From those letters, I personally connected with their closest Family members, and in some cases, developed life-long friendships with the parents of my aides. I also believe it might have further motivated the aides to learn as much as they could in this unique position.

★ F2F: Foxhole to Family and Family to Foxhole ★

Never was writing letters more important than in preparation for deploying to war and while serving in combat. In preparation, I wrote my Family what I called my "last letters home," which were intended to be read should something have happened to me.

Sitting at my dining room table and trying to find the words to express what I wanted them to know was excruciating but necessary. It was essential to me that they know how much I cared for them, how grateful I was that they cared about me, and to thank them for honoring my decisions to serve my country.

I also wrote personal letters to the leaders who remained at home, assuming responsibility for taking care of our Families while we were deployed. I wanted them to know that I cared about the challenges they would face without us there. I wanted to give them my full support and tell them we depended upon them and that they would be instrumental to our overall success.

While deployed, I also tried to find innovative ways to keep those at home encouraged and connected to us. We created quarterly videos, giving them an idea where we worked and how we lived. We also asked our Families to send us photos of their activities. About halfway through the deployment, we incorporated sharing Family photos at the end of our Monday evening battle update. Families sent photos of their children going to the prom, competing in sporting events, and celebrating special birthdays, and many sent photos of their pets to brighten our long days.

Taking just those few moments to laugh, smile, and enjoy a touch of home kept morale up and helped us get to know each other better. I enjoyed listening to the conversations that took place after the meetings. "Congratulations, man, I didn't know your daughter was the state champion in cross-country running!" or "My son wrestles, too. What weight does your son wrestle?"

As much as I might take pride in having taken care of my Soldiers' Families, let me share how they took care of me. Although I was married for a short period early in my career, I was single for most of the time. When we deployed to war, we depended on our Family members, specifically spouses, to take the lead on the home front. They also served at great sacrifice to their Family life and sometimes their own careers. Many had to quit their jobs and relocate, depending on their Family's needs.

Typically, the spouse of the senior officer of a unit has responsibility for shepherding the other spouses during deployments. In this capacity, they help keep Families informed on key events, provide tremendous support when tragedy hits a unit or Family, and keep the lines of communication working between the foxhole and Family.

As commanding general of my unit, I was the senior person but had no spouse. There were leaders above me who, because of this fact, were skeptical of my ability to care for Families while we deployed to Iraq. However, they didn't understand how I had networked and developed friendships with the spouses.

As a result of my connecting with them, a wonderful, caring spouse came to me and volunteered to fill the role of senior spouse for me while we were deployed.

I will be forever indebted for the personal sacrifice of time, energy, and effort this spouse offered in support of our team. Her selfless service was an example for other spouses to emulate and inspired in them an even greater sense of service. As a result of her efforts to show how much she cared, we had one of the strongest Family support groups in the command.

When you know each other better, you care for each other better.

★ No Greater Love Than to Care for Each Other ★

I was always amazed and deeply touched by the desire of our wounded Soldiers to return to their units and rejoin their buddies. No matter how critically injured, they cared about their team and not letting them down. Caring for each other is encompassed in the last line of our Warrior ethos, "I will never leave a fallen comrade."

On one of my visits with wounded Soldiers at the hospital in Balad, I met a Soldier who was on patrol when his vehicle was hit by an IED. The impact caused his vehicle to be tossed in the air like a toy and flipped upside down.

The Soldier was hooked to all kinds of machines, and there was a flurry of activity. As I approached the gurney he was lying on, his eye caught me and he tried to get up and salute. I reached out for him, placed my hand on his arm, and said, "Lay back, big guy, you do not need to get up. I appreciate your respect. We need to take care of you right now!"

He continued. "Ma'am, there was smoke and fire everywhere. It was the loudest blast I have ever heard. I was hanging upside down, ma'am. I knew I was going to die. I made peace with God. I knew I was never going to see my Family again, but then through the window, I could see my battle buddy.

"Ma'am, I started to scream to him, but I could hardly hear myself." (The blast had blown out his eardrums.) "I told him to get me out of the vehicle!" (He actually used a few flowery adjectives when speaking to me.)

"Ma'am, he was no bigger than you. I knew he couldn't carry me, so I told him to grab me by the back of my equipment and drag me by my a—! I did not care if he broke my neck. I think my back was broken because I could not move or feel anything. I didn't care if I ever walked again—I just wanted him to get me out of my burning vehicle! I wanted to live and see my Family again!

"Ma'am, I've never even broken a bone before. Everybody is being so good to me. I can't thank them enough. Ma'am, I want to stay here and recover. I want to get back to my guys. Don't let them send me to Germany, ma'am."

I knew he would have to be medically evacuated. His injuries were too serious to keep him at our hospital in Iraq. He was paralyzed from the waist down, although the doctors did believe strongly that his paralysis might not be permanent. I tried to reassure him. "I know you want to be back with your team, buddy. Right now you have to focus on you. We need to get you to the best care possible so you can rejoin your team later."

"Ma'am, I'm just a private and I can't do anything for anyone, but I know you can. Would you take care of my buddy? He saved my life, ma'am!"

"Command Sergeant Major and I will find him, and we will make sure he gets recognized for his valor. I promise you!"

I was so impressed that this junior Soldier wanted to make sure we gave credit where credit was due. What an awesome way to show others you care.

The next day my CSM and I flew to the base where the heroic Soldier lived. We held a battalion formation, and I spoke to the Soldiers about caring for each other. I told them how proud I was of each of them for doing so, expecting absolutely nothing in return.

When I finished, I called out the name of the Soldier whom we wanted to honor and asked him to step forward. He was completely shocked that we were recognizing him. His arm was in a sling, and he had a bruised face. He had visited the medic when he returned to the unit the day before but hadn't told anyone of his heroic actions. He was selfless and humble, a valued member of the team, and a true Warrior honoring our ethos. He represented all that we desired in our Soldiers.

I will neither forget the expression on his face and the look in his eyes as we placed a medal for valor on his chest—nor will I ever forget the thunderous sounds of cheering and clapping from his fellow Soldiers.

God love these men and women who are willing to sacrifice so much and ask so little.

At the end of our year in Iraq, I did my very best to go to the airfield and send off the Soldiers departing from our location, regardless of the time of day or night. They had just spent a year of their life, separated from Family, serving their country, and they deserved at least a thank-you.

How much do you care for others? How are you showing it? Does your organization encourage people to take care of each other, or is there an everyone-for-themselves mentality?

Studies have shown that people aren't concerned only with monetary rewards; they want to know they are appreciated. You don't have to rescue anyone from a burning vehicle or hand out medals to show your appreciation. Caring enough to acknowledge a contribution can be as simple and powerful as two words: *Thank you.*

When is the last time you said thank you in person or wrote a thank-you note?

Leadership Principle 28

Leave a Legacy

No legacy is so rich as honesty. ~William Shakespeare

I want it said of me by those who knew me best, that I always plucked a thistle and planted a flower where I thought a flower would grow.
~President Abraham Lincoln

Outlive your life! ~Max Lucado

A common question asked of me is, "What do I consider my greatest accomplishment during my military career?"

My answer? "Leaving a legacy."

Developing those I led and helping to positively shape their leadership style were very important to me. As a leader, I had a responsibility to coach, teach, and mentor. I didn't take that responsibility lightly. I believe my legacy involved everything and every person I touched, for good or bad, and building a legacy continues every day of my life. I want all that people see in me or hear from me to be honorable and worthy of passing on to others.

We have a symbolic military tradition of honoring our mentors and our legacy. When we are promoted, we are allowed to ask whomever we want to conduct the ceremony. Typically, we choose leaders whom we revere and call mentor. This was true for me. What also made this process very special was that the officer conducting the promotion would quite often give you his or her personal rank to wear on your uniform, referred to as "passing down our rank." I have done this countless times over the years for the officers whom I promoted.

There have been many special occasions where I was on the receiving end, as well. I'll never forget the evening that my four-star boss called me into the den of his house. He and his wife had generously opened their home for a holiday event for the entire staff, including the aide-de-camp and myself. I was a senior colonel and the boss's executive assistant. The aide and I were considered part of his personal staff.

We arrived early to make sure we could provide any help needed, and for the same reason, we were also the last to leave. On this evening all the guests had departed and the aide and I were helping with cleanup. All of the sudden, the boss walked into the room and said, "Meet me in the den in five minutes."

The aide and I looked at each other with curiosity and concern because the boss did not look happy. The evening seemed to have been a huge success, so we were perplexed as to what he was going to talk to us about. We entered the den, and the boss shouted to his wife to join us. I was thinking to myself, *Oh no. Something is clearly wrong. This is a serious group meeting.*

"I brought you together because I have something to say." He turned toward me, and he reached out his hand as if he wanted to shake hands with me. I moved my hand toward his. As I did, his face lit up with a huge smile and he said, "Congratulations, Becky!"

He placed two silver bullion stars into my hand. The threads were still hanging from them because he had just torn them off his own uniform!

I have been surprised few times in my life, and this was one of them. The army had selected me for promotion to brigadier general. My emotions ranged from shocked to humbled.

As reality set in, we all roared, hugged, cried, and high-fived each other. I can't imagine a better scenario for receiving this life-changing news—with my mentor, his wife, and my battle buddy.

I placed those stars in a small leather wallet, and a few weeks later made a surprise presentation to my parents. Holding on to that secret for those weeks wasn't easy, but seeing the expression on their faces in person was priceless.

When my mom opened the wallet, her mouth dropped and she just looked at me and said, "What does this mean?"

"It means what you think, Mom. I've been selected for general officer."

We shed tears of joy, laughed together—especially after I shared with them how my boss had informed me—and reminded ourselves of our blessings.

I am the legacy of my parents and of my boss and many other people who entered my life and shared their values, wisdom, and character with me. The leaders whom I chose as my mentors understood the importance of coaching, guiding, and nudging but not making decisions for those they mentored. They provided recommendations based on what they knew about a situation and their experience. The mentors I respected never held it against those they mentored when their advice was not taken.

How are you mentoring others? Are you teaching them how to think through their problems and creating a legacy you can be proud of?

★ What Would M6 Do? ★

During my military career, those who worked for me came to know me as "M6." I discovered that people had great difficulty spelling "Ma'am" in e-mails, and it often ended up as "Mamma" with the help of automatic spelling correctors. To simplify, I gave those who worked for me permission to address me as "M6" instead.

The military uses call signs to speak on the radio. My call sign as a battalion commander was "Mustang Six." The "Six" signified to everyone on the radio network that I was a commander. The "Mustang" identified the unit I commanded. So whenever I spoke on the radio and identified myself as "Mustang Six," everyone would know it was me—although, being the only female commander in the infantry division made it pretty easy to identify me without a call sign!

As a humorous side note, my peers affectionately came to know me as "Mustang Sally," and it was not uncommon for the song to be broadcast over the radio at the end of training exercises. I wasn't insulted by this title. In fact, I found it endearing, and I still smile when someone calls me and starts the conversation with "Mustang Sally!"

People began referring to me as "M6" on a regular basis, and it took on a life of its own. Today, I still receive e-mails from Soldiers I served with, the greeting addressed to me as "M6."

One such note came from one of the colonels who was a brigade commander for me in Iraq. We had served together before Iraq at Fort Drum, New York. He was a battalion commander, and I was the brigade commander. In his note, he let me know he had completed thirty years of service and was retiring. He didn't want a retirement ceremony, but his wife convinced him it was the right thing to do. I'm thrilled she did! His note read:

M6,

[My wife] and I discussed often and decided to do a retirement ceremony. I remain somewhat ambivalent. I did not send out announcements; I wanted low key. The ceremony will be this afternoon. I want to let you know that I will present my son with my ID tags—to include the medallion (Shield of Faith) with the Isaiah line which you gave us in theater. I will cite you by name.

God bless,

His son was eight years old when we served together at Fort Drum. For many years I kept a photo on my refrigerator of what I called my "Army Family," and it was a picture of me with sons and daughters of people who worked for me, including his son. We laughed that I fit right in with the kids! Now his son is entering Penn State and doing so with a shield of faith draped around his neck. How fitting to pass on our values and steadfast principles to his son, who shared our journey. One of the greatest rewards of leading is watching those you led carry the torch forward with determination, character, and high standards.

There are few greater gifts than when those I've worked with share their stories of leadership with me and remark about finding themselves wishing they could have asked me what to do. When time and distance don't allow that luxury, they tell me they relied on the principles they learned from me. In the quiet moments of their decision-making process, they asked themselves, "What would M6 do?"

Words don't do justice for how that makes me feel. I didn't bear any children, but I have to believe the emotions I feel are much like those of a proud parent.

As a battalion commander in Hawaii, I was blessed to have an incredible team. My command sergeant major was my right-hand man and confidant. He and I connected from the very beginning—we were both tough and demanding but loved our Soldiers.

When I took command, he was one of the first people I sat down with to discuss the status of the unit. We sat in his office and talked about our careers, our Families, and the unit. I noticed a small US flag, about four by six inches, framed on his desk. My curiosity got the best of me. "Command Sergeant Major, is there a story behind this small flag?"

"Yes, ma'am, actually there is. I am originally from Ecuador. My mother fled, with my brother and me, from Ecuador to New York City. My father was in the Ecuadorian army. After high school, I joined the US Army. When I was a young specialist four, I became a US citizen."

As he spoke, his voice cracked and filled with emotion. "I was all alone at the naturalization ceremony. No Family, but there was a young girl in attendance who gave me that little flag. It meant so much to me that I framed it. It was the most important day in my life."

He and I stood together in his office, with tears rolling down our cheeks. I was touched by his story and his authenticity. We became a solid, cohesive command team. During the two years we served together, from 1997 to 1999, he met and married a wonderful woman. In 2000, when I was stationed at Fort Drum, he called me with exciting news. He and his wife were having a baby!

"Ma'am, we wanted you to be the first to know. We are having a baby, a little girl, ma'am. We want to name her Rebecca, after you. Are you OK with this, ma'am?"

I was speechless. What an honor.

My legacy, personal and professional, exists because I genuinely care about people and I want to make a difference every day. My litmus test for how I live my life is whether or not I can honestly lay my head on the pillow each night and say, "No regrets."

I ask myself, "Is at least one other person's life better today because of my having been in it? Have I served, loved, and shown others that I care about them? Am I leaving a positive legacy?"

You can take the girl out of the army but not the army out of the girl, so as I transitioned to civilian life, my nickname of *M6* followed me. I am now Motivator Six, as my desire to continue to share stories, mentor, motivate, and leave a legacy also followed me.

Do the people in your life consider you someone they want to be like? What are you etching on the hearts and minds of your legacy?

Leadership Principle 29

You Have a Purpose in This World

Everyone has the power for greatness, not for fame but greatness, because greatness is determined by service. ~Martin Luther King

"For I know the plans I have for you," declares the Lord, "plans to prosper you...to give you hope and a future. ~Jeremiah 29:11

The purpose of life is not to be happy. It is to be useful, to be honorable, to be compassionate, to have it make some difference that you have lived and lived well. ~Ralph Waldo Emerson

I believe every person has potential and purpose. I also believe that every event that occurs in your life has purpose in your life, even when that purpose may not be immediately evident.

To recognize and fulfill your purpose, you must understand your own identity and accept that not only do you have a destiny, but you also help create it. In concert with what you have read on earlier pages, discovering and fulfilling your purpose is intimately aligned with the choices you make, the discipline you practice, the values you cherish, and the attitude with which you approach life's shifting sands.

Leadership Principle 29

★ Values Aligned with Behaviors Help Shape Your Purpose ★

The purpose of your life becomes evident when preparation meets opportunity and where knowledge combined with experience becomes wisdom. Your value system provides your foundation, the basis of your purpose. Many people claim certain values are important to them, but their actions are contrary to their words. Your purpose will take shape when your values and behaviors are aligned. In other words, when you truly "walk the talk."

What values are most important to you? Write them down on a three-by-five card and carry them in your pocket or purse for thirty days. Over those thirty days, monitor your actions, decisions, and responses. As you pull out the three-by-five card, assess whether your actions reflect the values you identified as being important. If you aren't sure, ask someone you know who will be brutally honest with you. Better yet, find someone you trust who may want to join you in this exercise and provide feedback to each other.

If your values and behaviors are not aligned, you need to make some adjustments. Either your values or your behaviors have to change.

When your values are etched on your heart and are sharp in your mind, they will be reflected in your behavior. Others will see you as authentic.

Remember, my top five values are discipline, faith, grace, service, and trust. Below I have written the behavior I want others to see in my life as a result of living my top values:

> Discipline—be a role model for others; live the standards.
> Faith—let go and let God be in charge.
> Grace—see the good in others and in all situations.
> Service—make a difference for those who can do absolutely nothing for me.
> Trust—be true to myself and others; stay real.

I attended a wonderful leadership conference a few years ago where we conducted the values drill described above. We were also asked to write a purpose statement for our lives in ten words or less. I'd never done so before. I thought about my life's experiences, passions, strengths and weaknesses, values, convictions, and desire to serve and lead. I developed the following purpose statement for my life: Inspire others to live on purpose and with purpose.

Live your values and believe in yourself. When you do, your life will have purpose, as will your relationships, work, and talents. I think most people want to know that their life is purposeful. Leaders help those they lead to discern their purpose.

I have often wondered if the high rate of post-traumatic stress (PTS) among our Soldiers returning home from war is sometimes a result of what they perceive to be diminishing purpose in their lives. When they are deployed, they have tremendous responsibility, they are part of a team that depends on them, and they perform focused missions. When they return home, the environment completely changes. It is the responsibility of both the individual Soldier and the leaders to come to grips with this issue. We must find ways to ensure our Soldiers are able to handle their shifts in purpose as they return to civilian or post-war military life.

Do the people who work for you find their work purposeful? What are you doing to create an environment that inspires purpose?

Just as individuals must determine their personal top values, so must leaders develop and communicate the purpose and values for their business or organization. By doing so, and allowing employee input, you provide vision, direction, and priorities, as well as create a productive, high-performing environment.

Are your company's core values publicized and practiced? Is there a purpose statement for the organization you lead?

★ A Crisis Today May Unfold Into Your Purpose for Tomorrow ★

Remember under Leadership Principle 5 when I shared with you the story about my high school coach being killed? At that time in my life, I lived to be in the gym and play sports. I knew I was destined to be a gym teacher and coach. I couldn't see or consider any other possibility for my future.

When she was killed, my life came to a screeching halt. I could barely comprehend what was happening. Emotionally, I failed to accept the finality of her death and was consumed with the "why did it have to happen?"

I had never before experienced someone dying, especially someone I was closely connected to on a daily basis and whom I revered. I wanted to grow up to be just like her. I thrived on her attention, feedback, encouragement, and correction—there was a lot of the latter! It was a very confusing time for me.

I never considered at the time of this tragedy that at some point in my future I would fall back on it for strength and wisdom, for the purpose of helping others experiencing similar, overwhelming circumstances.

Fast-forward to Iraq in 2005, where I found myself consoling Soldiers wounded in battle, struggling to sort through loss or pain. Sometimes the loss was emotional, sometimes it was the loss of an arm or a leg, and the toughest by far, was the loss of a battle buddy.

It wasn't until visiting my wounded Soldiers that I came to accept and understand what the loss of my coach had provided in my life. I was being prepared to fulfill my purpose as a commander in combat. I was better able to identify with the loss and pain my Soldiers were experiencing. The support my Family, friends, and teachers provided for me when my coach died was manifested in the care and understanding I was able to give my Soldiers.

On one of my visits, I stood at the bedside of a wounded Soldier who had just lost his battle buddy. Although strong in physical stature, with muscular arms the size of my legs, all expression and emotion was gone from his face. I knew in an instant he was lost, sad, troubled, and unable to cope with the events of the previous twenty-four hours.

As I did with many Soldiers, I placed my hand on him, so he could feel the human touch. I looked him in the eye to connect, but it was as if he was a million miles away. I thanked him for his tremendous service and sacrifice to our country, and I pinned a Purple Heart medal on him. He wasn't accepting my words. "Ma'am, why? Why did my buddy have to die instead of me?

"Ma'am, we were hit with IEDs and grenades. Everything was blowing up, and it was so loud. We fought back and we kept moving. We pushed through it. When we stopped, I was covered with blood. Ma'am, I thought I was dying, but I couldn't feel any pain."

He paused, swallowed hard, and dropped his head in defeat. "Ma'am, it wasn't my blood. It was my buddy's."

Was there any wonder his expression was lifeless? We read about PTS and struggle with comprehending the reality of the condition and how to effectively deal with it. Let me assure you, PTS is very real. Dealing with it is a complex puzzle, as we are each unique and react differently to crisis situations.

"Ma'am, why? Why my buddy and not me?"

I hadn't overtly prepared myself for this moment. However, as I responded to him, what I discovered was that the tragic death of my coach almost thirty years prior had prepared me for this moment. There was a sense of purpose that revealed itself to me, not only for my own life and this moment, but also for my coach's life and the impact it had on me, as well as so many others.

"I wish I could tell you why. I can't. No one will ever really know. I do know this: if you allow the death of your buddy to pull you down into a dark foxhole of doubt, then the enemy just got a second kill. Don't let the enemy win. Honor your buddy by continuing to live your life. Don't let him down." I was able to say the words with the conviction that they were true.

I believe that every event is placed in our lives for a reason. We are being prepared today for what we are going to deal with tomorrow. I had no idea that dealing with the death of my coach in high school was preparing me for helping my Soldiers in Iraq when they lost their buddies. But it did. I had experienced that foxhole and could relate to what they were thinking and feeling.

Does this story make you stop and wonder what opportunities you may have missed or misunderstood along the way? Are you motivated to pay more attention and be more aware of what is going on in your life and be more willing to identify, define, and embrace your purpose in life? Have you reflected on the shifts in your life and connected them with events that unfolded later? How are you leading yourself to discover and fulfill your purpose?

★ Turning Points ★

I believe serving others connects you to something larger than yourself and helps to continue to reveal the purpose for your life. Giving of yourself and your time, reaching out to others, and being a part of the fabric of your community helps define who you are, what you cherish, and the values you live by. The ethic of service, grounded in values, is what has given our nation its strength of character and made us a purposeful nation to other countries around the world. In the army, we referred to military service as an affair of the heart—being willing to live and die for each other.

As I served in the military, my thoughts would wander down the road: How long would I stay in the military? Where would my experiences take me? What rank would I achieve? However, my thoughts always came back to one very important goal. When it was all over, regardless of how long I stayed or how many promotions I was given, I just wanted to hear the words "honorably discharged." I wanted my friends and Family to be able to say, "Well done, good and faithful servant to our nation." I wanted to touch lives, serve others, and then watch those lives go on to succeed and touch others—perpetuating and leaving a legacy of service.

Along the way we all have doubts—am I in the right profession, the right place, and is this the right time for me? There are defining moments when we are reassured that we are, and our lives and our work are divinely validated. Some of my defining moments, which I call "turning points," were barely noticeable, and others were quite dramatic.

Early on at West Point I wanted to quit every day, but there were moments of validation that I was in the right place. One summer evening after a long, hot, physically demanding day, we were standing in formation on the parade field for an evening ceremony to lower the flag for the day.

As I stood at attention, sweat dripping down my neck and back, all the way down my legs, I was longing for home and my friends. All I could think about was how all my friends were on summer vacation and I was at boot camp from hell with no privileges. I couldn't even enjoy a cold cola to quench my thirst or call home and talk to my friends without waiting in line for hours at the pay phone. My "poor me" thoughts were interrupted by the sound of the army band "sounding retreat." Then I heard in the distance, "Bring your units to attention and present arms."

We were brought to "present arms," to salute while the flag was being lowered from the flagpole. With my M4 rifle gripped in my sweaty hands, my arms shaking from the push-ups and grass drills from our early morning physical training, I listened to the band. Out the corner of my eye I could see "Old Glory" being lowered. At that moment, in that place, all my thoughts went to those who had gone before me, who had served, lived, and died for our flag. Chills ran up, down, and across my body. I knew there was a purpose for my being at West Point.

As the moment played out on a hot summer day in 1977, I had no idea how many more times in my life there would be turning points to validate the purpose of my life and confirm my heart's desire to serve others and my nation.

Four years later, in January 1981, as a senior at West Point, the US hostages were released from Iran after 444 days in captivity. The former hostages were welcomed back and reintegrated at West Point. We made banners, hung flags, and then cheered as their Greyhound buses convoyed across base to the Thayer Hotel.

One of the hostages was a former neighbor of my Family when we temporarily lived in San Diego in 1966. I had the privilege of escorting him and his Family to the cadet mess hall. We had an incredible dinner to honor their service and sacrifice. The Glee Club sang from the balcony. As they belted out the song for each service (army, navy, air force), people from the appropriate service would stand at attention and sing with the choir. It was another turning point in my life. Again, my journey was being validated and my life had purpose. After dinner I ran back to my room to capture my thoughts and emotions on paper, and I wrote my parents a letter about the evening:

> *The famous, hallowed words of General Douglas MacArthur, "Duty, Honor and Country," had new life breathed into them tonight as we honored the hostages and their Families in the cadet mess hall. I met our neighbor and his Family at the steps of the mess hall. I gave them both big hugs. Everyone was crying. I shook his hand, stepped back, saluted, and said, "Welcome home, sir!"*
> *He smiled and replied with, "It's great to be home!"*

Leadership Principle 29

As we walked into the mess hall, the cheering was overwhelming. The excitement, concern and patriotism were omnipresent.

As the glee club sang our national anthem, it gave me chills and made me feel proud to be standing at attention and being a part of the greatest academy in the United States, in the greatest country in the world.

The whole experience added so much to my cadet career and my purpose in life.

I was twenty years old and filled with a tremendous sense of duty, honor, country, and purpose. I was proud to be a cadet and excited about being on graduation's doorstep. Within a few months, I was commissioned as a second lieutenant and set out on a journey with the purpose of serving my nation.

What have the turning points in your life been? Have they been subtle, or do you recall them clearly? Have you discovered your purpose in life?

Leadership Principle 30

Make a Difference: Go Beyond Success and Be Significant

A great man is always willing to be little. ~Ralph Waldo Emerson

When we do the best we can, we never know what miracle is wrought in our life, or the life of another. ~Helen Keller

Yesterday is gone. Tomorrow has not yet come. We have only today, let us begin. ~Mother Teresa

I think the majority of us wake up in the morning and plant our feet on the ground intending to have a good day, make the right decisions, be successful in our professions, and enjoy our relationships. Although there is nothing wrong with wanting to be or being successful, I think it is important to look beyond success and seek ways to make a difference.

I suspect some of you spend a little too much time thinking about yesterday with regrets of some sort. I also suspect that a few of you fail to spend enough time thinking about the future and all the possibilities. It isn't uncommon to get caught in that rut. Do you find yourself following the same routine every day and feeling blah about life?

To help me avoid getting into such ruts in my own life, I have found it helpful to search for ways to make a difference. I look for opportunities every single day, and they usually appear in the simplest of ways.

On a larger scale, it's enjoyable and rewarding to use successes and blessings to help others. Unfortunately, many people are successful, but few use their success to help anybody else but themselves. Are you using your successes to make a difference?

I believe when the desires of your heart and mind are to use your talents and resources for greater good, something bigger than yourself, then you begin to move beyond being successful to being significant. You will know you are making a difference by the way people respond to you and by seeing hope reappear in their eyes when you are part of the equation. There will be a tremendous emotion that fills your heart, and it will result in your being inspired to look for more opportunities to make a difference. Even more exciting, some of those you help will want to do the same for others, and that will ignite an even bigger spark in your own life.

How are you paying it forward and perpetuating goodness?

★ Sometimes Not Minding Your Own Business Is a Good Thing ★

I had just taken my seat on the plane, headed from Richmond to Dallas, with a connecting flight in Atlanta, when the pilot announced, "Ladies and gentlemen, due to a maintenance problem, we are going to be delayed." You could hear the whole plane sigh.

I fly often and make sure I have over an hour on the ground at any airport where I have to make a connection. It minimizes my stress and regrets for not having done so! I took out my iPhone and began to catch up on text messages and e-mails. My seat was on the aisle, and next to me was an elderly woman.

As we waited, I could hear her speaking to someone on her cell phone. She was very concerned about making her connecting flight. I could hear the strain in her voice as she questioned whomever she was speaking to, "Where will I stay if I miss my flight?"

When she got off her phone, I decided I had to try to help her. "Ma'am, I wasn't eavesdropping, but I did hear you speaking on the phone. You sound concerned about your flight. What time does your flight depart Atlanta?" She showed me her tickets. Not only did she have less than an hour, but she was also flying to the Caribbean, and there was only one flight a day!

I wanted to stay as calm as possible and to encourage her. I asked the flight attendant to look at her ticket, and although she also remained calm, it was easy to sense her concern. "Ma'am, it will be a very tight connection. You have requested a wheelchair in Atlanta, correct?"

She replied, "Yes. I did."

"Ma'am, you will have to wait until everyone gets off the plane and then the assistants will come on to help you get to a wheelchair."

I started thinking to myself and decided there was no way she would make her flight if she was the last one off the plane. I asked her, "Ma'am, are you able to walk off the plane without help?"

"Yes."

"I thought maybe you could. You look very strong and healthy. Did you order the wheelchair to help you get to your next gate?"

"Yes, I did. The flight goes only once a day. I don't know what I'll do if I miss it."

I wanted to get the attention of the other passengers because I was going to need their help. As I spoke, I intentionally got louder and louder, "Ma'am, what I have seen many times is that the other passengers who have plenty of time will stay in their seats and let others get off the plane first. As soon as we land, I will help you get off this plane and the other passengers will help, too!"

When we landed, I grabbed my carry-on bags in my left hand and led her right off the plane. As we walked up the ramp, I held on to her left arm to support her. I wasn't going to let her fall or miss her plane! As we went through the gate into the terminal, I grabbed an attendant with a wheelchair. I quickly let her know time was of the essence. She had a walkie-talkie on her belt. I told her to call ahead to the gate and let them know this passenger was headed their way.

She started to push the wheelchair but was dragging her feet. I leaned into her and said, "There is only one flight a day for this woman to catch. I need you to move out with a purpose!" She took off toward the gate.

I went back to my gate and asked the attendant to call the departing gate attendant. I wanted them informed that they had a passenger headed their way and to please hold the flight for her.

As my head hit the pillow in my hotel later that night, I thought about the woman I had helped. I felt good inside that I paid attention, gave the situation a little extra effort, and in some small way, may have made a difference in someone else's life.

★   Heart to Heart—No Language Barrier   ★

In 2006, while commanding in Iraq, I traveled south to visit one of our partner Iraqi units near the Iranian border. One of my responsibilities was to develop professional relationships with Iraqi military leaders. On this particular day, I met with the Iraqi colonel who commanded the supply distribution unit.

I spent the day focused on their training, Soldier discipline and readiness, and observing their warehousing operations that supported distribution of supplies to their units. The colonel shared with me his challenges through a translator. He told me how hard it was to retain Soldiers because the enemy threatened to kill their Families. They also dealt with other huge obstacles, including rationing of fuel, weapons accountability, maintenance of equipment, tracking of critical supplies, and a high illiteracy rate.

I toured all their facilities, including the barracks where his Soldiers lived. The Iraqi Soldiers had never seen a female general, but they were incredibly respectful and quite curious.

Why did I do this? I could have simply had the colonel brief me on his operations and been on my way. I chose to spend the entire day with him and circulate with his Soldiers, just as I would have with my own units, so that I could better understand his daily operations and coach and connect with him.

He told me about his brother being murdered, and how he, himself, did not wear his uniform in his local community because it increased the threat to his Family. I found myself thinking about the fear and uncertainty he must experience every day. I was impressed by his determination and commitment to his country.

We finished our day in his office at the headquarters building. The room was clean but quite bare. There were a few chairs, a table, some photos and maps on the wall, and the Iraqi flag on a pole in the corner of the room. Several other leaders, both US and Iraqi, gathered around the edge of the room. The colonel invited me to sit down in the chair next to him. A coffee table separated us. Two teacups and a plate of cookies were placed neatly on the table.

He gestured, offering me tea without speaking a word. I graciously accepted, and he poured me a cup of tea. I don't like tea and am usually very careful about drinking water when I do not know its source. However, the entire day was about building relationships and sharing our leadership thoughts and tactical expertise, and I didn't want to offend him.

As we sat together, I had an overwhelming desire to tell the Iraqi colonel how much I appreciated his willingness to be open and transparent with me, and how impressed I was with his patriotism. I wanted him to know that I could tell how much he cared about his Soldiers and his country. Serving during such tumultuous and uncertain times took courage, and I wanted to make sure he understood that this spoke volumes about him as a person and as a leader.

I placed my cup of tea on the small table, leaned into him, and with the help of the translator told him, "Sir, I would like to thank you for your service to your country. Every day you risk your life and the lives of your Family by being willing to serve while your country rebuilds its government and military."

Without having to say another word or needing a translator, I placed my open palm on my chest and tapped my heart several times. I could see in his eyes he knew exactly what I was trying to convey. "From my Soldier's heart to yours, thank you. You are making a difference for your country."

He began to speak quickly, but the translator kept pace with him, "Oh, no, please, *I* thank *you*. You left your country, your Family, to come here and to help my country." He tapped his heart and stood up, signaling to me to stay seated.

As he walked across the room, I wondered what would happen next. He went to the corner of the room, signaled to one of his Soldiers to assist him, and grasped the pole with his nation's flag on it. Together they took the flag off, meticulously folded it, and he walked back across the room to where I was sitting.

I immediately rose to my feet as he approached. As I stood, he raised his nation's flag to his face and gently kissed it. With tears rolling down his cheeks, and with outstretched hands, he presented his nation's flag to me.

Time stood still. Tears rolled down both our faces. The years that had prepared me for this moment were spinning through my head. Visuals of places I had been, people I had served with, and Soldiers I had led all flashed through my head. Things that did not make sense before became clearer to me. I knew at that very moment *we* were making a difference—my Soldiers, his Soldiers; my country, his country; my Family, his Family; my leadership and his leadership.

I was at the right place, at the right time, doing absolutely the right thing, and without any regret. The emotional bond we shared, as two fellow Soldiers willing to sacrifice for and serve others, welled up inside me. For a moment, I was back in time, on that hot, summer day at West Point, nearly twenty-five years prior. As I took in the faces of the people around me, I consciously validated my life, my purpose, my service. This was not about being successful. This was about being significant and making a difference.

Making a difference in someone else's life can be as simple as a smile, lifting a hand to help, or lending an ear to listen, especially when it might be easier to ignore the opportunity. Each day is a new day and a new chance to use what you've worked for and been given to lighten someone else's load. It's never too late to choose to move beyond success to significance.

PART III:

What Next?

Creating Your Own

Definition of Leadership

The United States Military Academy (USMA) leadership model was my foundation for becoming a leader. The mission of USMA is to graduate leaders of character, grounded in values, who are prepared to honorably lead America's sons and daughters and be dedicated servants to our nation. Some of our nation's most profound leaders and courageous heroes are West Point graduates.

The army provided me with field manuals for every aspect of my service, including leadership. Every organization should provide a framework of standards, core competencies, values, and expectations. Employees should know how they will be measured when it comes to performance and promotion.

At the same time, I think it's also important for you as individual leaders to develop your own set of expectations, your personal definition of leadership, and, if you chose to take it to that level, your leadership vision or model.

Taking the time to think about how you see your role as a leader will help solidify your leadership values and ensure their integration into your daily thoughts and actions. Taking the time to create a leadership model that you can share will extend what you believe to be important to the rest of your team.

★　STEADFAST Leadership Model　★

As a battalion commander, I developed a leader philosophy that I shared with every member in my organization. It was my way of communicating who I was, what my expectations were, and what principles were most important to me as a leader. To make it easier for all to remember, I called my philosophy *STEADFAST Leadership*. STEADFAST was an acronym:

Soldiers
Training
Excellence
Attitude
Discipline
Family, Friends, and Faith
Accountability
Safety
Teamwork

These principles merged nicely with the army's values of *LDRSHIP*:

Loyalty
Duty
Respect
Selfless Service
Honor
Integrity
Personal Courage

I would use and continue to share my STEADFAST principles with those I led throughout the rest of my military career.

Upon retiring and trying to determine a name for my post-military business, I decided to revise the STEADFAST acronym to fit the civilian and corporate worlds. On your journey through *24/7*, you've been introduced not only to my definition of leadership that is outlined at the very end of the book but also to the premises and principles behind my "STEADFAST Leadership" model:

Selfless Service
Trust and Tenacity
Encourage and Embrace
Attitude and Approachability
Discipline
Family, Friends, and Faith
Accountability
Standard Setter
Teamwork

★   Creating Your Definition of Leadership   ★

The fact is there is no single correct answer to the question "What is leadership?" There are likely as many and varied definitions as there are leaders, which is why I believe the study of leadership remains stimulating.

Life is an open leadership laboratory, and in one way or another, we are all students. My personal thoughts on the subject of leadership have changed over the years as a result of many influences—experience, relationships, responsibility, knowledge, culture, and research.

Each of you should create your own definition, put it to the test, and recreate as your leadership experiences evolve. Creating your own definition will help internalize your commitment to live according to your personal leadership principles. You owe that investment to yourself, and you definitely owe it to the people you lead now and in the future. Remember, we all have a responsibility to lead, and it begins by leading ourselves.

To help you get started on your definition of leadership, I will close this book by sharing with you my definition. These five simple but powerful components, developed and practiced over my lifetime, define how I continue to strive to lead others.

Leadership is:

The fusion of heart and mind,
in selfless action,
for the betterment of others,
to effectively accomplish the mission,
and make a difference.

About the Author

Becky Halstead, retired brigadier general, US Army, is a 1981 graduate of the United States Military Academy. Becky achieved a historic milestone as the first female graduate of West Point to be promoted to general officer. As the senior commanding general for logistics in Iraq, she was the first female in US history to command in combat at the strategic level. In Iraq she was responsible for leading over two hundred multidisciplinary units (twenty thousand military and five thousand civilians) providing supply, maintenance, transportation and distribution support to over 250,000 personnel serving in Iraq.

The culmination of Becky's career came in 2006 when she became the first female chief of ordnance and commanding general of the Army's Ordnance Center and Schools (equivalent to president of a university). Becky honorably served with the US Army and retired as a general officer in 2008.

Becky has over fifteen years of executive-level leadership experience, developing and training high-performing, complex, and diverse units capable of strategic planning and execution. She has a record of leading change, building successful teams in demanding environments (Afghanistan and Iraq), and creating innovative systems and programs to solve complex problems. In addition to an experienced leader and logistician, Becky is known as a highly effective communicator. She founded her own leader consultancy company, STEADFAST Leadership, with the intent of extending lessons learned in the military to the civilian world. She specializes in inspirational speaking, consulting, and advising, and serves as a member of multiple military, corporate, and nonprofit boards of advisers.

Becky was a recipient of the 2007 National Women's History Project award for "Generations of Women Moving History Forward." She also served as a commissioner on the President's Military Leadership Diversity Commission from 2009 to 2010. Becky's STEADFAST Leadership model was the subject of a 2011 Harvard Business School Leadership Case Study.

Rebecca "Becky" Halstead

Brigadier General, US Army, Retired
Key Assignments

Dates	Rank	Titles	Unit and Location
1977–1981	Cadet	New Cadet, Cadet, Plebe, Yearling, Cow, Firstie	United States Military Academy, West Point, NY
1982–1984	Lieutenant	Platoon Leader	69th Ordnance Company, Vicenza, Italy
1985–1988	Captain	Company Commander	Headquarters Company and 63rd Ordnance Company, Fort Lewis, WA
1989–1991	Captain	Personnel Assignments Officer	Personnel Command, Alexandria, VA
1991–1992	Captain	Aide-de-Camp	Combined Arms Support Command, Fort Lee, VA
1992–1993	Major	Student	Command and General Staff College, Fort Leavenworth, KS
1993–1995	Major	Support Operations Officer and Battalion Executive Officer	526 Forward Support Battalion, 101st Air Assault Division, Fort Campbell, KY
1995–1997	Major	Logistics Staff Officer	Office of the Deputy Chief of Staff for Logistics, Pentagon, Wash, DC
	Lieutenant Colonel	Assistant Executive Officer to the Deputy Chief of Staff for Logistics	Office of the Deputy Chief of Staff for Logistics, Pentagon, Wash, DC
1997–1999	Lieutenant Colonel	Battalion Commander	325 Forward Support Battalion, 25th Infantry Division, Schofield Barracks, HI
1999–2000	Lieutenant Colonel	Student	Industrial College of the Armed Forces, Fort McNair, Wash, DC
2000–2002	Colonel	Brigade Commander	10th Division Support Command, 10th Mountain Division, Fort Drum, NY
2002–2003	Colonel	Executive Assistant to the Combatant Commander	Southern Command, Miami, FL
2003–2004	Colonel	Deputy Commanding General	21st Theater Support Command, Kaiserslautern, Germany
2004–2006	Brigadier General	Commanding General	3rd Corps Support Command, Wiesbaden, Germany, and Balad, Iraq
2006–2008	Brigadier General	Commanding General	Ordnance Center and Schools, Aberdeen Proving Ground, MD

www.beckyhalstead.com

Made in United States
North Haven, CT
14 February 2022

16102123R00183